D0636322

MS HARRIS'S BOOK OF GREEN HOUSEHOLD MANAGEMENT

MS HARRIS'S
BOOK OF
GREEN
HOUSEHOLD
MANAGEMENT

CAROLINE HARRIS

JOHN MURRAY

First published in Great Britain in 2009 by John Murray (Publishers)
An Hachette UK Company

1

A CIP catalogue record for this title is available from the British Library

ISBN 978-1-84854-008-8

Typeset in Horley Old Style MT by Servis Filmsetting Ltd, Stockport, Cheshire
Book design by Janette Revill
Printed and bound by Clays Ltd, St Ives plc

The paper used to manufacture this book has been sourced from a Forest Stewardship
Council accredited paper mill in Finland.

John Murray policy is to use papers that are natural, renewable and recyclable products
and made from wood grown in sustainable forests. The logging and manufacturing
processes are expected to conform to the environmental regulations of the country
of origin.

John Murray (Publishers)
338 Euston Road
London NW1 3BH

www.johnmurray.co.uk

For my parents, June and Peter, who have taught me
so much of what I know and value.

CONTENTS

INTRODUCTION

T he idea for this book began to form while I was staying in a Cornish cottage with my family a couple of years ago. It was a lovely place. Slate floors in the kitchen and cosily battered antique furniture.

A leafy garden with a sand pit, and a little cove of beach two minutes down the hill. But under the sink, in place of my familiar battalion of eco-friendly bottles, I was confronted with a gaggle of big-manufacturer brands, all bright greens and yellows and blues, with their hypochlorite bleaching agents, antibacterials and synthetic perfumes, and a host of other chemicals whose effects on our health have yet to be gauged.

I ended up using the more benign-looking ones (there wasn't a health-food shop or supermarket nearby), but it made me realize a couple of things. First, that I'd already changed my ideas considerably from a few years before, when buying anything environmentally friendly seemed like a luxury. And second, that if only I knew how, I could have cleaned the cottage with just a few household basics such as vinegar and baking soda.

What I needed, I decided, was a green household compendium. It should inform me about all the eco-friendly options – from saving water and energy to ethical clothing, growing your own veg and cutting down on waste – but not in an overwhelming way. It should bring together hints and tips based on traditional housekeeping methods, from a time before we got used to so many synthetic chemical cocktails, but also take into account our modern lifestyles with their slimline laptops and dry-clean-only fabrics. It should be presented in a way that made for sensible, useful reading – something you could turn to for helpful reference – but be entertaining and not preachy.

It should be, if you like, a kind of Mrs Beeton for the climate-changing twenty-first century, but more fun to dip into over a cup of (fairtrade) coffee. The name – *Ms Harris's Book of Green Household Management* – started out as a pastiche, but it seemed fitting and so the title has stuck.

In writing it I've consulted many different sources, from centuries-old publications in the British Library to the wealth of diverse information on the web, and from parents and friends to experts at eco-related organizations. Our home has become, at times, something of a laboratory as I've experimented with laundry alternatives and ways of using greywater, and installed our Electrisave energy consumption meter. There have been great successes – our vegetable plot is perhaps our happiest achievement – and also failures, including the marmalade pan that boiled over and taught me how *not* to clean sugar off a ceramic hob.

My knowledge has increased enormously, and as a result I'm much more confident about the steps I'm taking in a greener direction – my hope is you'll feel the same after reading this book and having it there to consult on your kitchen shelf. Through trial and error I've fathomed out a lot of what works and what doesn't. It's one thing to be told, 'Try baking soda for cleaning,' but quite another to understand its various properties and the easiest ways to use it. That's the kind of information I've attempted to put in this book – the practical steps of how to do things.

Like me, most people would like to be at least a bit greener in their homes and lifestyles, but often don't have the necessary knowledge or skills. After decades of being sold supermarket aisles-full of chemical products that promise instant, no-effort results, we've forgotten the crafts of household management. There are so many things I had no idea about before I began working on this book. Do you know how to make a furniture cleaner from kitchen ingredients? I couldn't have told you at the start of my researches but now I wouldn't think of using anything except an olive oil and vinegar mix on our stripped-wood banisters.

Of course, you don't have to prepare all your own cleaning mixtures or laundry powders. Eco brands are now making their presence felt and a very useful range of products is readily available. Even the multinationals are bringing out greener options. However, simpler, cheaper alternatives are usually just as good, and many of the ingredients, such as vinegar and salt, have been used in food for centuries and more – making them the safest kind of chemicals with which to shine your home.

Saving energy and water can seem even more daunting than swapping to eco-friendly cleaners. Partly, this is to do with the size of the problem, especially when it comes to climate change. Can switching the TV off standby really prevent catastrophic floods and droughts? Well, no, and certainly not if just a few people are acting on their own. But as the cleaning up of our rivers in the UK shows, concerted efforts can and do bring results. If more of us make changes in our own lives, and show that we want a different attitude to inform government, business and world political decisions on the environment, then, with luck, something of value will be achieved. And even if we don't manage to persuade anyone else, we will have made the choice of changing our own behaviour and ecological footprint.

Perhaps, after that high-mindedness, this is the right point for a confession – I love to spend longer than I strictly should in our power shower, with energy-wasting hot water cascading down (five minutes uses about the same amount of water as a bath). I know it's wrong (and in my defence I'd like to point out that the power shower was here when we moved in) but I can't help it. Still, it's not as though I use it anything like every day, so maybe it counts as only a partial green sin (› page 231 for more about bathing and showering less frequently).

There are plenty of occasions when I forget the green rules – when I'm tired, for example, I have a tendency to wander up to bed leaving the broadband router on all night – and I don't follow all of the tips in this book all of the time. You don't have to be perfect (or an austerity fiend) to be a green householder, but simply try to do what you can.

If you have green leanings it's all too easy to get tangled up in guilt and dilemmas about whether you're a terrible person for having a dishwasher (that's another confession – we have a dishwasher) or whether it's OK really because, if you scrape the plates rather than rinsing, dishwashers can actually use less water than doing it by hand.

Too much guilt can lead to an unhelpful state of paralysis. One thing I'd like this book to do is to relieve some of the panic and palpitations (or total denial) that can accompany reading or hearing about the dire consequences of not recycling our tins or insisting on flying to our holiday destinations. The advice here is practical and do-able, and you don't have to do it all at once. Developing a greener lifestyle is an ongoing process – there are layers of greenness, and many different areas in which to apply its principles creatively, once you start to look into it all.

Before I took my own first steps I'd had a vaguely growing awareness of eco issues for some years, but while working hard and late and living the singleton (and then couple) lifestyle, I hadn't actually put a great deal into practice apart from recycling the newspapers and wine bottles. What changed everything was having a baby.

New parents are bombarded with advice about making sure everything is sterilized and clinically clean, but at the same time frightening evidence is emerging about the build-up of toxic chemicals in young children. So I was torn between a desire to protect my baby from the onslaught of germs and fear of making him into a chemistry lab. My solution was to look for alternatives to bleach, lysol and triclosan – and worry less about bacteria.

For my next step, I thought I'd do the right thing and opt for re-usable nappies – an altogether tougher assignment, I found. Here's another confession – we lasted nine months, then somehow slipped into disposables.

Our mistake was possibly to be too keen too early. Clive (who refuses to be called my partner so I suppose I have to call him my boyfriend) and I put in our order with a promising local nappy laundry before our son, Ethan, was born. But when he came along, all tiny and milk-fed, the folded cloth nappies and huge-looking waterproof wraps didn't quite seal things in as you might want. We used shaped nappies for a while, then went for one of the new biodegradable disposables. (To learn more about the nappy conundrum, → Chapter 14.)

And that's about the point I'd reached when we went on our Cornish holiday. Since then we've made some big changes, including moving from London to Bath. But we don't have a cutting-edge eco home here. It's a Victorian mid-terrace house in need of more insulation. We don't generate our own electricity; we don't have a reedbed greywater filter. What we have done is tried to live in the kind of greener way that most people could do in most homes, without having to totally transform them.

We've saved some money (on energy, for example, and by growing our own salads and vegetables) and spent some money (mainly on redesigning the garden, and buying organic products).

We've developed new habits, such as always looking to see if we can re-use something before putting it out for recycling or in the bin, and we've rediscovered creative skills, including making our own Christmas cards.

Green household management might seem like a challenge but it's not too great a one. A bit of enthusiasm, a few ideas, adapting to different ways of doing and thinking about things are really all that's needed. Being greener doesn't have to be all hair shirts on the one hand, or simply switching to eco-consumer brands on the other. There is another way, and you might even have some fun if you venture along it.

Caroline Harris
Larkhall, Bath
September 2008

1

WHAT IS GREEN HOUSEHOLD MANAGEMENT?

G*reen household management is smart household management. It's about making your home welcoming, people-friendly and environmentally friendly. It's about running your house (or flat, or*

house-share) in a way that reduces your waste and carbon footprints, cuts your utility bills and unnecessary household spending, and shuts the door on many potentially harmful chemicals. It's about being creative, challenging old habits and enjoying trying to do things in a different way.

Making your home greener doesn't need to involve spending loads of extra time on chores, or loads of extra money on so-called green products (although some choices, such as organic food, do tend to be more expensive). It doesn't mean throwing out everything in your house and starting again from scratch, and it doesn't mean signing up to the belief that everything natural is good and anything invented after the Victorian era is automatically to be distrusted.

WHAT'S IN THIS BOOK

The main focus of what you'll read here is the practical day-to-day running of your home. Things like food, clothing care and laundry, cleaning, waste management, energy and water use, and planning celebrations – the stuff you do in the regular household round. The aim of this book is to be a source of useful advice and skills. It includes the most effective methods and products that I and others have discovered, where to find them, and websites to browse if you want to investigate any subject further.

There are tips on buying appliances and removing fruit juice stains; on making your own marmalade and cleaning your computer; on choosing greener nursery furnishings and making a DIY wedding bouquet.

The advice combines traditional techniques and twenty-first-century innovations, and applies them to our modern homes, with their iPods and stainless steel fridges. Whether you have a tiny urban flat or a house with a large garden, and whether you're a student, parent or full-time career-person, the information in these pages will help you to negotiate a route to greener living.

THE LOST ARTS OF THE HOUSEHOLD MANAGER

Most of us are now painfully aware of the need to care for the environment and reduce greenhouse gas emissions. We do think about the environmental impact of the choices we make for our homes. A growing number of resources and initiatives are available to help us, but the prospect of transforming the way we keep house can still be daunting.

It doesn't help that we've become deskilled, and lost touch with many traditional household arts. Just as ready meals mean we have

The basics of green household management

Less is more – use less, live more is a key concept of much green and conservation thinking.

Cut carbon emissions – by reducing energy use, consumption and waste, and choosing energy-efficient appliances.

Detox your home – by using simpler cleaning formulas and, where possible, furnishings and finishes with fewer treatments that could contain potentially harmful chemicals.

Reduce water use – cut the strain on water resources and save carbon emissions at the same time.

Choose organic, local and sustainably produced foods – and learn the delights of cooking from raw ingredients.

Reduce, re-use, repair, recycle – cut back on the waste that comes into and goes out of your home.

Choose fairtrade – look at where the goods you buy come from, and whether they've been produced ethically.

Be creative – find your own green solutions as you go along, and enjoy doing it.

less need to cook, quick-fix household cleaners and cheap clothing mean we don't need to know how to use simple mineral or plant-based cleaning methods, or even sew up a hem.

Moving to a more sustainable, less oil-dependent and chemical-filled household often (but not always) means turning to older, simpler, more home-made ways of doing things. This doesn't mean harking back to the days before washing machines or vacuum cleaners (although carpet sweepers have their place, → page 25), but if we want to be greener in our modern houses, it's useful to get to grips with some of these basic skills – cooking with raw ingredients, sewing, composting, growing at least some of our own food – and see how to adapt them to our own needs.

Thrift and craft

Green thinking has brought some old-fashioned ideas out of the closet – 'living within our means', for instance, which could be translated today as 'sustainable development', and 'make do and mend' and the 'cottage industries' of home-based crafts that are finding new devotees.

In researching this book I encountered blogging communities of craftspeople who are experimenting with natural dyes and spinning, while not long back knitting was suddenly *the* thing to be seen doing. Household management doesn't need to be limited to cleaning and meal provision; there are huge possibilities for being creative, from making preserves, to growing flowers for cutting, to designing your own gift cards, wrapping paper and home furnishings.

In the green household, everything can become a resource. 'Old stuff' is no longer just something to be chucked away, but something to be thought about, re-used, swapped or made over. All of which means that thrifty living doesn't have to be austere or dull – far from it.

CHANGING THE HABITS OF A LIFETIME

Don't try to do it all at once. That's the first thing I'd say. Choose a bit of 'greenery' that you feel most drawn to, or that you figure will make most difference to your home comfort/your bank balance/ the environment and go for that first. I started off with cleaning products and organic fruit, vegetables and baby clothes, and moved on from there. I made changes in some areas only once I had begun to research this book – and there are others where our household is still a work in progress.

Changing habits means making informed decisions. When we're running on automatic, it's easy to fall into bad old ways. Some of the changes will probably seem like a lot of effort to begin with – but look back after a few months and you'll see that many green household strategies have become your normal way of doing things. (Give it a while and you'll remember that re-usable shopping bag pretty much all the time . . .)

Green householder's tip:

For local support, see if your area is part of the Transition Towns movement (www.transitiontowns.org). Transition communities are growing up around the UK and worldwide, with local people coming together to address the issues of Peak Oil and climate change practically, from growing their own food to sharing skills and lobbying for improved public transport.

The time problem

You might feel there aren't enough hours in the day to be the complete green household manager – and you'd be right. I'd rather be out in the garden than cleaning the house, and mending gets done only when there's a heap of it and I've enough energy to tackle it rather than curl up on the sofa.

Some strategies – including energy-saving fixes such as installing insulation or draft-proofing (→ Chapter 3) – are one-offs. Others, such as always seeing what you can re-use, are more of an ongoing enterprise, but take just a few minutes.

It's really up to you what kind of green householder you choose to be – energy-efficient aficionado, baking-and-sewing supremo, or grow-your-own guru. If your entire household decides to take up the challenge, you can play to each one's strengths.

If your partner (or housemate) isn't interested . . .

Moving to greener ways of doing things is a change and so likely to be resisted unless your family or housemates can see the benefits. It may be that not everyone in your household is as convinced of the need to be green as you are, although the arguments in favour are impressive.

▼ Saving money can be a great incentive for the environmentally sceptical. In advance of making changes, explain how much they are likely to save you, and plan together what to do with those savings. Check energy bills and weekly shopping receipts to see how it's going, but bear in mind that price increases may make the savings look less than they are. For energy, for example, check the number of kilowatt hours used, which should be listed on your bill.

♥ Make sure you explain why you're calling on members of the household to make changes, and that they know how to do what you're asking them to do. It's no good banning certain products unilaterally if you haven't explained exactly why, and discussed replacements.

♥ Use the competitive instinct to your advantage – if internal competition works in your household, green challenges, such as who can save the most greywater, or come up with the most creative use for a cereal packet liner, might be a way forward.

♥ If your wife, husband, boyfriend, girlfriend or housemate is stressed and always busy, limit what you're asking for. Maybe he or she could help with one weekly task to start with, such as putting out the recycling (nearly the same as putting out the rubbish), or something relaxing and satisfying, such as picking strawberries.

♥ Give lots of praise and positive feedback – and, tempting as it may be, try to avoid anything approaching nagging. (For tips on encouraging children, → page 382.)

BALANCING GREEN IMPERATIVES

When I started writing this book, some friends of friends made the very valid point that since climate change is now recognized as the greatest threat facing our planet, shouldn't we focus all our efforts on reducing fossil fuel consumption and cutting greenhouse gas omissions? Isn't a broader greenness in danger of diverting crucial attention and resources from the real big issue?

Some of you reading this book may well agree and want to concentrate on energy above all else – although it's worth remembering that other green principles, such as reducing waste and cutting water consumption, can also lower carbon emissions. But for those of us who feel it's important to adopt a balanced approach that takes in all of the environmental, health and ethical impacts, trying to be green can be something of a juggling act.

For example, you may feel instinctively that re-usable nappies are naturally better than disposables, but if you buy a lot of them, wash at high temperatures and use a tumble dryer, they could be worse in terms of energy use. Then there's the organic food miles dilemma – do you buy organic beans that have come from Africa and are supporting farmers there, or pesticide-sprayed ones from a local farm?

It's impossible to satisfy every single green diktat in all your choices. None of us is perfect, so I reckon the thing to do to stay sane – and not fall into a fit of green paralysis – is to make the best possible choice you can at the time, given the information available and what is most important to you.

IS IT REALLY GREEN?

Some of the attractive-sounding green claims on product labels are informative, but others are more for marketing hype than helping you find what has truly green credentials. I've included some of the main marques to look out for, but new products and sites are always springing up, and information becoming available. I'll try to post updates on the Ms Harris website, www.ms-harris.com, and do leave your own findings and comments to inform others.

The best measure of the greenness of any product or process is life-cycle assessment (LCA) – environmental analysts actually add up all the product's impacts through its entire life, from raw materials, production and use to disposal or recycling. This method is being strongly encouraged by the European Commission and is already used as the basis for some eco-labels. As it becomes more widely used, the information generated should begin to show what really are the greenest options (there may, of course, be surprises).

How to look after this book

This book is intended to be kept in your kitchen – or somewhere else where it comes easily to hand in a domestic eco-crisis or for everyday reference. Its pages may, through regular use or occasional mishap, become stained or creased. Don't worry if this happens: it means that the volume has been put to good use. In a similar spirit, feel free to write your own notes, or adaptations to recipes and instructions, in the margins.

When pages become stuck together, hold them briefly in the steam of a boiling kettle and ease apart. Running the handle of a spoon in between the stuck pages may also help. You might like to make your own cover from wallpaper scraps or decorated brown paper.

If, for whatever reason, you no longer find this book useful, please try to re-home it sensitively. Pass it on to a friend or relative, swap it through a site such as www.readitswap.co.uk or www.bookmooch.com, or release it into a suitable wild habitat with a Bookcrossing ID number (www.bookcrossing.com).

2

GETTING TO GRIPS WITH GRIME

Now, given that I'm writing a book about household management, you might be forgiven for believing that my own home is a temple of cleanliness, gleaming from vinegar-washed window to broom-swept wood floor. This, however, is not exactly the case. I like my house to be what I'd call presentable, and I also want it to be cleaned without potentially damaging or environmentally persistent chemicals. I just don't want to spend too many hours in the week doing it.

In fact, the level of shine and tidiness in our home is embarrassingly closely linked to the imminent arrival of guests. Like many people, I'm usually too busy working/running around after a young child/making the most of life while I can to dwell for that long on the business of keeping the house spick and span.

So while some of the methods in this chapter may take a little more elbow grease than the spray-on über-cleaners advertised on TV, the idea is not to make you a slave to the cleaning cloth. To this end, I've started off with 10 simple, environmentally and time-friendly hints.

TOP 10 EASY ECO-CLEANING TIPS

1. Baking-soda oven cleaner

Remove all the oven shelves, wipe or brush out any loose bits, then shake the baking soda thickly over the bottom and spritz with water. For the sides, mix a thick paste of baking soda and water and daub it on. Leave for several hours or overnight, occasionally dampening with more water. In the morning, wipe out the baking soda, scouring away any stubborn spots (most grime will just lift off). Wipe with a clean cloth, then spray with vinegar, or use a vinegar-soaked cloth, to dissolve the remainder.

2. Vinegar-spray shower descaler

The best eco-friendly way to keep showers free of limescale is to dry them off after use, but to remove existing limescale, spray white distilled vinegar from the top of the glass (or tiles) down and leave for at least 15 minutes, or overnight. Rub over with a cloth or a knitted scouring pad, have your shower, then dry off the glass panels. If your shower cubicle is really caked, repeat as necessary.

3. E-cloths and other microfibre cloths

I'm a fan of these. The construction of the fibres means you can clean up quickly and easily with only a touch of water. They even mop up grease. I know microfibre is a synthetic material, but they last for ages. Just make sure to wash them before they get smelly – if you leave it too late, boil them in a pan of water.

4. Citric acid or vinegar toilet reviver

I've found that toilet stains can be hard to remove with gentler commercial eco toilet cleansers, but with this method you can

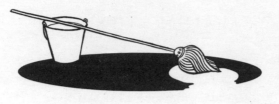

get rid of stains *and* limescale, which is where the bacteria build up. Every couple of months, pop two tablespoons of citric acid – available from pharmacies, 'bath bomb' suppliers, or online – in the toilet pan (you can substitute half a cup of vinegar, but I don't think it works quite so impressively). Leave overnight, or while you're away. Much of the limescale will simply float off, while the rest can be removed with a toilet brush.

5. Handy towels
Keep old towels and, if you live on several floors, have one within easy reach on each. They're invaluable for quickly mopping up water spills, toddler accidents and potential stains.

6. Paintbrush dado rail duster
For hard-to-reach places, a decorator's paintbrush is better and quicker than a vacuum cleaner nozzle, or even a duster. Make sure to do your brushing before you clean the floors, not after.

7. Lavender-oil instant lavatory wipe
Lavender oil has antiseptic qualities, so use a few drops in water to dampen a cleaning cloth (never use essential oils undiluted, because they are potent and can irritate the skin, → page 33). Alternatively, you could use vinegar – scented if you like, for example with the lemon vinegar recipe (→ page 36).

8. Baking-soda fridge deodorizer

Baking soda absorbs odours, so put a small cup of it in the fridge. When it's no longer working, use it for a scouring job, such as cleaning the sink (you can also scatter baking soda in the bottom of your rubbish and compost bins to neutralize nasty smells). Clean your fridge regularly with a solution of baking soda and warm water.

9. Wiping not rinsing

Instead of running litres of water into a basin, bath or shower to rinse off the cleaner, wipe with a clean cloth dampened in fresh water instead. It not only uses less water, it's quicker too.

10. Carpet sweepers

With an old-fashioned mechanical carpet sweeper – not one of the battery-powered cordless types – you can quickly clean up crumbs, hair and grit, which is better than lumbering out the vacuum cleaner or leaving them to be ground into the carpet. Carpet sweepers also work on wood and lino floors. Try to get one with bristle brushes.

GREENER CLEANING

So what's the problem with conventional cleaners? The issue is, no one knows exactly how safe – or unsafe – many of them are. Manufacturers are required by law to list constituents above a certain concentration on the label, and ingredients such as disinfectants, enzymes and perfumes, but there are many other things they don't have to admit to. Safety data isn't available for most of these, and we wouldn't really know what manufacturers were talking about if they did list them. There are, after all, about

100,000 chemicals in use in household and consumer products, and some cleaners can have as many as 30 ingredients.

Greenpeace's Chemical Home campaign worked with manufacturers to identify ingredients that could be hazardous, and persuade them to remove these (you can read the report at www.greenpeace.org.uk/toxics/chemicalhome). Some products have now been given a clean bill of health; however, in others you may still find chemicals that Greenpeace and the Worldwide Fund for Nature (www.wwf.org.uk) regard as potentially harmful.

As with much else in adopting a more eco-friendly way of living, a guiding theme of green cleaning is 'less is more'. The idea is to reduce the number of unidentified chemicals around your home, in order to make it a more hospitable place to live. One way is to switch to eco brands, but it's possible to tackle most day-to-day cleaning tasks with even more minimalist options: baking soda, vinegar and leftover lemon halves, or even just plain water on a cloth. They're cheap, relatively harmless (although → notes on pages 34–6), have been used for centuries and occur naturally or are made through fairly simple processes – and using them means you know exactly what you're introducing into your home.

Cleaner's tip:
If you want to explore eco brands, names to look out for include Ecover (www.ecover.com), Bio-D (www.biodegradable.biz) and Clear Spring (www.faithinnature.co.uk). You could also try supplier websites such as www.greenpeople.co.uk, www.just-green.com and www.daylesfordorganic.com

Chemical versus natural

Whether it's cleaning products or food additives, it can be all too easy to adopt a mindset of 'all chemicals bad, all natural products good' – but it isn't that clear cut.

What we usually mean when we talk about 'chemicals' in an eco context is synthetic chemicals – which are man-made as opposed to coming from naturally occurring sources – and products of the petrochemical industry. Strictly speaking, compounds such as sodium chloride (aka salt) and active plant ingredients, like the citric acid in lemons, are chemicals too.

A good number of synthetic chemicals are very useful, and some are even life-saving, but many are untested, or haven't been around long enough for their long-term effects to be known, including the impact they might have on health in a cocktail with other chemicals. 'Green chemistry' is a relatively new discipline (see York University's Green Chemistry Centre of Excellence at www.york.ac.uk/ res/gcg/site/) that seeks to help industries and manufacturers make the substances they work with safer and more sustainable, and the processes involved more energy-efficient.

On the other side of the equation, not everything 'natural' is safe, and the same goes for substances that have been around a long time. Plant-based compounds can be poisonous (hemlock) and carcinogenic (tobacco), and we wouldn't want to go back to lead water pipes. Also, ingredients or materials may have a natural source, but have gone through energy and chemical-intensive processes as they are refined.

Open a window not an air freshener

A number of studies have found that the air in many homes is more badly polluted than the air outside, even in a big city. Stain-resist coatings on carpets, formaldehyde given off by MDF, brominated flame retardants on furniture, curtains and mattresses, pesticides and coatings on new clothes, synthetic fragrances in fabric conditioners, fumes from household cleaning products, volatile organic compounds (VOCs) from paints, glues and nail varnish – all of these and more can contribute to a chemical cocktail in your home.

Given all this, why would you want to open a synthetic, chemical-based air freshener? Some work by 'numbing' your sense of smell, while others simply cover odours with a strong fragrance carried in a solvent. The ones you plug in – so they use electricity, too – are perhaps the worst green offenders.

Instead, open a window, use baking soda to absorb and neutralize smells (→ page 34), or hang up posies of fresh-scented herbs, such as mint or lemon balm, which can also help to repel flies.

Cleaner's Tip:

You can find out more about chemicals that are of concern – and ways to avoid them – in What's in This Stuff? *by Pat Thomas and* The Toxic Consumer *by Karen Ashton and Elizabeth Salter Green. Also see the CHEM Trust website at www.chemtrust.org.uk.*

HOME HYGIENE

Ever since it became widely accepted that bacteria and viruses cause illnesses – not an 'imbalance of the humours', as our forebears believed – we've had a love-hate relationship with the germ world. On the one hand, we've become increasingly convinced that we have to exterminate every single one of them at all costs, while on the other we drink 'friendly bacteria' to help our digestion.

For as long as humans have been around, we have coexisted with bugs, and we have an immune system that does a pretty good job of keeping all but the nastiest in their place. One argument even suggests that the modern mania for disinfecting our homes has had a detrimental effect on our bodies' defence systems.

In my home, I now opt for cleanliness above disinfection. This means following simple home-hygiene practices rather than dousing everything with chemicals.

- ♥ It's worth avoiding unnecessary antibacterials, such as triclosan, and opting for thorough hand-washing with soap instead. The advice is to rub hands for 10 to 15 seconds, and make sure you dry them properly afterwards.
- ♥ Clean the kitchen often, keep surfaces well wiped, and wash and dry chopping boards thoroughly. If you really want to use something to help disinfect, you could try vinegar, or salt solution.
- ♥ Thoroughly cleaning a surface can remove 99 per cent of microbes, but remember to rinse out cloths in fresh water between cleaning tasks so you're not simply moving bugs between surfaces.
- ♥ Store raw meats and fish separately from cooked, and away from salads or other foods that are eaten raw. Keep separate chopping boards for them.
- ♥ Germs and moulds like damp, warm conditions. Kitchen and bathroom cloths and sponges can become bug heaven if you're

not careful. Dry tea towels and other cloths after use, and change them frequently.

❊ *Cleaner's tip:*
❊ *You can zap the bugs on kitchen sponges and cloths by putting*
❊ *them in the microwave on high for a couple of minutes, or*
❊ *boiling them in a small pan of water (add a quarter of a*
❊ *lemon for a pleasant aroma). Disinfect grubby cloths by*
❊ *putting them in your washing-machine maintenance wash*
❊ *(→ page 250), or by pre-soaking them before a*
❊ *lower-temperature wash.*

Your cleaning tool kit

Cleaning cloths: Microfibre cloths (→ page 23) are my prime kitchen and bathroom cleaning cloths, but you can use pretty much any piece of soft cloth, including old T-shirts and baby muslins.

Lint-free cloths: These are cloths that won't leave fluff all over the surface – so not towels, for example. They're especially useful for glass, mirrors and computers. Use special microfibre glass cloths, or save the ones that come with spectacles and sunglasses.

Tea towels: I am fast approaching the conclusion that it is impossible to own too many tea towels. For drying washing-up or salad leaves, or lifting pan lids – I use them all the time.

Scourers: I have a knitted copper pan scrubber; this type lasts a long time and is kind to pans and most surfaces. For a renewable, biodegradable (and cheap) alternative, see the loofah scrubbies from www.choosethealternative.co.uk.

Brushes: A dustpan and brush are pretty much essential, plus a broom if you don't want to be bending down all the time. Old nailbrushes can become scrubbers; toothbrushes are good for inaccessible nooks and for cleaning metal. Clean your plastic brushes in the dishwasher, or sanitize by soaking in percarbonate laundry bleach (the milder, powdered kind that's often sold as 'oxygen' bleach). Ageing curved washing-up brushes will clean off toilet limescale more effectively than many toilet brushes.

Mop and bucket: To make an impromptu mop, wrap a cloth around a clean broom. When Ethan was small, and throwing food everywhere, for a while we used a mop with clip-on disposable wipes. Now I'm trying to redeem myself by using it with recycled T-shirt cloths instead.

Vacuum cleaner: Since they use electricity, vacuum cleaners aren't as green as carpet sweepers, but they do lift dust effectively, and help to remove hazardous household chemicals and allergens along with it. A high efficiency particulate air (HEPA) filter traps much smaller particles than an ordinary filter. Make sure you are buying a genuine HEPA filter – it will include test results on the label – and keep it clean to prevent dust blowing back.

Containers: If possible keep products in their original packaging so you retain all the relevant information about the contents. Decant bulk buys into clearly labelled jars. A spray bottle makes vinegar easier to use, but don't be tempted to recycle a bottle from a conventional cleaning product because it could still contain traces of the previous contents.

Cleaning with kitchen chemicals

Most dirt and stains will respond to an armoury of simple kitchen chemicals and household minerals. As a general rule, start off by using the most benign substance available. This will often be plain water with a cloth or scourer. The next step up is a mild option, such as baking soda, vinegar or washing-up detergent. This is where I usually stop – one of these will get rid of most dirt. If it doesn't work straight away, try leaving it on the stubborn mark or greasy gunk for a while and see if it shifts then.

In most cases, I use these chemicals individually, partly because I'm too lazy (or busy) to concoct cleaning recipes, but also because I'm then less likely to mix something dangerous or unusable by accident. Never combine baking soda and vinegar in a sealed container, for instance – the result could burst the bottle.

Safety notes

As with all cleaning substances, store household minerals away from children, in an inaccessible cupboard. Keep the versions of kitchen chemicals you use for cooking apart from those bought for cleaning, which may not be of edible grade. I buy different brands and make sure they're stored in different containers.

Essential oils: These plant oils may come from a natural source, but they are highly concentrated and potent. They contain complex mixtures of chemicals, which can have strong effects on human and animal physiology – so treat them with respect.

Never put undiluted oil on the skin, or where it could come into contact with the skin, because some oils are highly irritant and can burn. Always check up about a particular oil before using it – thyme oil, for example, is poisonous, while others should be avoided during pregnancy – and, to be on the safe side, keep essential oils away from food preparation surfaces.

Cleaner's tip:
Just because household minerals and kitchen chemicals are likely to be safer for health and relatively easy on the environment doesn't mean they will be kind to your hands. Some can irritate the skin, so always wear gloves when you use them.

YOUR KITCHEN CHEMISTRY SET

Baking soda
(aka bicarbonate of soda, sodium bicarbonate)
This mineral salt is mildly alkaline and will neutralize many strong odours, as well as being probably the most useful all-purpose cleaner – there are a huge number of hints online, including at www.bakingsodabook.co.uk. Buy it in large-size packs from supermarkets, hardware stores and eco suppliers.

Uses: As a gentle abrasive, to absorb and eliminate odours, to treat stains on fabrics and clear small drain blockages.

Vinegar
(contains acetic acid)
White distilled vinegar is the most useful type, because it won't stain. Some people scent vinegar with a few drops of essential oil. I like to use it neat, or as lemon vinegar (→ recipe on page 36). Don't use vinegar on unglazed pottery or marble and never mix it with products containing sodium hypochlorite.

Uses: To dissolve limescale, cut through grease, remove tarnish from metal, clean dirt from wood, treat odours and stains on fabrics and clear small drain blockages (with baking soda, → page 40).

Plant-based detergent
Modern plant-based eco detergents tend to biodegrade more quickly than conventional petrochemical-based options. Using a concentrated detergent will cut down on packaging, but make sure

you only use small amounts instead of the usual squeeze; diluting can help. Some people prefer a liquid soap – the recommended type is pure castile soap, especially Dr Bronner's (www.drbronner.com). However, soap is less effective in hard water.

Uses: As a degreaser and general cleaner.

Lemon juice
(contains citric acid)
Citric acid is stronger than the acetic acid in vinegar. I wouldn't recommend going out and buying up the world's entire lemon crop for cleaning purposes, but the remains of lemon halves that you've juiced, and the odd cut lemon that's going musty in the fridge, can be rescued for cleaning.

Uses: To dissolve limescale, as an antiseptic, to remove tarnish from copper and rust marks (with salt), as a stain remover and bleaching agent.

Salt
(aka sodium chloride)
Choose fine table salt, which you can get in large packets.

Uses: As a gentle abrasive, to remove tarnish from copper, and rust marks (with lemon juice), as a mildly disinfecting scrub.

Washing soda
(aka sodium carbonate, soda crystals)
A cousin of baking soda; this is a strong alkali and should be reserved for tough jobs. You should definitely wear gloves as it can be an irritant. However, it is a useful alternative to solvents

containing volatile oroganic compounds (VOCs). Do not use on fibreglass or aluminium, or on waxed floors. Dri-Pak (www.dripak.co.uk) soda crystals are available from supermarkets.

Uses: As a strong degreaser that will even cut through wax, to unblock drains.

Olive or other vegetable oil
Refined oil is best for cleaning purposes.

Uses: As a wood polish, wood cleaner (with vinegar), to polish stainless steel.

RECIPE: *Lemon vinegar*
✳ ✳ ✳ ✳ ✳ ✳ ✳ ✳ ✳ ✳ ✳ ✳ ✳ ✳ ✳ ✳

I've used this as a substitute for rinse aid in the dishwasher, and for cleaning windows and kitchen surfaces. Unwaxed lemons are best, otherwise you may end up with sticky wax in your vinegar.

You will need:

> *Several unwaxed lemon halves*
> *White distilled vinegar*
> *1 pan with a lid*

Put the lemons in the pan and add enough vinegar to come at least halfway up. Bring to the boil with the lid on, then turn off the heat and allow to steep for a couple of hours. Strain the lemon vinegar into a glass jar. Keep in a cool, dark place.

As well as these basics, you may want to keep some of the following stain-zappers handy for treating stains on clothes and fabrics (→ page 266).

Glycerine

Also known as glycerol, this is a solvent, and also used in some types of cake icing. It's useful for softening up old and dried stains. Plant-based glycerine is available from Neal's Yard Remedies (www.nealsyardremedies.com).

Soda water

The bubbles can help lift a stain. Soda water is mildly acidic and is especially useful for carpets.

Milk

The problem with milk is that you have to wash out the residue – don't put it on shoes, carpets or anything non-washable. But if you want to go really natural, milk can be used for ink stains, and sour milk for mildew and mould. To make sour milk, add a teaspoon (5ml) of vinegar to half a cup of milk.

Cream of tartar

As well as being used in cooking, cream of tartar can be substituted for lemon juice as a stain remover. The advantage is you can make it into a paste, which can be spritzed with water to keep it damp and working, then brushed off when dry. Cream of tartar (aka potassium bitartrate) is a natural byproduct of wine fermentation.

Cornflour or cornmeal (dry polenta)

Ground maize is highly absorbent, and can be useful for treating stains on carpets and spots on dry-clean-only fabrics. Brush or vacuum off gently as the cornflour takes up the pigment or oil, and put on more if necessary.

Disinfectants from natural sources

Many cleaning materials have some antibacterial effects – such as soap and vinegar – but an array of herbs and plant extracts may also be used as disinfectants. Not all of them are scientifically recognized, but their properties are well known to herbalists and have been passed down through generations. However, these are potent substances, so they also carry caveats.

♥ Tea tree oil
This comes from the Australian tree *Melaleuca alternifolia* and has long been used by Aboriginal peoples. Modern tea tree oil is a powerful extract with antiseptic, antibacterial and antifungal properties, but it can be an irritant and there are concerns that it could, like other disinfectants, increase the resistance of superbugs. The oil degrades in light and air, so keep it in a cool, dark place in a tightly sealed bottle, and don't use oil that is more than six months old.

♥ Lavender oil
Another long-established antibacterial oil, this is also used as a moth and insect repellant and to aid sleep. Like tea tree oil and a number of other plant oils, it is subject to regulation. In cleaning, I use it only as a toilet disinfectant.

♥ *Herbs*

Sage, thyme and rosemary are particularly well known for their antiseptic properties. Sage and thyme extracts should not be used during pregnancy. For more about herbs, their uses and safety advice, consult a herbal such as *Jekka's Complete Herb Book*, by Jekka McVicar.

What to use for different tasks

If you look online, you'll probably find a confusing array of recommendations for what to use for the same job. That's because many of the greener cleaning alternatives can be substituted for one another.

Action	Cleaner
Degreasing	Soap Detergent Vinegar Washing soda
Deodorizing	Baking soda Vinegar (for odours such as urine and fish)
Disinfecting/antibacterial	Soap and detergent Salt Vinegar Lemon juice Some essential oils, such as tea tree and lavender (→ page 38)

Anti-mould/antifungal	Percarbonate ('oxygen')
	Bleach solution
	Tea tree oil
Limescale removal	Cloth and a little water
	Vinegar
	Lemon juice
Abrasive	Baking-soda paste
	Fine table salt

How to use baking soda

Baking soda is the mainstay of my kitchen and bathroom cleaning. It makes a gently abrasive paste that is suitable for many surfaces, including ceramic and stainless steel, but may scratch softer materials such as acrylic, laminate and enamel. If in doubt, try it first in an inconspicuous area.

I don't actually bother mixing a paste. Instead, either shake a little baking soda over the offending glued-on gunge and rub at it with a damp cloth, or else wrap a damp cloth over your forefinger and dip this into the baking soda – more economical for small marks. For extra grease-shifting action, mix in a drop or two of detergent or soap. When the grime is really stuck hard, I shake on the baking soda, sprinkle over some water and leave overnight – the gunk often just lifts off in the morning.

Baking soda can leave a milky residue, so make sure you've wiped it off well with a wet cloth. For really shiny surfaces, spray on a little vinegar afterwards. This reacts with any remaining baking soda to make a fizz, producing water and carbon dioxide, and helping to cut through grease.

KITCHEN SURFACES

For wiping down tables and worktops after meals a microfibre cloth is often enough. A dry cloth works better for crumbs, so they don't all clog together.

Stainless steel

Try water and a microfibre cloth first. Crusty deposits will often come off if you dampen them and leave for a while, or cover with a moistened cloth. Baking soda should be fine on most satin-effect stainless steel, but is not so good for shiny stainless. Always rub satin stainless steel in the same direction as the grain, and dry thoroughly after cleaning to help prevent patchy watermarks.

Wipe off finger marks quickly, because the acids can corrode the surface. You should keep lemon juice and salt well clear of steel, because they can rust it. If you do get small rust marks, however, I've found you can whittle them away with a scrub of a little lemon juice and salt – but, remember to clean off thoroughly.

Cleaner's tip:

To get a soft sheen on satin finishes, use a little oil – mineral oil (such as baby oil) is usually recommended but I've found that refined vegetable oil works fine. Avoid olive oils and unrefined oils because the compounds in them may corrode the metal. Put a tiny bit of oil on a soft cloth and work all over the surface, wiping off any excess. This can help protect against finger marks, but next time you wipe with a microfibre cloth, some oil will be removed.

Ceramic hobs

We inherited a ceramic hob with our house, and I clean it with a damp microfibre cloth after pretty much every use. A little baking soda deals with glued-on patches, and to remove shiny, opalescent mineral marks – or at least reduce them – squeeze over lemon juice and leave for a few hours or overnight.

Sugar is the real enemy of ceramic – if it melts and then cools, it fuses to the glass. If you have a jam overflow or similar sugar accident, remove the pan at once, turn off the heat and try to scrape off as much as possible with a hob scraper or thin metal fish slice before it cools. If necessary, warm the hob up again. Don't be tempted to chip away any really hard patches, because you'll also remove flakes of the ceramic surface. Instead, you could try several applications of baking soda, moistened and left overnight.

Sinks

Use a paste of baking soda for stains and deposits on stainless steel and ceramic sinks. Be more careful with Corian, although the matt surface especially should take the gentle abrasion of baking soda. Enamel and acrylic surfaces can be dulled by scratches, and made harder to clean, so stick to a little detergent, and try vinegar or lemon juice on stubborn stains.

Cleaner's tip:

If you have some stained laundry that you need to treat with percarbonate bleach, soak the items in the sink and you'll get rid of stains there at the same time.

Worktops

Be careful what you put on worktops. Cast iron and copper pans can leave marks, especially if damp. Invest in trivets or mats to protect surfaces from hot pans – for emergency protection use a folded tea towel. Wipe up spills as soon as possible and keep surfaces dry – especially around edges where mould can attack the sealant.

Laminates

We have an ancient wood-print laminate worktop, which stains very easily. I once made the mistake of trying some baking soda on it, but all I succeeded in doing was removing more of the pattern. Instead, I now use lemon juice, which is excellent for getting rid of the black marks left by cast-iron pans when I forget to put them on a mat.

Wood

It's especially important to keep wood dry. It should be re-oiled every three months, or when the water no longer stands up in beads around the sink. For more advice on oiling worktops see www.diydoctor.org.uk. Osmo TopOil (www.osmouk.com), available from green construction stores and flooring suppliers, is a natural wood protector. Avoid anything abrasive, including baking soda.

Granite

Granite may be very hard but the polish that makes its surface gleam is more delicate. Clean with a little detergent and a soft cloth dampened in warm water, then buff dry with a soft cloth or old towel. You could try a razor blade or ceramic hob scraper for glued-on gunk. Avoid abrasives – even microfibre cloths are lightly abrasive so to be on the safe side don't use these – and don't leave lemon juice or vinegar on the surface for any length of time.

Cleaner's tip:

If your washing-up drainer is getting caked with limescale, rub half a lemon over it and leave – it'll come up all shiny. You can also use an old lemon as a pan scourer to remove white lime deposits.

Getting rid of grease

What do you do about serious grease, of the kind that gets deposited on a cooker hood? Natural citrus solvents degrade quickly in the environment, but they produce strong fumes, containing volatile organic compounds (VOCs), that give me a headache and may cause an allergic reaction if you are sensitive. Instead, I use baking soda mixed with a little detergent.

To make a microwave easier to clean, first heat a bowl of water in it, with either a few lemon slices or a teaspoon or two of baking soda. The steam will help loosen the debris, and the lemon or baking soda will remove smells.

BATHROOMS

Bathrooms may not produce the grease associated with cooking areas, but they present their own problems, which can usually be tackled with the same cleaning materials that you use in the kitchen.

Limescale

Light droplet marks will rub off with a just-damp cloth, and others can be removed with a little baking soda. For stubborn areas, squeeze on lemon juice or rub with half a lemon, leave for a short while, then wipe clean. A clogged shower head can be soaked in vinegar overnight. (For easy shower cleaning, → page 23.)

Chrome taps

Use a microfibre cloth or baking soda to clean, then buff with a soft cloth, such as an old towel.

Scum rings

Ceramic and resin baths can be cleaned with baking soda, but go easy on enamel (see notes about enamel sinks, → page 42). For greasy marks from bath oils, mix in a little detergent if necessary.

The toilet

Pour half a cup of vinegar in the pan for general cleaning, and use a spray to get under the rim. Leave for a couple of hours, then clean with a brush. (For tough stains, → page 23, and for a disinfecting lavender wipe, → page 24.)

The mould problem

Black mould thrives in damp conditions. There are huge numbers of fungal spores in the air, but you can outwit a lot of mould by keeping down condensation. After showers or baths, wipe down the shower cubicle and anywhere the wall meets the shower or bath. To ventilate the room, turn off the heating and open a window for a 10-minute blast.

If you do get mould, clean it off as soon as you see it – before it starts eating into the silicone sealant. A vinegar wipe seems to help, or mix up a solution of percarbonate bleach, or a teaspoon of tea tree oil in 250ml/½ pint/9fl oz of water. You can work on stubborn and tough-to-reach areas with an old toothbrush and a paste of vinegar and fine salt.

DUST

A gram of household dust contains, on average, something like five million fungal spores, seven million bacteria, 8,000 algae and 12 mites, and that's before you get to the chemicals, fluff and skin cells. Lightly dampen your dusting cloth so it picks up the particles.

Unprotected mattresses and pillows can hold frighteningly large numbers of dust mite skins and faeces after a few years. Wash pillows at 60°C or above once a year or so. You could also vacuum your mattress and cover it with a protector – high-thread-count organic cotton can be an effective barrier. Zap adult dust mites in cuddly toys by putting the toys in the freezer for a day.

If you or your family suffer with asthma or allergies, see www.asthma.org.uk and www.allergyuk.org for advice.

RECIPE: *Window cleaner*

✳ ✳ ✳ ✳ ✳ ✳ ✳ ✳ ✳ ✳ ✳ ✳ ✳ ✳ ✳

You will need:

> *500ml/1 pint/18fl oz water*
> *3 tablespoons vinegar*
> *Small squeeze of detergent*
> *1 microfibre or similar cloth*
> *1 or more lint-free drying cloths*
> > *(although old tea towels or T-shirts will do)*

Mix the water and vinegar, then add the detergent. Wipe enough on the windows so it doesn't dry immediately. Go round the edge of the pane first, getting into the corners.

Dry off the windows thoroughly to prevent streaking, and don't use a cloth that has previously been in contact with oils.

Mirrors are usually less dirty than windows, so a damp microfibre cloth is often enough – but make sure to buff them dry to help prevent streaking.

Cleaner's tip:

In the past, newspaper inks contained hydrocarbon solvents such as kerosene, which boosted their buffing power. Most are now soy-based and so polishing windows with scrunched-up newspaper is not as effective as it used to be.

FURNISHINGS

Wood

Most of the time wood simply needs a dust, or an occasional wipe with a damp cloth. Only polish when really necessary. Never use silicone products – they leave a residue that goes milky if you put a wax or oil-based polish on top and are almost impossible to get off.

You can mix a wood cleaner and light polish by combining equal parts of oil – such as olive oil – and vinegar. Wipe on with one cloth, and buff off with another. This will strip dirt and grime but can also affect some wax surfaces, so be careful where you use it. Don't put this mix, or other oils, on limed wood, as it will remove the matt chalkiness.

Varnished wood doesn't need a wood polish, but if you have waxed furniture, nourish it about once a year to protect against dryness and cover small scratches or wormholes. Use a beeswax-based polish; there are quite a few on the market, but check for other ingredients, such as solvents.

Use mats to protect wood from heat and watermarks. If you do get marks, you could try rubbing with a little toothpaste, which is mildly abrasive, then covering any lightened patches with shoe polish and finishing with wood polish. Wood doesn't react well to being too near a radiator, or in a damp atmosphere.

Fabric upholstery

Vacuum or brush out dust and debris regularly, and beat cushions (preferably outdoors). If you have removable covers, wash them all at the same time to reduce the risk of variable fading. Treat any stains first – but test the treatment on an inconspicuous area (→ page 264).

With marks on non-removable upholstery, first decide if it's worth attempting to remove them yourself or whether it would be better to trust the job to a professional cleaner. If you decide to go ahead, check any labels you can find for cleaning instructions. For spot-cleaning treatments for specific stains, → pages 266–71. To clean with detergent, make a froth with about half and half detergent and water whisked together in a bowl. Spread this on the mark with a cloth or soft brush. Then rinse and blot with a clean damp cloth and dry with a towel, pressing into the fabric.

Leather

Dust leather, and occasionally wipe over with a damp (but not wet) cloth. Milk can be used to remove some marks, such as ink, but clean well afterwards. For other stains, try rubbing with a drop or two of glycerine, or sprinkling with cornflour (→ page 37). For a deeper cleaner, mix 100ml/3½fl oz of white vinegar with a teaspoon of olive oil.

FLOORS

Carpet and rug care

Vacuuming helps to prolong the look and life of carpets, removing the grease and grit that gather around the base of the tufts, as well as chemical residues. Go over the same patch several times for a thorough clean. In between, try using a carpet sweeper to remove surface debris (→ page 25).

With a loop-pile rug, or a shaggy rug that is hard to vacuum, turn it face down, preferably on a hard floor. Beat the back, then sweep up the dust and debris that comes out. In dry weather, use the old-fashioned method – hang it over the washing line and beat it. Deodorize rugs and carpets by sprinkling them with baking soda, leaving for a few hours and then vacuuming off.

Mop up spills quickly by treading an old towel on to any liquid. A useful general method is to pour over soda water – the fizzing will often help to bring the stain to the surface – and blot again, or sprinkle the area with cornmeal. This is generally better than salt, which can leave a residue. Allow to dry, then vacuum up and treat any remaining stain. You can also try spot-treating stains (→ pages 264–71).

Detergent is difficult to remove fully from carpet fibres. If you do need to use it, follow the method for fabric upholstery on page 49. You can find environmentally aware professional cleaners through www.ecocarpetcare.co.uk.

❋ *Cleaner's tip:*
❋
❋ *Ask house guests to leave their shoes at the door. This will reduce the*
❋ *amount of cleaning you have to do, cut down the bugs and chemicals*
❋ *that might be trodden in from outside, and keep floors looking good*
❋ *for longer. I'm thinking of investing in some organic cotton waffle*
❋ *slippers for visitors who don't want to go barefoot, or socked.*

Natural floor coverings

Coir, jute, seagrass and sisal are, in fact, less hard-wearing than wool, and they react badly to getting wet. Vacuum regularly, and blot spills as soon as they happen.

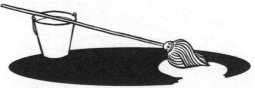

Vinyl, lino and tiles

These are generally easy to sweep and mop. The ancient vinyl flooring in our kitchen is lumpy and scratched, and seems to act like a dirt magnet. Because it's a tough customer, I like to use a two-stage clean: first, I mop with a solution of washing soda (half a cup to 500ml/1 pint/18fl oz of water), then I follow up with a linseed oil liquid soap. You could use a little washing-up detergent instead, but I really like the smell of the linseed. (Don't use washing soda on waxed floors, because it will peel the wax; on most floors you will probably find you don't need it.)

Wood

Wooden floors, whether varnished or waxed, can easily be scratched by dust. Try to sweep or vacuum in line with the wood grain, and use a dustpan and brush to get into inaccessible corners.

If a floor is not too dirty, clean it with a cloth or mop dipped in water and wrung out until it's almost dry. An old T-shirt is good for this.

For muckier floors, add a squeeze of washing-up liquid, or linseed, or other wood soap. On waxed floors, any water droplets will leave cloudy spots, so buff dry with a dusting cloth on a broom to help avoid this. Treat laminate floors as for varnished wood.

Cleaner's tip:

For toddler and pet accidents on hard floors, wipe up the urine, spray with a little vinegar and dry off. This will deodorize and disinfect.

METALS

- ♥ Lacquered brass and copper should just need wiping, or cleaning with a little washing-up liquid in water for stubborn grime.
- ♥ Acid-plus-salt is an effective tarnish remover for brass, bronze, copper and aluminium. Either put some salt on an old lemon half, or mix a paste of fine table salt with vinegar, and rub on. Clean off thoroughly and buff to shine.
- ♥ A soak in a solution of half-and-half water and white vinegar in a glass or ceramic bowl will brighten up small brass, bronze and copper objects. Leave for a few hours, or overnight, then rinse off with warm water and rub dry. You could also use ketchup or Worcestershire sauce – their acid content makes them effective metal cleaners.
- ♥ Silver can be tricky. It will tarnish in contact with salt, acid and sulphur – so boiled eggs and rubber gloves aren't silver-friendly. It doesn't like stainless steel or dishwashers either, as I discovered when we mistakenly put a silver-plated spoon in the cutlery basket. Frequent use and hand-washing with mild detergent will keep silverware looking good.
- ♥ I've successfully used a mix of 1 teaspoon baking soda and 1 teaspoon flour, with a damp cloth, to clean tarnish off highly polished silver, but some modern silver plate is so thin you could be in danger of polishing through it. (Don't use baking soda on aluminium, because it could corrode.)
- ♥ Discoloration can be cleaned off stainless steel knives with baking soda, but if you have carbon steel knives this won't do them any good – they need to be scrubbed with a scouring pad,

dried well and then lightly oiled. Cooking knives benefit from regular sharpening with a steel or whetstone – you could check online videos if you're not sure how to do it. Very blunt knives will need professional regrinding; ask your local cookware shop or butcher for recommendations.

PEST CONTROL

It's good practice not to attract vermin in the first place, so store food in air-tight containers or mouse-proof cupboards, and keep food on tables covered against flies. If you suspect small visitors, make it a policy to wipe and sweep up all crumbs and food debris, and dispose of them in a bin with a tight-fitting lid, before you go to bed. Use a lidded caddy or similar covered container for kitchen scraps and take it out to your compost heap frequently. Alternatively, a bokashi bin ferments kitchen waste indoors (→ page 179 for details).

For ants and mice, the first thing to do is to search out any nesting spots, and block up holes they could come through, although this is not always easy in an older terraced property where mice, for example, can migrate between loft spaces.

You can buy humane mousetraps (bait them with peanut butter) but they should be checked every few hours so trapped mice don't starve. Then you need to decide where to release the mice – far from home, they will probably meet their end pretty quickly in the outside world. PETA (People for the Ethical Treatment of Animals) has commended the RADAR trap, which kills mice quickly and humanely with carbon dioxide (see www.uk.rentokil.com).

Mint is a deterrent for flies, ants, fleas and mice. Mix a teaspoon of peppermint oil with 400ml/¾ pint/15fl oz of water and spray round skirting, kitchen cabinet bases, door openings and other places where evidence has been found. You could also scatter ground cloves where ants are visiting.

Unless you have a serious problem, beware of using pesticides, even if they are from a natural source, because they can kill beneficial insects as well as the ones causing you trouble.

GREENER CAR-CLEANING

We do have a car, which we bought a while before Ethan was born, although we try to keep its use strictly to trips that would be hard to do another way. We're not very good about cleaning the car – mostly the rain does it for us – but when we do, we simply use a squeeze of plant-based washing-up liquid in a bucket of warm water. Try to use greywater (→ page 240) from a bath, shower or paddling pool if you can, and don't add too much detergent or it'll take ages to rinse off the foam.

To get rid of bugs and bird poo on the windscreen, scatter a little baking soda on the damp glass and rub off (don't use this on the paintwork). I find an old washing-up brush is very handy for hard-to-get-into areas, such as around the window seals and wheel trims.

Rinse well and make sure any grit is washed off before you start rubbing dry with a soft cloth – you don't want to grind it into the paint surface. Finally, polish with a chamois, or faux chamois, leather.

How to practise green home hygiene

Do you really need all those synthetic disinfectants? Aim to reduce the chemical load in your house by moving to eco cleaners and tried-and-tested home remedies.

Dispose of any hazardous chemicals safely, so they don't leach into the water system.

Use simple kitchen chemicals and minerals so that you know exactly what substances are coating your worktops and furnishings.

Stock up on baking soda, white vinegar and a vegetable oil for cleaning – and keep those old or squeezed lemon halves.

Make sure you have the tools you need – from cloths and rags to brushes and a dustpan.

You'll often need less than you think you do – a little water may well be enough, and a drop of concentrated detergent goes a long way.

Treat strong natural ingredients, such as essential oils, with respect.

Try out the easy eco tips at the start of this chapter – and add more that you've found really work.

3

ENERGY ETIQUETTE

These days, as well as overseeing the housekeeping budget, home management involves looking after your household's carbon and water usage. Our homes produce more than a quarter of the UK's carbon

emissions – that's more than our cars. Building more carbon-neutral homes, and retrofitting older buildings (adding energy-saving measures, such as insulation and greener heating), will play a part in reducing the 'carbon houseprint'. But, in many cases, there's not a great deal that can be done to make existing houses substantially more energy-efficient – at least, not without huge disruption, cost and uproar from individuals and conservation groups.

Just think about Bath, where I live, with its sweeping Georgian crescents and elegant terraces. Who would want those walls clad (either inside or outside) with enough insulation to make a real difference? This is one of the issues identified by the Centre for Alternative Technology in *Zero Carbon Britain* (www.zerocarbonbritain.com). Basically, it means it's over to us concerned citizens to keep down the energy use in our own homes, and insulate where we can.

In this chapter I'm assuming that major changes, such as installing solar energy panels, aren't exactly everyday household jobs for you, so the emphasis is more on what you can do easily, with just a trip to a hardware shop or a fairly quick online order.

How much can you cut?

By taking energy-saving steps you could cut your bills by as much as a quarter, and save around 1.5 tonnes of carbon dioxide a year. See what you could do by completing the home energy check at www.energysavingtrust.org.uk.

To estimate your carbon footprint – the total amount of carbon dioxide you or your household are responsible for producing each year – log on to an interactive calculator such as Act On $CO2$ at www.direct.gov.uk, the more detailed www.resurgence.org/carboncalculator (you will need a year's gas and electricity bills, car mileage and other details) or www.cat.org.uk/carbongym, which is the Centre for Alternative Technology's version.

Home Information Packs (HIPs)

If you're selling a house or flat, you need to provide a Home Information Pack, which includes an Energy Performance Certificate (EPC) or energy assessment. This rates the property's efficiency from A to G (A is the best) and gives the buyer advice on making energy savings. You can put this together yourself, or ask the estate agent or your solicitor to arrange it – but it needs to be sorted out before the property goes on the market.

The assessment covers such things as the heating system, double-glazing and insulation. See www.homeinformationpacks. gov.uk for more details and www.epcregister.com to find an accredited assessor.

HEATING

Household heating is the really big one, accounting for about two-thirds of energy bills. How much you use is influenced by the kind of home you live in – urban terraces and small modern houses tend to be more energy-efficient than rambling old detached properties – but also by energy spending patterns. While the energy we use for cooking is going down, the figure for heating is on the rise – partly because of central heating, and partly because we've become used to indulging ourselves with T-shirt temperatures in the middle of winter.

Central heating strategies

♥ Lower your thermostat by 1°C – which can cut 10 per cent off your annual energy bill. I've been trying to lower by about a degree a year, from 20°C to around 17°C. A temperature of 18°C to 21°C is recommended for older people, but babies don't need a sauna – in fact, 16°C to 20°C is the current advice.

♥ Get to know how your timer and thermostat work – dig out those instructions.

♥ Set the timer so your heating comes on about half an hour before you get up or come home, and goes off about half an hour before you go out or before bedtime (a declining temperature can help your body prepare for sleep).

♥ If you need the heating on all day, make sure you're not keeping water hot for all that time, too. With a combined heat-and-water timer, set a shorter time for everything to be on and use the override button when you want extra heating. You could also use the water override to switch the water heating off in the evening once you've finished with showers and washing-up.

- ♥ The main thermostat switches off all the heating when the temperature has reached the preset figure. Keep warm or cold draughts away from the thermostat, and don't turn off nearby radiators or it won't get an accurate picture of your house temperature.
- ♥ Invest in some thermostatic radiator valves (TRVs), which allow you to control the temperature in individual rooms. You can get them for less than £10 each, although you may need to factor in the cost of a central heating engineer. The valves switch the radiator off when the room has reached the temperature level on the dial (usually 1 to 5).
- ♥ Turn radiators off or down in rooms that are not being used, but make sure you close the door, so heat isn't drawn into that room from the rest of the house.

Keeping heat in

Insulation, insulation, insulation – that's the key phrase for the energy-conscious householder. It's the number-one way for most people to cut household carbon emissions.

Here are some lower-cost options, from zero to tens of pounds (OK, up to hundreds if you go for *really* expensive curtains).

Keep doors closed
If you have a lobby, closing the door will help create a buffer zone to retain heat – especially if you haven't got around to draught-proofing an ill-fitting front or back door. Inside the house,

keeping doors closed will retain heat where you want it and reduce draughts.

Don't open windows with the radiator on

If you need to air a room, switch off the heating, throw open the windows, shut the door and leave it for a few minutes. On a safety note, if you're using a portable gas or paraffin heater, do make sure there's enough ventilation in the room.

Fix draught-excluders to doors, letterboxes and windows

About 30 per cent of the heat lost from your home can be due to gaps and draughts. Go to your local DIY or hardware shop for everything from O-tubes for doorframes to brushes for letterboxes and keyhole covers. I rely on the *Reader's Digest Complete DIY Manual* for advice, but for sash windows you may want to get a professional to put in a fine brush strip. Check on a cold, windy day that the draught excluder forms a tight seal.

Install reflective radiator panels

These are particularly helpful on uninsulated external walls, through which 25 per cent of the heat lost from your home could be escaping. The ones with fins, from a specialist such as www.ecofirst.net, are most effective (from £10 per standard radiator), but you can also find plastic foil sheets in DIY shops – or make your own. Cut a sheet of cardboard slightly smaller than the radiator and cover with foil (extra-wide will make your job easier), with the shiny side out. Double-sided tape will fix it behind the radiator.

Block up unused chimneys

Get a chimney balloon (see www.chimney-balloon.co.uk, from under £20) or use scrunched-up newspaper so that air can still circulate for ventilation.

Hang heavy curtains or install insulated shutters

Opt for interlined floor-length curtains (they have a fleecy layer between the outer fabric and lining, but are expensive) or choose a thermal-reflective lining. For second-hand, try www.thecurtainexchange.com. Don't draw them over radiators – use shorter curtains instead, or, if there's room, tuck the curtain in behind the radiator.

Energy budgeter's tip:

When we stripped back to bare floorboards, we found a draughty gap between the floor and skirting board. Measure up and buy quadrant beading from a hardware shop, leave it in the room to acclimatize (so it won't shrink once you've fitted it), then paint it and nail to the skirting board (not floor). You'll need a mitre box to cut the corners.

MAKE: *Caterpillar draught excluder*

✳ ✳ ✳ ✳ ✳ ✳ ✳ ✳ ✳ ✳ ✳ ✳ ✳ ✳ ✳

This kind of 'sausage' draught excluder is especially useful when you've taken up carpet and are left with a big gap. Customize it with a cute caterpillar face for children, or make a striped version with several pieces of fabric – remember to allow 3cm/1in on each for the seams. For sewing basics → Chapter 11.

You will need:

> *1 piece of medium to heavyweight fabric*
> *Felt-tipped pen or sewing marker*
> *Tape measure*
> *Ruler*
> *Sharp scissors*
> *Pins*
> *Needle and sewing thread*
> *Sewing machine*
> *1 leg of an old pair of tights, mended so there are no holes (optional)*
> *Rice or dried beans to fill (about 3kg/6½lb)*
> *Buttons, wool or other decoration (optional)*

1. Measure the width of the door space, remembering the caterpillar should extend beyond the door itself. Flatten out your fabric, wrong side up, and line up your tape measure along its grain. Using your marker or pen, mark out the width you've measured plus 3cm/1in for seam allowances (so for a width of 80cm/31½in you want 83cm/32½in). Draw a line with the ruler.

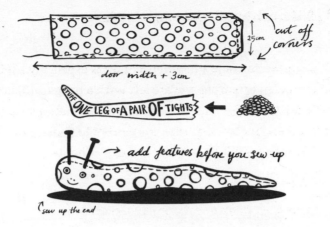

25cm ↕ cut off corners

← door width + 3cm →

STUFF ONE LEG OF A PAIR OF TIGHTS ←

→ add features before you sew up

sew up the end

2. At right-angles to this, measure lines of 25cm/10in at both ends, then another line joining them (which in this example should also be 83cm/32½in, if you've got your angles right). Cut out the fabric rectangle.

3. Fold the fabric in half lengthways, wrong side outermost, and pin and tack round three edges, leaving the final short edge open. Machine-sew a seam along these three sides, 1.5cm/½in in from the edge. Snip a triangle off the sewn corner, then press the seam (→ page 318). Turn your caterpillar the right way out, using a knitting needle or pencil to push out the corners.

4. You can either fill your draught excluder directly, or put the filling in the leg of a pair of tights, so it's easier to remove for washing. If you are going to sew on a caterpillar face, do this before filling – but check it will look right when filled out. Model it on a children's book, such as *The Very Hungry Caterpillar*.

5. Finally, fold in the open end and sew closed by hand with over-and-over stitch (→ page 311).

Greener insulation materials

Whatever insulating option you can afford is definitely better than nothing. Putting in loft insulation can cut 20 per cent off your fuel bills. Insulation will also make your house or flat (especially a top-floor apartment) more comfortable by reducing temperature fluctuations. If you can, opt for recycled materials such as cellulose, renewables such as wool, or, if those aren't possible, a plentiful naturally occurring source, such as rockwool.

Cavity wall, floor and loft insulation can cost several hundred pounds, so find out about grants through your local authority and the Energy Saving Trust postcode grant-finder (www.energysavingtrust.org.uk). When insulating a loft, build a raised platform over the top for storage, well above the level of the insulation material so it doesn't become compacted. If you're living in rented accommodation, use the possibility of grant finance to help persuade your landlord that the work is worth doing.

Also see the Centre for Alternative Technology tipsheet, at www.cat.org.uk/catpubs (pay-and-download area), and Construction Resources (www.constructionresources.com).

Material	Good because. . .	The disadvantage is. . .
Cellulose	it's made from recycled newspaper and can be blown in, so is great for awkward places and getting round pipes. There's also a pourable version (Warmcel) for	loose cellulose doesn't perform well in damp areas. Spraying should be done by a professional and must fill the whole space (so you could lose the loft area for storage).

	DIY use, and one with jute that comes in flexible planks. Cellulose is reasonably priced.	
Sheep's wool	it uses surplus fleeces and takes less energy than other insulation materials to produce. Sheep's wool is becoming more widely available – you can get Thermafleece (www.secondnatureuk.com) from some B&Q stores.	it's quite expensive, and potentially harmful chemicals may have been used to treat it for pest and fire resistance. (Thermafleece contains no permethrin or pyrethroids.)
Flax	it's a renewable resource and absorbs moisture well, helping to protect against mould.	it can be expensive and is not so widely available.
Cork	it's renewable, and could support cork farmers, who have lost trade because of the move to plastic and screw-top wine bottles. Ideal for floors and lining walls internally.	it's mainly used in sheets, although granular cork is available.
Rockwool	it can be used as an alternative to foam for cavity walls, and is often made from byproducts and recycled material.	it's irritating to handle (the installer will need to wear protective gloves and mask), and it takes a lot of energy to manufacture.

Personal insulation

Otherwise known as jumpers. Invest in thick socks and slippers so your feet don't chill on cold floors, and if you sit down for a lot of the day (at a computer, for instance), get up and move around regularly. Maybe go out for a walk or do the shopping to boost circulation, and you'll feel the difference when you get back.

HOT WATER

This is the second largest user of household energy. Here are some ideas for saving on water heating.

- ♥ *Lag your hot water tank* or you could be wasting three-quarters of the energy used to heat your water. The lagging needs to be at least 75mm/3in thick. (Modern tanks have efficient foam jackets already.)
- ♥ *Check your hot water tank has a thermostat* and set it to no more than 60°C, or the water will be unnecessarily hot.
- ♥ *Lag your hot water pipes,* especially if you notice it takes a while for your water to run through hot. Lagging pipes between the boiler and hot water tank will bring most benefit, as well as those under ground floors and in lofts.
- ♥ *Fix leaking hot-water taps* because they could be dripping away half a bath's worth in a day (→ page 235).

MONITORING YOUR ENERGY

My plan to get my boyfriend Clive involved in energy-saving was to make it competitive. I bought us an Electrisave, an energy monitor that you attach to the cable from your meter. It not only displays how much electricity is being used but converts that into the cost both in hard cash and carbon dioxide. Once it's fitted, you can have fun tracking down what's really eating up the pounds and raising the global temperature.

It took me less than half an hour to install and programme it, although if your cabling is more complex, you may need an electrician. The trickiest bit was finding the right size of screwdriver. In the end, I used a commemorative teaspoon from my old school – the crest fitted perfectly.

These kinds of monitors cost around £50, but you can also hire them (see www.electricity-monitor.com), buy with friends and family, or shine a torch on your electricity meter and see the difference as you try switching things on and off. (Well, it could help to pass a rainy Sunday . . .)

'Everyone out, everything off' is our household mantra (most of the time, anyway). This is the simplest approach – when you're leaving a room for more than a few minutes, turn everything off that uses energy, including your computer, the TV, the radio, the radiator. Switch off the lights even if you're going out for just a few minutes. After a while it'll become routine – like brushing your teeth or remembering to take your door keys.

Guzzler or vampire?

Guzzlers:

Electric showers, kettles, electric cookers, immersion heaters, room heaters (bar, fan and oil-filled all use around the same), washing machines, dishwashers, toasters and irons.

These will send your energy monitor or electricity meter whirring. An average dishwasher, toaster and iron all use electricity at a rate of about 1 kilowatt per hour, while heaters and kettles use twice this. Electric showers gorge themselves on 8 kilowatts an hour.

Energy-efficient appliances will help. You can get energy-saving kettles – they boil quickly, keep the water hot and make sure you heat only the amount you need – from online eco stores, such as www.ethicalsuperstore.com. Use washing machines and dishwashers sparingly, but make toast in the toaster – it's more efficient than using the grill.

Vampires:

Extractor fans, computers, conventional lightbulbs, TVs, DVDs and hi-fis, fridges, chargers and answering machines.

These may use 100 watts an hour or less, but it all adds up. Sometimes these machines have a useful purpose – fridges, for instance – but others take without giving much back. Most of us know about not leaving the TV or DVD on standby, but what about cordless phones, iPod chargers, electric clocks and digital boxes? Turn these off when they're not in use (remember the mantra). It can be a pain waiting for your cable TV to reboot, but you could always make yourself a quick cuppa. An energy monitor, or detective work, will help you track down what's still switched on.

COOLER REFRIGERATION

Refrigeration used to be a luxury, and in a way it still is. Today UK households spend around £1.2 billion a year on cooling and freezing food, which is almost as much as the electricity consumed by all office buildings.

To help your fridge or freezer work at its best, make sure you site it carefully. Keep it away from ovens or dishwashers that could warm it up, and positioning it under a glass roof where the sun blazes through isn't a great idea, either. See that there's a good airflow above and behind, and keep the condenser coils – the metal spaghetti at the back – free of dust and gunge, because this can reduce efficiency by nearly a third.

Fridges can be kept safely at 4–5°C, while the recommended temperature for freezers is –15 to –18°C. If either is getting caked with ice, defrosting will help regain efficiency.

Energy manager's tip:

When you need to defrost a meal, take it out of the freezer the night before and put it in the fridge. It'll keep the fridge cooled and defrost slowly. Heating dishes up from frozen uses more energy.

BUYING NEW APPLIANCES

Shiny appliances have become desirable status symbols rather than simply functional objects. Before you buy, it's worth asking yourself (and co-buyee, if you have one) a few searching questions.

☞ Do you want a new one of these because you really need it (because the old one broke down and can't be fixed, or you've moved house), or because you've seen a gorgeous new model you fancy?

⌁ Will lower carbon emissions from the new appliance cover the energy cost of making it and disposing of the old one? (It quite possibly will. Replacing an old, inefficient fridge could save £45 a year in electricity bills.)

⌁ Do we really need a TV/fridge/cooker that big?

⌁ Does the new one have an impressive energy CV, with an EU A-rating and maybe even an Energy Saving Trust badge, and does it compare well with similar products on www.sust-it.net?

⌁ What will you do with the old one (→ page 210.)?

Making your choice

In all cases, it's worth going for the best quality you can afford. This doesn't necessarily mean opting for the most expensive, however. Often, bigger price tags are for more functions, larger capacity and different finishes. If you're on a limited budget, it can be worth choosing a more modest model from a better manufacturer.

Fridges and freezers

Bigger is not better – fuller is better. Don't be tempted to buy a huge fridge or freezer if it will always be nearly empty. These appliances work best when three-quarters full.

Fridges and freezers sold as frost free can consume up to 30 per cent more electricity – so it might be worth using some of your own energy instead and choosing one that you defrost yourself. Make sure it relies on hydrocarbons (HCs) for cooling, not polluting HFCs (hydrofluorocarbons).

Televisions

The largest plasma TV screens can guzzle as much energy in 10 hours as a fridge uses in a whole year. The best options – for clarity, eyes and energy use – are LCD screens, although they take more energy than old-style cathode ray tubes to produce.

By 2011, when the analogue signal is switched off, we'll all need a digital TV receiver. This could be through a satellite or cable provider, a Freeview set-top box or an integrated digital television (IDTV). IDTV means you won't be tempted to leave the set-top box on, but if your telly still has plenty of life in it, a Freeview box could be a better option than adding to the jettisoned-TV mountain.

Ovens and hobs

Gas hobs are more carbon-efficient than electric hobs, except for the induction type. But if you're routinely using all five rings on a range, you need to think about streamlining your cooking.

Fan-assisted ovens use less power than conventional ones, and distribute heat more evenly. A double oven that offers one smaller option can be useful if you bake cakes or often cook small amounts.

Appliance buyer's tip:

Look for good reviews in Which? *(www.which.co.uk) or* Ethical Consumer *(www.ethicalconsumer.org). A top energy performance is important, but the energy label doesn't tell you anything about the appliance's reliability, ease of use, effectiveness or whether it's going to cost a huge amount to get repaired.*

Water heaters and boilers

Immersion heaters are the most expensive to run – especially if you don't have a timer. Combi boilers, which heat water on demand alongside central heating, used to be restricted to flats, but they can now cope with larger households and could be worth investigating if you don't use a lot of hot water. Condensing boilers, which are now compulsory except where they would be impossible to fit, reclaim heat that would otherwise be lost through the flue (see the www.boilers.org.uk site).

You could also think about a combined heat and power (CHP) boiler – common in Scandinavia – which uses some of the heat to generate electricity. Envocare, an information website run by a group of environmentally concerned individuals (www.envocare. co.uk/combined_heat_and_power.htm), has a helpful introduction to these boilers.

If your boiler is less than 10 years old, it's probably better simply to make sure the thermostat and timer are up to date and working properly.

Washing machines

Extra-large drums can be a boon, saving on energy and water, but only if they're run fully loaded.

Check that there is a proper 30°C cotton cycle, to give your clothes a really good wash at low temperatures. Don't be too concerned about whether the machine is hot or cold fill. Manufacturers claim cold fill is more efficient for low-temperature washes and bio powders, and that it's more economical to heat the water in the machine than to use the inefficient hot-water systems in most UK homes. Even with hot fill, little hot water will actually reach the machine from your tank.

When plumbing in a new washing machine, or moving into a new home, make sure the waste water pipe is connected to the sewerage system, not the surface water drainage system that the guttering flows into, otherwise your washing machine water could be flowing untreated into rivers. See www.whitegoodshelp.co.uk for helpful articles.

Some potentially exciting innovations, such as steam washing machines, are becoming available at the top end of the price range. (For how to get the most from your washing machine, → page 248.)

BATTERIES AND RECHARGING

Why do we still buy disposable batteries? They create hazardous waste and eat up money. Some children's toys even come with tiny, unreplaceable batteries that mean the entertainment loses its appeal when they run out.

The problem is that the AA battery in particular has become ubiquitous, found in so many gadgets that it can be hard to keep up with making sure they're all in working order (the Centre for Alternative Technology shop sells devices that revive them).

Clive and I are starting to convert to nickel metal hydride (NiMH) rechargeable batteries (about £3 each for up to 1,000 charges), which are better for most purposes than nickel cadmium ones, and don't contain poisonous cadmium. We've also invested in a solar-powered charger (from £12): just a few hours of sunshine gets the batteries going again. When it's cloudy, you can always use a mains charger instead.

Energy manager's tip:
Don't leave digital cameras, mobile phones or electric toothbrushes charging on the mains overnight. Plug them in when you're at home and switch off the chargers as soon as they've done their job. For battery tips see www.greenbatteries.com.

Battery alternatives

Wind-up, solar and USB-driven radios, torches and emergency mobile-phone chargers are increasingly available, as are iPod chargers and hand-driven media players, such as Trevor Baylis's Eco. You'll find them in eco stores and outdoor shops. To buy online, try www.windup-products.com.

LIGHTING

Lighting accounts for about 10 per cent of the energy we consume in our homes, but the amount we use will soon be much less, since the government plans to phase out high-energy incandescent bulbs by 2011. The use of low-energy bulbs is backed by some compelling statistics – they last up to 15 times as long as tungsten bulbs, and use a quarter (or even less) of the electricity, so over its lifetime, a single energy-efficient bulb could save £100.

The main type of low-energy bulb is the compact fluorescent lamp, or CFL for short. These are thin, coiled fluorescent tubes that you can buy 'bare' in shapes such as candy-like twirls, or sets of spikes (these are the cheapest and most efficient), or covered in a frosted casing so they look more like conventional bulbs. You may need to hunt down certain types and sizes, although the range available from eco stores, electrical suppliers (especially online shops) and supermarkets is improving all the time – you can now find candle bulbs and flat circles for wall lights as well as reflector spots and substitutes for halogen downlighters.

Since CFLs use less energy, you will need to buy a lower wattage to replace existing bulbs. The tungsten equivalent is usually marked on the box.

Tungsten	CFL
25W	6W
40W	7W to 11W
60W	11W to 18W
100W	20W to 25W
150W	32W

For an interesting opposing view on CFLs versus incandescent bulbs, see Andrew Steer's Techmind blog at www.techmind. org/energy/dontbanthebulb.html.

How to make the most of CFLs

The two main issues with CFLs are size and quality of light. CFLs are bigger than their tungsten equivalents, and this can cause problems, especially with kitchen and bathroom spotlight fittings (look for adaptors from online suppliers). I almost got in trouble when we put new wall lights in the hall. Our local Waitrose had the right kind of low-energy bulb (an E14 golfball), but it only just fitted in the glass shade.

Many people don't like the slightly institutional light that eco bulbs can give – even with 'warm white' the glow simply isn't as friendly as that generated by energy-guzzling tungsten – but it can be softened, depending on how you use the bulbs.

- ♥ Try milky glass shades to diffuse the light, or styles of shade that enclose the bulb.
- ♥ You can get fully dimmable low-energy bulbs that work with an ordinary electronic dimmer switch, including those from Varilight (www.varilight.co.uk).
- ♥ Colourful, translucent shades alter the tone of the light – one restaurant I visited had some great-looking purple pendant shades, and unless you looked closely, you wouldn't have realized the light was coming from an energy-saving bulb at all.
- ♥ Introduce low-energy bulbs gradually, to get used to them. Start off with the lights you use most – such as in hallways. This is where most savings will be made.
- ♥ CFLs don't get as hot as tungsten, because more of their energy goes into light, not heat. This means shades made from delicate,

heat-sensitive materials, such as felts, papers and silks, become an option. Look at Oliver Heath's interiors website www.ecocentric.co.uk.

♥ For security lights, try photosensitive, dusk-to-dawn CFLs that come on when it gets dark and switch themselves off at sunrise.

CFL safety

CFLs contain a tiny amount of mercury – around 5 milligrams per bulb – but over their whole life cycle they release less mercury into the environment than when fossil fuels, such as coal, are burnt to produce the energy for old-style tungsten bulbs. The Royal Society of Chemistry has an informative article about this (www.rsc.org/chemistryworld). It's worth remembering, too, that fluorescent lights have been around for years in kitchens and offices, so any health issues are likely to be well known and documented.

However, if you do break a low-energy bulb, open the windows for 15 minutes or so, and sweep the debris (don't vacuum it) into a plastic bag. Wear rubber gloves and use a damp cloth that you don't mind throwing away to mop up any last bits – or else a damp paper towel (recycled, of course). Put this in the plastic bag and seal it up. Since this is classed as hazardous household waste, don't put it in the bin but check with your council where to take it (usually your local recycling centre). Or try the hazardous waste disposal postcode finder on the National Household Hazardous Waste Forum website (www.chem-away.org.uk).

LEDs – the energy-efficient lighting of the future?

Light-emitting diodes (LEDs) are used in traffic lights and torches, and they're billed as the next big thing in energy-saving home lighting. They've been too expensive until recently, but you can now get replacements for halogen downlighters for about the same price as the CFL equivalent.

LEDs are not perfect – it's hard to get a good white, and currently they have a focused beam and low light output. They're good for uplighters, downlighters and decorative lighting, such as Christmas tree lights, and for mood-lighting effects.

If you're trying them out, it's best to replace all the bulbs on one circuit at the same time, because LEDs could be damaged by mixing them, in particular when the halogen bulbs fail.

Energy manager's tip:
Some people have been put off CFLs because the bulbs didn't last as long as advertised. This is due to the use of lower-grade parts. Always keep receipts and take non-functioning bulbs back to the retailer.

Ways to use less energy for lighting

♥ Fit electronic dimmers and lower wattage lamps. Modern dimmers (not the old resistor kind) reduce the amount of power being used, although not as much as replacing with an energy-efficient bulb. Dimming a traditional bulb halfway will reduce its energy use by 40 per cent, and also extend its life.

- ♥ Have fewer lights. Be brave – buck the trend for multiple downlighters. See how few lamps you can get away with – often it's more important to have good lighting in the right place, such as directly above the chopping board, or where you'll be reading or sewing.
- ♥ Make the most of natural light. Throw open blinds and curtains when it gets light, and decorate rooms with lighter colours. You could also think about installing a 'sun pipe' if there's no way to get natural light from a window – there's a very interesting forum on the subject at www.greenbuildingforum.co.uk.
- ♥ Choose alternative lighting. Have an occasional candle-lit dinner – with beeswax or sustainably produced soy candles (but be careful to position them away from anything that could catch fire, and where they can't be knocked over, especially by fascinated children). Use solar lights in the garden and try a Sun Jar (widely available online) for gentle night-time light.

GREEN ENERGY

With domestic energy for the average UK household responsible for six tonnes of carbon dioxide a year, it's worth thinking about how the electricity we use is generated. Micro-generation, where households and communities supply their own power and heating, has great potential, but if you aren't ready to install your own mini hydro station, you could try going on to a green tariff.

There are three main types – tariffs that put a unit of renewable electricity into the grid for every unit (or proportion of a unit) that you use; ones that invest in renewable electricity generation, research and environmental causes; and ones that offset carbon emissions with projects such as tree-planting. Low-carbon tariffs may also include nuclear-sourced electricity.

The government sets targets for the amount of renewably sourced electricity all energy companies must provide, but some companies have been caught out selling this as their green tariff, rather than doing more. It can be hard to work out how green the various alternatives actually are, and which is best for you – although Ofgem's new accreditation scheme (www.ofgem.gov.uk) should make the choice easier.

As a start, read the consumer guide to green tariffs at www.energywatch.org. I also found the Green Electricity Marketplace website (www.greenelectricity.org) helpful. For a hard-hitting report and detailed comparison of green tariffs (published in January 2007), see the National Consumer Council's *Reality or Rhetoric? Green Tariffs for Domestic Consumers*.

If you opt for a green electricity company, rather than a conventional power company's green tariff, you'll need a separate gas supplier. Some companies offer a green dual fuel option, while Equigas (www.ebico.co.uk) offers a 'fair price' ethical tariff.

GOING NON-ELECTRIC

Ah, the sound of a strimmer on a Sunday morning, crashing through a still, sunny day . . . By choosing manual, natural or mechanical options, you can often reduce noise pollution as well as energy use.

Out: *Electric or petrol lawnmower*
In: *Push-along mower, or meadow*

If you have a small garden, think about a manual mower. For larger areas, you could cut a few paths, leaving most of the grass to grow longer, or else plant a wildflower meadow. This will need cutting just once a year, and you could even try your hand at using a scythe (see www.thescytheshop.co.uk if you're tempted).

Out: *Electric hedge-trimmer*
In: *Shears*

Unless you have a huge length of hedge, try clipping it with a pair of shears. They are quieter and so much more satisfying to use than an electric trimmer, and I find them easier to handle.

Out: *Electric razor*
In: *Wet shaving*

To keep razor blades sharper for longer, dry them after use and don't keep them in a damp atmosphere – blades can lose their edge through water corrosion. Avoid badger-hair shaving brushes and disposable razors.

Out: *Cordless phone*
In: *Old-style cord phone*

You can choose between modern functional versions or something with retro chic appeal, and they don't emit radiofrequency radiation (RFR). Try Graham & Green (www.grahamandgreen.co.uk) or Skandium (www.skandium. com) for newly manufactured design classics. If buying an old phone, check it's compatible with modern phone lines.

How to reduce your footprint to a more delicate size

Keep heat in and bills down by insulating and draught-proofing.

Turn down your central heating, fit TRVs and learn how to use all the controls effectively.

Switch off anything you're not using, and everything when leaving a room.

Be a smart and thrifty appliance user by following energy-saving tips.

Scour the house for energy vampires.

Research the greenest options when you buy new appliances.

Start moving to energy-saving lightbulbs now, and make the most of natural light.

Switch to a recommended green electricity tariff.

Don't be a slave to electricity! Go charger-free and take the hand-powered and natural route.

4
EATING MORE SLOWLY

W e're a divided nation. On the one hand, we're a land of fast-food-addicted can't-cook-won't-cookers with a vegetable aversion. On the other, we're loving our organics, pootling along to farmers' markets and tending our new allotments. And it's not just a question of class and cash – plenty of well-paid people buy most of their food in packets, even if the packets are posher and the food is perceived to be of better quality.

Up until the middle of the twentieth century, people knew pretty much exactly where their food had come from and what to expect from it. Today, the issues around food have become complex, bewildering and worrying. With all the food scares, food miles and health advice to think about, it's enough to bring on a headache (and that's without the gluten intolerance). So how can we make it all simpler?

One of the guiding principles of green household management is to buy more raw produce. If we choose it carefully and cook more of our own meals, we can re-learn about the food we eat, and value it – and its producers – more highly, and so enjoy our food with a clearer conscience.

Slow Food

In 1989, Italian journalist Carlo Petrini was appalled to see a McDonald's opening near the Spanish Steps in Rome. He set up the Slow Food movement (www.slowfood.org.uk and www.slowfood.com) as a bastion against the takeover of fast food, fast life and industrialized homogeneity.

Today, with 80,000 members worldwide, the movement champions food that tastes good, is produced in a sustainable way and doesn't exploit its producers. In particular, it promotes local specialities and the endangered species of the food world (about three-quarters of European food-product diversity has been lost since 1990, and 30,000 vegetables have become extinct).

But it's really the *idea* of Slow Food that has been so influential. The name conjures an instant image.

FINDING SOURCES YOU TRUST

In an ideal world, we would all think about food from seed to saucepan, from plot to plate, and from ocean to oven. Shopping for food doesn't have to begin and end with the supermarket. It can be much more fun than that. We can be ethical and gourmets at the same time, because much of the most delicious food comes from smaller farms, artisan producers and shops that are full of enthusiasm for what they are selling.

When we buy food, we're well along the production chain, and often have no direct connection with the original farm or fishery.

Here are some questions to bear in mind.

- Where and how was this food grown, reared, caught, slaughtered, and what were the conditions?
- What has been the impact on the environment and the health of those involved in the process?
- How was it processed after it was harvested, caught or killed, and in how many places?
- How has it been packaged, and how far and by what means has it been transported?
- Who is getting the majority of the purchase price (in many cases, the final whack added by the retailer is the largest chunk) and is it benefiting the people who produced it?
- Is this food safe and healthy to eat, free (as far as possible) from pesticide or other chemical traces, with good levels of naturally occurring vitamins and minerals?

Practically, one of the best ways to be sure about what you're eating is to find food sources – shops, brands, farms or other direct suppliers – that you can trust. Food labelling has improved, and certification schemes, such as the one run by the Soil Association, are enormously helpful. For an online, searchable version of *The Organic Directory*, see www.whyorganic.org.

Supermarkets, whatever your other reservations about them may be, are stocking more organic and fairtrade products, and working to reduce their carbon emissions and environmental impact. *The New Green Consumer Guide* by Julia Hailes has a useful supermarket survey from 2007.

BUYING LOCAL, BUYING LOOSE, BUYING ORGANIC

These three principles can help to guide your choices – often they work in harmony, but they won't always coincide. It can be hard sometimes to know what you should be buying to tick all the green boxes, but try not to give yourself a hard time. All any of us can do is be guided by our own household circumstances and concerns, and the information available at the time.

Buying local

Buying from the UK is a great first step; choosing from within about 40 miles of where you live – where that's possible – is even better. Locally sourced produce means fewer carbon emissions. It also means buying seasonally, when produce is at its best and most nutritious. Ideally, however, local food isn't just food that has travelled a shorter distance to the shops, it should also contribute positively to the local community, by being produced and processed sustainably in the area and giving people more control over what they can buy and eat. See www.soilassociation.org/localfood for more information.

Food miles have become a big area of debate. Air-freighting certainly adds to the carbon footprint of produce, but there are many factors to weigh up, from the amount of energy it takes to ripen  commercial tomatoes in the UK, to the right of farmers and workers in the developing world to earn a decent living in decent conditions (see www.oxfam.org.uk). When deciding whether to buy foodstuffs from overseas or not, one option might be to buy only what won't grow in the UK climate – and make sure it's fairtrade.

Neighbourhood greengrocers, fishmongers and butchers are under great pressure from supermarkets, so if you discover good specialists, it's worth supporting them. Those who are genuine will be only too happy to answer any questions you may have. Other options are farm shops, farmers' markets and local box delivery schemes. Look out for roadside signs advertising local eggs, honey and pick-your-own fruit. If you buy directly, it cuts out some of the middle men and means producers are likely to get a better return – which in turn makes it more viable for them to continue raising the crops and rearing the livestock you want to eat.

Provisioner's tip:

To choose a local box delivery scheme for vegetables, fruit, dairy and meat products, try the postcode finder at www.vegboxschemes.co.uk. Localfoodshop (www.localfoodshop.com) is the first virtual farmers' market – you can buy online direct from a range of suppliers in your area. Try to opt for a scheme that is run or controlled by farmers, or by a neighbourhood food co-op, so you know the money is going back to the producers.

Buying loose

Thirty-five per cent of plastic waste comes from packaging. One of the annoying things about supermarket organics is that they are often unnecessarily packaged – the argument is that it's to keep them separate from non-organic produce. Cut down by buying fruit and veg loose. Greengrocers' brown paper bags are great for packed lunches and the compost heap, but try to go easy on them as they take trees and energy to make and transport. With an organic box scheme, much of the produce comes unbagged in a re-usable crate.

Buy store-cupboard foods, such as rice, in bulk where possible – ask local shops if you can place bulk orders through them. Think about setting up a food co-op with friends or neighbours so you can buy from a wholesaler. Suma, based in West Yorkshire, has a huge range, from chickpeas to chocolate and more (www.suma.co.uk); for customers further south, try Essential (www.essential-trading.co.uk). In London, you can take your own containers to Unpackaged (www.beunpackaged.com); try talking suppliers in your area into doing the same, even if it's only for a few items. (For more about storage, → page 112.)

Buying organic

Growing evidence suggests that, as well as being environmentally friendly, organically cultivated food is better for you. Research has shown it to contain more vitamins and minerals, and more antioxidants, than non-organic produce, while eating organic food is the best way of reducing your exposure to harmful pesticides.

The term organic is governed by EU law. Organic produce must fulfil strict standards that cover issues such as the way farmers treat the soil, animal welfare, use of chemicals and antibiotics, care for the local environment and wildlife, and human health. It will be labelled as organic (so if it isn't, it doesn't meet the organic criteria). Organic food must be non-GM (GM crops cannot, currently, be grown commercially in the UK) and not irradiated (a practice used to lengthen shelf-life). For more information, see www.aboutorganics.co.uk, www.soilassociation.org and www.whyorganic.org.

❖ *Provisioner's tip:*
❖ *You can tell how organic prepared foods are by how they're*
❖ *described on the label. To have the word 'organic' in its name, a*
❖ *product must contain 95 per cent or more organic ingredients.*

Confused by the symbols on the packet?

Logos and eco-labels are mushrooming over our food products and are useful guides, but they can take a bit of deciphering. There are, for example, around 15 accredited UK organic certification bodies and each has its own code, although they must all satisfy minimum criteria set by Defra. Sometimes the certification body's logo doesn't appear at all, instead you will see the UK organic code number (Organic Farmers and Growers is UK2, for example).

The Soil Association
The leading UK certification body and organic food and farming charity. The Soil Association's criteria are generally regarded as the toughest. They have the highest animal welfare standards (www.soilassociation.org).

Organic Farmers & Growers
Another major organic certification body, which aims to make going organic more achievable and practical for farmers (www.organicfarmers.org.uk).

Fairtrade

The most recognizable logo, guaranteeing that disadvantaged producers in the developing world are getting a better deal. Use of the mark is licensed by the Fairtrade Foundation (www.fairtrade.org.uk).

LEAF

The Linking Environment and Farming (LEAF) marque appears on food from farms that have been independently assessed as following the principles of integrated farm management, developed by LEAF. It is an assurance of high environmental standards, with reduced reliance on chemicals (www.leafuk.org).

Freedom Food

The RSPCA's farm assurance and food labelling scheme is dedicated to improving welfare standards for farm animals (www.rspca.org).

Lion

The lion stamp on eggs shows that the chickens have been vaccinated against salmonella (this covers 85 per cent of UK eggs), and other food safety practices have been followed (www.britegg.co.uk).

EATING ON A BUDGET

In the UK we have become used to spending a much smaller proportion of our income on food than we did even a quarter of a century ago (15 per cent in 2006–7 compared with 25 per cent in the early 1980s), and to finding cheap, plentiful, year-round produce. Going green with your food can mean spending more, if you replace like with like, but may not be as expensive as you think.

For the estimated four million Britons on low incomes, this kind of healthy eating is all but out of reach (see www.fareshare.org and Dr Hillary Shaw's www.fooddeserts.org). But even if you have a modest budget, and as prices rise, you can still take steps to eat healthily. You can keep the cost down if you spend time researching what is best to buy from where and planning meals. Here are some ideas that we are trying at home.

- Include more cheap staples in your diet, such as pulses ($\rightarrow$ page 135).
- Reduce the amount of meat you eat and buy cheaper cuts ($\rightarrow$ page 106), and plan menus so the meat lasts for several meals.
- Use lower-priced seasonal vegetables and make the most of gluts.
- Be creative with leftovers ($\rightarrow$ page 149).
- Grow your own fruit and vegetables from seeds or bare-root plants (for fruit bushes), which don't cost very much money. (For advice on growing your own, $\rightarrow$ Chapter 6.)
- Set up a food co-op buying group to make bulk purchases ($\rightarrow$ page 91).

THE SHOPPING LIST

A shopping list saves time, saves arguments, saves money, saves food from going in the kitchen waste bin. We have a rolling list – literally, the back of an envelope, although some people use a

blackboard or magnetic whiteboard on the
fridge. We write down everything that we're
running out of or want to stock up on, and then
work out what we're planning to eat each day,
often based around what is left over from earlier meals.

Since we both work from home, and have excellent local shops,
we tend to buy vegetables, fruit and dairy products daily. If you
work late, supermarkets can seem the only option, but shopping at
lunchtime might be another possibility, depending on the outlets
within an easy distance. Alternatively, you could try direct online
ordering for staples and a delivery box for a stock of fruit, veg and
other perishables.

Buying fruit and vegetables

For maximum nutrition – and maximum taste – the minimum time
should elapse between picking and the crop reaching your plate.
This can be achieved by growing your own, shopping frequently
(even daily, especially with the tender produce of summer) or
buying directly.

Supermarkets do our quality control for us, so what we buy
there is usually in perfect-looking (some might say too
perfect-looking) condition, although it may have taken some days
to reach the shop. If you're buying loose, check over your
purchases carefully. Organic produce often has blemishes, but this
does not mean it is of lower quality.

- Look for plump specimens. Avoid wilted greenery and dull,
  wrinkly skin, on aubergines for example.

- Give them a squeeze. Onions, potatoes and apples should feel hard, and tomatoes firm (depending on variety). Don't be rough with mangoes or avocados, which can bruise.
- Some blemishes are fine. On apples and other tree fruits, scabbing and small bruises are no worry, but blackish areas or dapples could mean rotten patches in the flesh. A hole may indicate a small visitor, but often this affects the core only. You can always cut damaged areas out.
- Check the bottom of the punnet. With soft fruits, those underneath could be starting to mould.
- Rub off soil to check the condition beneath. A little scabbing shouldn't affect the flavour of potatoes but can sometimes go deeper. Watch for cuts in the flesh, from harvesting.
- Fruits should be fragrant. Scent will help you determine whether mangoes, melons and tomatoes are ripe enough. Watch for musty, mildewy scents from tomatoes, and a nail-varnish remover tang from over-ripe melons and kiwis.

Get the most from your organic vegetable box

According to The C-Change Trust, the best delivery schemes can save you 98 per cent of the carbon footprint for the food you buy, compared with supermarket shopping.

- Find a scheme that's really local. The green credentials of supermarket box schemes, for example, are at present questionable.

- Experiment with your box – try out different options or combinations over a few weeks to find what suits you.
- Rethink your order if the cauliflowers are getting you down. Box schemes do their best to be creative, including using some imports during April and May (the period known as the Hungry Gap), when last season's stocks are finishing and there isn't enough new season's local produce, but if you're finding items going mouldy because you're not using them quickly enough, either reduce the frequency of delivery or try a smaller box.
- Investigate what else you can get delivered at the same time – from washing-up liquid to sustainably caught fish.
- Take some time to find recipes you really like for the produce in your box. Try online, or books such as Jane Grigson's *The Vegetable Book*, Madhur Jaffrey's *World Vegetarian*, Viana La Place's *Verdura*, or *Sarah Raven's Garden Cookbook*.

Provisioner's tip:
At pick-your-own farms you can do your own quality control as you
harvest, and often get better fruit and vegetables at a better price.
Check about pesticide use. To find farms in your area go to
www.pickyourown.org/unitedkingdom.htm.

Choose organic alternatives

These 10 fruits, vegetables and cereal products are the crops that the Pesticide Action Network (www.pan-uk.org) has calculated are likely to give the highest consumption of pesticides in the diet of typical UK consumers – so these are ones to focus on when deciding what to buy organic.

Flour	Grapes
Potatoes	Strawberries
Bread	Green beans
Apples	Tomatoes
Pears	Cucumber

According to experts, other organic products it's beneficial to buy include milk, peanut butter and ketchup.

SAY NO TO PLASTIC BAGS

In the UK we use approaching 18 billion plastic bags a year, or 290 for each of us, and most go into landfill (or end up on beaches) without a second use. Things are changing, however, as shopping areas and towns are lining up to go 'plastic bag free' and retailers are starting to charge for plastic bags. Switching to paper or degradable plastic isn't really an improvement, because paper takes more energy to produce, while compostable bags made from cornstarch bioplastic require land and intensive farming. The longer-term answer is to have bags or other shopping carriers that can be re-used many times. (For more about plastics, → page 216.)

♥ Colourful string Turtle Bags (www.turtlebags.co.uk) and tough parachute nylon Onya bags (www.onyabags.co.uk) fold up small when not in use, and can be carried in a pocket or handbag.

- ♥ Small items, such as toothpaste or tights, don't need a bag at all.
- ♥ A rucksack is a good option, or a fashionable tote. You could also try baskets, or an ever-more-stylish wheelie shopper.
- ♥ For supermarket visits in the car (which obviously you'll be keeping to a minimum), put some cardboard boxes in the boot.

Provisioner's tip:

Would you like your town, village or city to ban plastic bags? Modbury in Devon was the first UK town to stop issuing plastic shopping bags, led by BBC camerawoman Rebecca Hosking. Find out more at www.plasticbagfree.com.

MAKE: *Shopping bag*

Re-use an ailing denim skirt, especially one with belt loops, by transforming it into a courier-style shopper. The loops are to thread the handle through, but if your skirt doesn't have them, you can still make the bag – look at the bag projects on www.sewing.org and choose a pattern for handles from there. (For sewing basics, → Chapter 11.)

You will need:

An old denim skirt	*Needle and sewing thread*
Felt-tipped pen or sewing marker	*Sewing machine*

Tape measure

Sharp scissors

Pins

Bias binding

Scarf (not a woolly one)

1. Turn the skirt inside out and smooth it flat, then mark a line across its width about 40cm/16in from the top of the waistband and cut along this with sharp scissors.

2. Pin, tack and sew a seam 1.5cm/½in from the cut edge. To neaten, sew the two layers together with a zigzag stitch or finish with bias binding (see the Home Sewing Association's 'Learn to Sew' articles on www.sewing.org).

3. Press the bag flat, then open it out and press the seam to one side, ironing on the wrong side of the fabric.

4. Hold the bag inside out from one of the corners, so the seam you've just sewn runs vertically. Open out the fabric equally to either side, so you have a triangle with the seam down its centre. Measure 7cm/3in from the triangle's point and mark a horizontal line. Sew along this line through both layers, and repeat on the other corner.

5. Push the triangles in towards the bottom seam and secure them to it with a few hand-stitches.

6. For the handle, or strap, thread the scarf through the two side belt loops and tie in a knot round each one, letting the ends trail artfully.

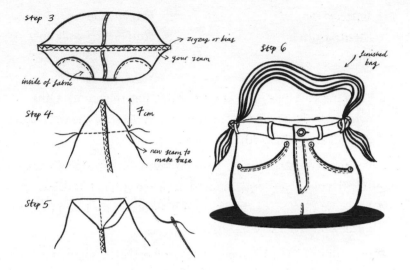

step 3
→ zigzag or bias
→ your seam
inside of fabric

Step 4
7cm
→ new seam to make base

step 5

step 6
✓ finished bag

A YEAR OF SEASONAL FRUIT AND VEGETABLES

If you buy fruit and vegetables when they are in season, quality should be high and prices relatively low. In this list, January includes winter produce that came into season at the end of the previous year.

January

Cabbages, sprout tops, kale and cavolo nero
Cauliflower
Chicory and radicchio
Jerusalem artichokes

Purple sprouting broccoli
Champagne rhubarb (forced)
Late pears, such as Conference
Seville oranges and other citrus fruits (imported)

February
Greenhouse lettuces

March

Nettles

Watercress

Chives

April

Early baby salad leaves

Radishes

Sorrel

Spinach

Wild garlic

Dandelions

May

Asparagus

New season carrots

New potatoes

Wild rocket

June

Broad beans

Lettuce

Peas

Cherries

Gooseberries

Elderflowers

Wild and cultivated strawberries

July

Artichokes

Beetroot

Cauliflower

Courgettes

French and runner beans

Garlic

Onions
Beetroot
Cauliflower

Raspberries, blueberries and
   currants
Chanterelle mushrooms

August
Aubergines
Broccoli
Chard
Cucumber
Fennel
Sweetcorn
Apples (early varieties)

Apricots
Blackberries
Damsons
Plums
Ceps (porcini)
Oyster mushrooms
Autumn raspberries

September
Borlotti beans
Cabbages and kale
Chillis
Peppers
Squashes and pumpkins

Apples
Elderberries
Greengages
Pears
Hazelnuts

October
Celeriac
Apples for over the winter
Crab apples

Quinces
Sloes
Walnuts

November
Brussels sprout tops
Chicory and radicchio
Jerusalem artichokes
Kale and cavolo nero

Parsnips
Swedes
Chestnuts

December

Brussels sprouts	Champagne rhubarb (forced)
Spring greens	Citrus fruits (imported)

Preparing fruit and vegetables

Fruit and vegetables will need either peeling or washing, with the final rinse under running water. For non-organic produce, this is to wash off pesticides or other chemical residues that still remain on the surface, and for organics, to get rid of soil and the bugs it contains. Soaking earthy potatoes before scrubbing makes it easier to clean them.

If you happen to buy some bagged salad leaves or herbs, you should re-wash these and keep them in the fridge, to reduce any risk of salmonella or E coli contamination (another good reason for avoiding them in the first place).

Provisioner's tip:

Vegetables such as spinach and broccoli will keep their nutritional level best if stored at low temperatures, such as in the fridge. The nutrients in fruits don't deteriorate as much over time, even at room temperature.

Five wild foods

A trip out to forage for your own food is an attractive idea, but you need to be sensible about where you look for it. Avoid busy roadsides, for example, and the edges of possibly pesticide-sprayed fields. Also, don't take all the berries or leaves off a plant, and never dig one up by the roots.

Blackberries

Everyone's favourite, these delicious berries are found in woods and on waste ground. There are about 400 microspecies in the UK, with flavours ranging from earthy to winey to tangy. The earliest berries, at the tips of stems, are the fattest and best. (For a blackberry and apple jam recipe, → page 144.)

Nettles

In March, when nothing much else is growing vegetable-wise, you can gather the new green tips of stinging nettles by snipping with scissors – wearing thick gloves, of course. Blanch them for delicate nettle and ricotta gnocchi, or make nettle pesto.

Jack-by-the-hedge

This is also known as garlic mustard, or hedge garlic. Check a wildflower guide to identify it. The bright green, heart-shaped and toothed leaves come up around the same time as nettles, and are good in salads and salsa verde.

Sweet chestnuts

These are found in parks and woodland from late October. Children enjoy spotting the prickly cases, but make sure they wear gloves to pick them up. Open them carefully to find the heart-shaped nut inside.

Wild thyme

Many herbs grow in the wild, from marjoram and fennel to mint and lemon balm. With tiny leaves and pinky-purple flowers, wild thyme nestles in the grass, especially in limestone and chalk areas. The best way to identify it is to rub the leaves between your fingers. The resulting smell is unmistakable.

MEAT AND POULTRY

I should come clean at this point: I don't eat meat, poultry or
game, although Clive and Ethan do. When I was a student
I became a vegetarian, mainly because I was shocked by the state
of animal welfare (or the lack of it in intensive rearing methods).
I didn't miss meat, but eight years later I lapsed, becoming one of
the many veggies who've turned 'fishatarian', and that's where I've
stayed ever since.

Were I making the veggie decision today rather than in the 1980s,
it would be less cut and dried because it's possible to buy meat from
well-reared animals that have been kept and fed according to a
free-range, organic regime, and slaughtered with care. However,
factory farming is still by far the most widespread source of meat and
dairy produce – check the findings of investigative and campaigning
charity Compassion in World Farming (www.ciwf.org.uk). When
buying, bear in mind that welfare standards for animals reared
abroad may be considerably lower than those in the UK.

Another factor is that perhaps we should all be eating less meat
anyway to help stretch the world's food supply, since meat
production takes a lot of energy and land resources. Also, cutting
down on the amount of animal protein we consume reduces the
risk of heart disease and colon cancer.

Provisioner's tip:

If you are a caring meat-eater, try Hugh Fearnley-Whittingstall's
The River Café Meat Book, *Rose Prince's* The New English Cookery
and Fergus Henderson's Nose to Tail Eating.

Good meat-buying practice

♥ *Buy meat from well-reared animals.* Caged chickens may have been kept in a space no bigger than a sheet of A4 paper, while on an intensive pig farm it's regarded as acceptable for up to 15 per cent of pigs to die prematurely. Buying organic, and using known, trusted suppliers, can help ensure the animals and birds have lived a decent life.

♥ *Look for British animals and traditional or newly rediscovered breeds.* UK sheep farmers find it hard to sell their lamb in the domestic market, especially once the animal is a little older. Buying British means the meat – or animals – will have travelled less distance (although long journeys may still be involved). Traditional and rare breeds often have more distinctive flavours.

♥ *Be wise to ambiguous labels.* 'Local' doesn't necessarily mean free range – it could be a local intensive farm. It may also simply mean reared in the UK, rather than down the road – so check. 'Barn-raised' chickens haven't lived as cosy a life as it sounds – it's a good step up from caged birds, but conditions are still cramped.

♥ *Practise 'nose-to-tail eating'.* This means using all the parts of the animal that are tasty and nutritious. Try less popular – and often cheaper – cuts and perhaps even offal.

♥ *Learn more about meat and meat cookery.* Which meats and recipes do you like most? What cuts of meat are best for which types of cooking? How can you make meat and poultry stretch further?

How to recognize a good piece of meat

This is the advice I've gleaned from expert sources. Butchers are beginning to put information online, such as Lancashire supplier Tom Higham (www.butchertom.com).

♥ Meat should look dark red (for beef) or deep pink (for lamb and pork) – not brown or grey. Look at the meat in natural light, near a window, if you can, because lighting can change how the colour appears.

♥ Good meat will have a sheen, but not be wet or slimy.

♥ Well-hung meat is hard to find, but if you have a local butcher, ask how the carcasses have been treated. Hanging for the right length of time helps to make the meat more tender and improves its flavour.

♥ Don't be scared of fat on meat. Bear in mind that fat helps the meat to stay moist during cooking, and is where much of the flavour lies. With beef, look for marbling – fat in veins through the flesh – as a sign that the animal has grown slowly. If you are worried about eating fat, cut it off once the meat is cooked – or eat less meat.

♥ Chickens and turkeys are not the only birds to be intensively reared – geese and even guinea fowl may have been farmed for fast growth, so check with the butcher or on the label.

♥ If you are buying meat pre-packed, remove the packaging and pat the meat with paper when you get home. Store it in the fridge, covered on a plate, away from cooked foods and produce you will be eating raw.

Provisioner's tip:

Supermarkets tend to sell relatively few cuts of meat. To lower your
food bill, try some of the cheaper cuts used in traditional recipes,
such as beef brisket or chuck steak, scrag or neck end of lamb, or
belly of pork. These usually have a higher proportion of connective
tissue or fat than prime cuts, and are best suited to longer cooking,
often in stews or casseroles.

FISH AND SHELLFISH

On holiday in a small Portuguese village a few
years ago, we were delighted to find a local
fisherman selling fish from a van, and dined
happily on fresh-caught sardines grilled over
the barbecue. Most of the time, buying fish is a more fraught
affair. The Food Standards Agency (www.eatwell.gov.uk) tells us
to eat more fish, especially oily species containing omega-3 fatty
acids – but, on the other hand, ocean pollutants such as dioxins,
mercury and polychlorinated biphenyls (PCBs) build up in their
fat (for what to avoid during pregnancy, → page 371). Add to this
that pretty much all our favourite species, from cod to monkfish,
have been over-fished, with the United Nations reporting that up
to 78 per cent of the world's fisheries are 'fully exploited',
'over-exploited' or 'seriously depleted'. Then there are the
pressures of global warming, the problems of bycatch (the large
numbers of unwanted fish and marine animals caught in trawler
nets) and the scourging of the seabed by scallop dredging.

All these factors have made me want to make extra efforts to
ensure that my fish-eating is as ethical as it can be.

Good fish-buying practice

♥ *Avoid over-fished species and locations.* The Marine Conservation Society's website, www.fishonline.org, has detailed information, and you can download its *Pocket Fish Guide* to take shopping with you as a handy reminder of what's good to buy and what to steer away from.

♥ *Buy sustainably caught fish.* Fishing methods matter. Look out for the Marine Stewardship Council eco label (www.msc.org) and for line caught fish. Line fishing is generally more sustainable than trawling with nets.

♥ *Look for local.* The label should say something like 'caught by day boats' and state where the fish was landed. Inshore 'day-fishing' takes place in coastal waters from small boats. The fish is fresher than from boats that have been at sea for days and the fishermen tend to use responsible methods.

♥ *Try something different.* Line-caught mackerel (see www.linecaught.org.uk, an association of hand-line fishers in the South West) and Cornish pilchards are great oily fish. Gurnard, pollack, black bream and grey mullet are also caught in British waters, and often overlooked. Crayfish (langoustines) aren't cheap, but are more sustainable than all but the best farmed prawns.

♥ *When buying salmon, choose farmed organic.* Stocks of Atlantic wild salmon are too low to feel comfortable eating them. Organic salmon are still affected by sea pollutants, but the best farms are trying to change the tarnished image of aquaculture. Some are now certified by the Soil Association (see www.whyorganic.org).

Provisioner's tip:

Fish is not cheap, so make the most of it by learning how to cook it well. Fish *by Sophie Grigson and William Black has details of species and techniques as well as recipes.* The River Cottage Fish Book *by Hugh Fearnley-Whittingstall is worth a look, and gather online tips from FishWorks at www.fishworks.co.uk.*

How to recognize good fish and seafood

Mitch Tonks founded the award-winning FishWorks shop and restaurant chain (www.fishworks.co.uk). Here's his advice on buying fish.

- ♥ Ask the fishmonger what's best on the day. Any good fish-monger will know and recommend the right cut – a nice piece of haddock from the thick end of the fillet for a steak, for example, or a whole fish on the bone for roasting and keeping moist.
- ♥ Inspect the whole fish to check freshness – the eyes should be clear and bright, the smell should be of the sea, the gills should be red not brown and the flesh firm. It's harder to judge the freshness of fish that has already been filleted and pre-packaged, so buy from a trustworthy source.
- ♥ Buy the freshest fish you can. It's far better to cook this simply with herbs and olive oil than to mask an older piece of fish with rich sauces.

PANTRIES AND LARDERS

We have a north-east-facing utility room with a thick plastic roof, no heating and chunky stone walls on all sides. In summer it's the warmest, brightest room in the early morning, but in winter it serves as a great cold store – very handy for Christmas. Of course, you don't need a space like this in order to have a pantry or larder. However, ideally the cupboard should be on an external wall and have some ventilation (but make sure it's mouse-proof).

Provisioner's tip:

Tomatoes are at their most flavoursome when kept at room temperature. Mushrooms are better out of the cold, too, and stored in a paper bag, not plastic. For herbs, snip off the bottoms of the stems and put in fresh water.

The word 'pantry' comes from the Old French *paneterie*, or bread store. I'd define it as a store cupboard for foods that don't need to be kept chilled. Dark is good, cool is good – but these foods won't go off just because it's not freezing. A well-stocked pantry means you won't have to keep nipping to the supermarket to buy the ingredient you forgot. Shopping ahead of time also makes it easier to buy as many organic and fairtrade products as possible, since you're not having to make do with what's on offer from the only store that's open. Traidcraft's online shop (www.traidcraft.co.uk) offers a good range, while at www.fairtrade.org.uk there's a comprehensive list of fairtrade products, from Co-op muesli to Fruit Passion juices.

'Larder' comes from the Old French *lardier*, or the place where you keep your fats. Old-fashioned larder foods are the ones that today we keep in the fridge – cheese, yogurt, milk, eggs and fats, plus quick-to-deteriorate ready-mades, such as mayonnaise and fruit juices.

Pantry foods

The following is my own personal stock list, which you may want to use as a starting point and adapt for the style of cooking you prefer.

Grains, flours, pastas and other staples
Arborio or other risotto rice, basmati rice, brown rice for salads
Soup barley and/or farro (spelt grain)
Couscous
White plain flour, white self-raising flour, stoneground wholemeal bread flour, spelt flour
Spaghetti, penne or other shaped pasta
Potatoes (the greenest staple there is – they are often locally grown and don't need processing)

Pulses

Puy lentils, Egyptian red lentils
Chickpeas
Black turtle beans, cannellini, borlotti, black-eyed beans

Tins

Italian tomatoes
Sardines, and skipjack tuna (which should really be line-caught
   and MSC-certified, but – confession here – mine often isn't)
Coconut milk

Jars and bottles

Capers
Lea and Perrins Worcestershire Sauce
Dijon mustard, English mustard
Tomato ketchup (an essential accompaniment to some meals)
Soy sauce
Thai fish sauce
Red wine, white wine and cider vinegar, rice vinegar
Cooking and salad oils (→ page 116), sesame oil

Herbs and spices

Dried oregano, dried chilli (other herbs are best fresh)
Cumin seeds, ground coriander, turmeric (or the spices you use
   most – do a regular audit to clear out old, tasteless leftovers)
Saffron
Cinnamon sticks, vanilla pod (this can be washed, dried and
   re-used if you want to be thrifty)

Dried porcini mushrooms
Flaked sea salt, black peppercorns

Baking ingredients
Unrefined caster sugar, light muscovado sugar
Baking powder, baking soda (for cooking, not cleaning!), cream of
  tartar
Cooking chocolate, cocoa

Fruit, nuts and seeds
Raisins, dried apricots
Pine nuts
Pumpkin seeds, sesame seeds

Larder foods

Organic milk
As well as encouraging more humane milk production, organic
standards can mean higher levels of nutrients, such as omega-3
fatty acids and conjugated linoleic acids, and there is a possible
link to reduced incidence of eczema in children.

Artisan cheeses
We now have a wide and delicious range of specialist cheeses in the
UK. A few are available from supermarkets but production is often
limited, even of award-winning cheeses, so farmers' markets and
specialist cheese shops are your best option.

Eggs

More free-range and organic eggs are now sold than battery-produced ones, which has to be a good thing. Free-range and organic hens should have access to outdoor space for at least eight hours a day, although with larger flocks of many thousands a study found that this doesn't always happen. The Soil Association requires smaller flocks, organic feed and no yolk colourants.

Provisioner's tip:

If you're unsure how the hens have been kept, check the first number of the code stamped on the eggs. Organic is 0, free range is 1, barn 2, caged 3. 'Best before' dates must be a maximum of 28 days from laying.

CHOOSING COOKING OILS

When you're deciding on an oil for high-temperature cooking, the smoke point is all-important. This is when you'll see vapour above the oil, and usually notice a change in the smell. The oil begins to degrade at this point, and can produce carcinogenic compounds.

Refined oils have higher smoke points. Sunflower oil and rapeseed oil are good at high temperatures, and some people use avocado oil, with a smoke point of 271°C (520°F), in woks. Hemp and flax oils (rich in omega-3 fatty acids) are best unheated, while extra virgin olive oils can be used for lower-temperature cooking, but vary widely. See www.cookingforengineers.com for more smoke points.

WHAT NOT TO BUY

It would be easy to say, 'Avoid all processed foods,' but for most of us that's not realistic. So here's a general rule of thumb – short ingredients list with simple names you recognize, good; never-ending ingredients list with lots of chemical names and numbers, bad. Below are some ingredients that often skulk in prepared foods and you might like to avoid.

Palm oil

Found in foods from chocolate to chips. Large-scale palm oil production is destroying forest and peatland habitats in Malaysia and Indonesia. Campaigning organizations suggest pressing supermarkets and others to sell only sustainably produced oil.

Hydrogenated fats

These are more solid versions of vegetable oils, used as a substitute for saturated fats (which we're advised to cut down on for our health), but hydrogenation can leave traces of transfats, which raise cholesterol levels.

Soya

A source of cheap protein used for processed foods and animal feed. Huge tracts of land are now under soya cultivation, and much soya is GM. Supermarkets are working with Greenpeace to call for an end to soya taking over rainforest areas, and are also trying to keep out GM products, which British consumers clearly don't want.

Large amounts of salt and sugar

Watch for salt levels given as grams of sodium – multiply by 2.5 to get the amount of salt. Look on ingredients lists for other names for sugars, such as fructose, glucose syrup, hydrolysed starch and invert sugar.

E numbers and other food additives

Some of these are natural and/or necessary (yeast, for example), while others are at best cosmetic (such as food colourings, hiding the fact that otherwise the product wouldn't look very appealing) and at worst linked with health or behavioural problems (such as some combinations of food colourings). Try to avoid artificial sweeteners.

WHAT ARE THE BEST STORAGE CONTAINERS?

I must admit here to a small obsession with the 'lock-shut' style of plastic containers that come in different stackable sizes, although I also love collecting glass jars and decorative tins to re-use (Italian amaretti and panettone tins are the best).

- Glass is great for long-term storage. It won't react with the contents, or take up the smells, it's scratch-proof, long-lasting and easily recyclable. You can collect and re-use old jam jars (Bonne Maman and Duchy Originals are particularly attractive) and even store food in the freezer – but they must be sterilized before re-use (→ page 144). Kilner jars – glass containers with a rubber seal closed by a thick wire catch – are also excellent for food storage.

- Ceramic is long-lasting, but takes a lot of energy to produce because of the high firing temperatures. Try to re-use pottery jars where you can, although plastic seals and cork lids can suffer with time.

- Plastic is lightweight, often non-breakable and relatively cheap, and you can buy shapes to suit, but it uses petrochemical resources, and can become scratched and absorb odours. Plastics may leach chemicals – polypropylene and polythene are deemed the safest for food. See page 218 and the kitchen plastics guide at US eco site www.care2.com/greenliving.

Provisioner's tip:

Clingfilm is unnecessary. Cover pastries, dry foods and rising dough with a clean tea towel, and put a mesh food cover over cakes.

For the fridge, place a plate over a bowl – or a bowl over a plate.

For sandwiches, wrap with re-used brown paper bags and carry in a sandwich tin, or try Wrap-N-Mats, which I found at www. thechildmindingshop.co.uk.

Trust your eyes, nose and tastebuds

Up to a quarter of the food waste that goes into landfill each year from producers, retailers and consumers is reckoned to be still edible. The use-by dates on perishable foods are important so you can avoid anything dangerously old, but 'best before' dates tell you when produce is past its prime, not that it'll have gone bad after this. It's worth refining your own inbuilt food safety sensors, to check home-made foods and to make sure you're not throwing away food unnecessarily.

Look – to see if there are any spots of mould, or if the texture has changed.

Sniff – to check for sourness or any unpleasant odours.

Taste – if it passes both the previous tests, by trying a tiny amount on your tongue. It shouldn't fizz or have any nasty flavours or aftertastes.

How to turn your supersized plateful into a gourmet nibble

Buy from local farmers and producers.

Choose organic – for your own health and that of farm workers, and the greater wellbeing of the environment and the animals we eat.

Buy loose, raw, unprocessed ingredients rather than packaged, pre-cooked and pre-prepared food.

Search out sources you can trust.

With meat and poultry, eat less, but better; keep fresh fish to a couple of times a week.

If you don't have local shops you'd like to support, try a box scheme or online supplier – or push your nearby supermarket to stock the foods you want.

Take a good look, sniff and (if allowed) prod at what you're buying, and ask questions about where it has come from.

In general, the shorter and more understandable the ingredients list on prepared foods, the better (check health information such as salt and fat levels, too).

Keep a well-stocked pantry – it will mean you have more options for meals in a hurry.

Save jam jars for storage containers.

5

MADE IN YOUR KITCHEN

One of the big advantages of home cooking from raw ingredients is that it means you know exactly what's going into your meals. You choose the produce, so you know how fresh it is and where it's

come from; and there's no place for artificial preservatives, fillers or colourings. It's also a great way to get children more involved with meal-making, and can even persuade them that foods they wouldn't otherwise try really are tasty. (Ethan loves putting the toppings on his pizza, and gets very excited at the prospect of eating the results.)

Cooking for yourself also means you can make the most of in-season produce and save on packaging, but you'll need to watch the carbon emissions. We do a lot of home cooking, and inherited an eight-year-old ceramic hob, which accounts for a sizeable chunk of our electricity bill.

Two strategies make it easier to maintain a green kitchen, and mean your eating is cheaper, more energy-efficient and less prone to waste. The first is planning in advance, and the second is making the most of what you have.

FORWARD PLANNING

Ideally I like to know what I'm going to be cooking over the next few days or even a week, especially when we'll be having visitors. It means I can get ahead – chickpeas can be put in to soak and entire dishes made in advance (with double quantities for freezing). I can devise meal schedules that mean extra mashed potato from one day can be used to make fishcakes the next. This can often help to save energy, as it takes less to re-heat a meal than to cook it from scratch. Of course, often things don't happen that way – there are times when my planning operates smoothly, and others when I'm rushing out to catch the shops before they close because it's only just dawned on me that I don't know what I'm making for supper.

LOWER-CARB COOKERY

One way to reduce your kitchen carbon emissions is to prepare several meals at once. If you know you'll need to use the oven, see if there's something else you can cook at the same time – put in some meringues or a crumble with the roasted vegetables (for a crumble topping you can keep in the freezer, → page 132).

It's also more efficient to cook larger quantities. This will give you lunch or supper the next day, or something in the freezer for a night when making dinner from scratch is too much hassle. In fact, risotto cooks faster in larger amounts as the rice retains the heat – and you can use any leftovers to make risotto fritters.

Cook's tip:

There are concerns about some of the chemicals used in the manufacturing of certain non-stick coatings in pans and fast-food wrappings, and stain-proof finishes on clothes. Stop using non-stick pans if the surface begins to degrade. When buying new, think about alternatives, such as metal-finish cake tins and enamel baking trays. You can line these with unbleached baking parchment, or use the old-fashioned method and butter a cake tin lightly, then dust flour over to coat it, tapping the side to give an even layer.

RECIPE: *Oven-roasted tomatoes*

This is an ideal way to double-use an oven and make the most of a glut of tomatoes if you're growing your own or they're going cheap. They're great for sandwiches, couscous salads, sieving to make passata, or as the basis for a tomato soup. You can roast other veg in a similar way.

For cherry tomatoes, leave them whole; for larger tomatoes cut in half cross-wise and squeeze over a bowl to remove the seeds. (This is something even young children can help with, as long as you don't mind tomato juice over the kitchen table.)

Ingredients:

Tomatoes
Olive oil
Sea salt
Freshly ground black pepper

Put the tomatoes on a baking tray, cut side up, trickle over some olive oil and lightly season with salt and black pepper. Place in a ready-heated oven, between 110°C/225°F/gas mark ½ and 180°C/350°F/gas mark 4, and roast for around 45 minutes for higher oven temperatures (about half this for cherry tomatoes) or up to two hours for cooler ovens – or until softened, reduced in size and starting to colour.

Other ways to reduce kitchen carbon emissions

🍎 *Put the lids on pans.* They'll heat up to boiling much quicker, and then you can turn the heat right down low for a simmer. This works for pasta, soups, vegetables and stews. Listen for the telltale rumbling sounds to avoid overspills (this is where glass lids come in handy). If you're reducing a sauce or frying, don't use the lid – although for soft, sweet, slow-cooked onions, covering the pan works well.

- *Match the pan size to the contents and ring.* Use the smallest pan you can – except for frying, where food needs plenty of space. Avoid jets of gas flame leaping up the sides.
- *Stack up.* A steamer will cook several vegetables on one ring. Learn some one-pot meals, such as risottos, chillis and knife-and-fork soups.
- *Don't keep peeking.* Opening the oven door makes the temperature plummet.
- *Use the grill, not the oven.* Where it's an option, the grill is more efficient.
- *Use retained heat.* Get used to switching the ring off a little before the food is ready – this works especially well with a heavy-bottomed pan and electric hob. To steam rice, turn off the ring after the water has reached boiling point. You can often switch the oven off early, too.

FREEZING

Pickling, salting, smoking, bottling, drying, canning – all traditional techniques for preserving food; ways of stretching the plenty of the summer and autumn over the less bountiful months of the year. Now, thanks to the Inuit and Clarence Birdseye, we have freezing.

When big chest freezers started colonizing people's garages in the 1970s, a host of recipe books and manuals appeared, telling us how to make the most of the technology by freezing fresh produce and making dishes for the freezer. These days, it seems to be assumed that either we know exactly how to use them, or we'll fill them with shop-bought ready-made foods. So here are a few recipes to keep your freezer replete.

RECIPE: *Tomato sauce for pizzas and pasta*

⁜ ⁜ ⁜ ⁜ ⁜ ⁜ ⁜ ⁜ ⁜ ⁜ ⁜ ⁜ ⁜ ⁜ ⁜

Ingredients:

Olive oil
2 cloves of garlic, crushed with a knife, peeled and finely sliced
400g/14oz tin of plum tomatoes
Sea salt
Freshly ground black pepper
A handful of fresh basil leaves

Heat a little olive oil in a pan and cook the garlic gently until soft. Add the tomatoes, some seasoning and about half the basil leaves. Mash the tomatoes in the pan and simmer for about 20 minutes, with the lid off, until thick and smooth. Check the seasoning and add the remaining basil. When cold, pour into sterilized jars with plastic-coated lids (→ page 144), or kilner jars, and freeze.

RECIPE: *Laksa soup*

⁜ ⁜ ⁜ ⁜ ⁜ ⁜ ⁜ ⁜ ⁜ ⁜ ⁜ ⁜ ⁜ ⁜ ⁜

Laksa is a South-East Asian soup, with noodles, vegetables and sometimes prawns, that makes a quick supper if you use a coriander paste you have previously frozen in small jars. The recipe below makes four jars of paste.

Coriander paste ingredients:

2 red chillis (this makes a mild paste – use more for a hotter version), finely chopped

4 stalks of lemongrass, chopped (tough outer leaves removed)

6 cloves of garlic, peeled and roughly chopped

2 shallots, peeled and chopped

10cm/4 in piece of ginger root, peeled and chopped

3 finely pared strips of lime zest, cut into thin slivers

1 large bunch of coriander, leaves and stalks roughly chopped

2 teaspoons turmeric

A little vegetable oil (olive oil is too strongly flavoured)

Blitz the chillis, lemongrass, garlic, shallots, ginger and lime zest in a food processor for a few seconds. Add the coriander and turmeric and process to a paste, adding a little oil if the mixture gets too stiff. Split between four sterilized jam jars with rust-proof lids (→ page 118) and freeze.

To finish the soup, defrost a jar of the paste and select around 600g/1lb 5oz of at least two types of vegetables – you could try one of the seasonal combinations suggested below. Serves two with plenty for second helpings.

Soup ingredients:

1 defrosted jar of laksa paste

A little vegetable oil

500ml/1 pint/18fl oz vegetable stock

400ml/¾ pint/14fl oz can of coconut milk

2 tablespoons Thai fish sauce (nam pla), or light soy sauce

1 teaspoon light muscovado or other unrefined sugar (optional)

100g/3½oz dried noodles, such as vermicelli or egg noodles
Juice of 1 lime
About 600g/1lb 5oz vegetables (see combinations below)
Garnishes (see below)

Summer combination:

300g courgettes
50-100g/2–3½oz (weight after podding) fresh broad beans or
    peas
100g/3½oz French beans
100g/3½oz cherry tomatoes, halved
About 10 raw shelled prawns (optional)

Autumn combination:

300g/10½oz butternut or other squash
200g/7oz broccoli (or purple sprouting broccoli in winter)
100g/3½oz late-season cherry tomatoes, halved

For garnishes:

A handful of coriander leaves, roughly chopped
A handful of mint leaves, roughly chopped
Crushed peanuts, strips of cucumber, crisp beansprouts, shredded
    spring onions (all optional – choose whichever you like, or leave out)

Chop the vegetables into large-ish bite-sized chunks. If using
squash or broccoli, steam these until the squash is tender but not
falling apart (10–15 minutes) and the broccoli is starting to soften
but still has some crunch. Save the water to cook the noodles
later.

Add a tablespoon of oil to a large heavy pan over a medium heat. Fry the laksa paste for a few minutes, stirring until it's fragrant but not turning brown. Add the stock and coconut milk and bring to the boil (add sugar if none of your vegetables are particularly sweet).

Add the Thai fish sauce or soy sauce, along with slightly slower-cooking vegetables such as courgettes. Simmer for about 5 minutes. Meanwhile, cook your noodles in the steamer water.

Add the other vegetables to the sauce according to their cooking times, finishing with a few minutes for the prawns (optional). Err on the side of under-cooking for the vegetables, but make sure the prawns are fully cooked. Take off the heat, add the noodles and stir in the lime juice. Serve into bowls, topped with your chosen garnishes.

RECIPE: *Crumble topping*
✤ ✤ ✤ ✤ ✤ ✤ ✤ ✤ ✤ ✤ ✤ ✤ ✤ ✤

I like the extra texture given by the oats here, which provide some soluble fibre and give a homely kind of crumble, not a fancy-looking restaurant version. These quantities are enough for two crumbles made in 1 litre/2 pint dishes.

Topping ingredients:
*   240g/8½oz flour (plain or self-raising)*
*   180g/6½oz butter, cold and diced into small cubes*
*   Small pinch of salt (leave out if you're using salted butter)*
*   6 tablespoons light muscovado sugar*
*   3 tablespoons unrefined caster sugar*
*   50g/1½oz soft porridge oats*

Put the flour and salt in a large bowl and rub in the butter, using the tips of your fingers. The finished mixture should resemble the oats. Add the sugar – the muscovado gives richness but you can experiment with different combinations of fine-textured sugars. Stir in the oats and separate the mixture into two batches. Put both in the freezer, but if you're making a crumble straightaway, take one batch out after you've prepared your fruit.

To finish your crumble . . .
I like the combination of vanilla and orange juice with most fruits – and with rhubarb you can add some orange zest as well. For apples, try ground cinnamon or allspice instead of the vanilla for more of an apple strudel flavour.

Crumble ingredients:

>*750g/1lb 10oz washed fruit (peeled and sliced where appropriate, the weights given are for prepared fruit), such as blackberry and apple, plum and apple or rhubarb*
>*light muscovado sugar to taste*
>*20g/³/₄oz butter*
>*1 vanilla pod*
>*Juice of half an orange*

Set the oven at 190°C/375°F/gas mark 5. If using apples, warm them in a pan with the butter, sugar and vanilla pod for a few minutes. Otherwise, butter the crumble dish and toss together the fruit and sugar in it; push the vanilla pod down into the fruit. Add the orange juice and any other flavourings.

Sprinkle the crumble topping over the fruit and bake for 25–35 minutes, until the fruit is bubbling and the topping is turning golden brown. Serve with custard, cream or crème fraiche.

SAVING ON PACKAGING

Whether it's deli foods such as hummus and pesto, or your own yogurt, making foods yourself, and then storing them in glass jars, can help to cut down your packaging footprint.

RECIPE: *Home-made yogurt*

⁜ ⁜ ⁜ ⁜ ⁜ ⁜ ⁜ ⁜ ⁜ ⁜ ⁜ ⁜ ⁜ ⁜ ⁜

First you need some yogurt 'culture'. You can get this from a shop-bought plain, live yogurt. Save a few spoonfuls from your first batch to make the next one. These quantities give 500ml/1 pint/18fl oz of regular yogurt, of 250ml/½ pint/9fl oz of an extra creamy version.

Ingredients:

500ml/1 pint/18fl oz whole milk (or semi-skimmed if you prefer)
1 generous tablespoon live natural yogurt

Heat the milk to boiling point, removing the pan from the heat as the milk froth is rising. Leave to cool until it's about the temperature of a hot bath (the yogurt culture needs to be at 38°C/100°F to work best, but much higher than this will kill it). Put a little of the milk in a cup or small bowl with the yogurt and beat with a fork until creamy, then pour this mixture back into the milk.

Turn the milk and yogurt mixture into a bowl, cover and wrap in a clean towel. Place the bowl somewhere warm, such as an airing cupboard (with a cooler temperature it will take longer to set) for eight hours or overnight. The yogurt will keep, covered, in the fridge for up to a week.

For extra creamy yogurt, when the milk comes to the boil, turn the heat down and simmer until it has reduced by a third to a half. Use the same amount of yogurt culture and continue as for regular yogurt. (Add cream at the cooling stage to make it even more luxurious.)

Cook's tip:

Make flavoured yogurts by mashing fresh berries with a little icing sugar and mixing with the cooled yoghurt. Put the berry mixture through a sieve to get rid of the pips. You could also freeze portions of compotes (such as apple, plum, quince or rhubarb) to add to the yogurt.

COOKING WITH PULSES

Pulses (beans, dried peas and lentils) are the Cinderellas of cooking – they work hard, being a wonderfully thrifty source of protein, minerals and fibre, but are rarely seen in culinary high society. However, they are surprisingly adaptable, taking up the flavours of other ingredients, and are a staple of cuisines from India to South America, and from North Africa to Italy. Tuscans were once known as *mangiafagioli*, or 'bean eaters', because they relied on them so much.

From a health point of view, pulses contain both soluble and insoluble fibre and are recommended for heart health and diabetes management, since they have a low glycaemic index. Beans are also high in folate and iron. What puts a lot of people off, I believe, is that they think beans are a hassle, and don't know what to do with them.

How to prepare beans and lentils

You can buy organic pre-cooked beans in tins, but cooking them yourself will almost always give you a tastier result and a better texture. Most pulses need two stages of preparation – soaking, and then a fairly long cook – but it's a simple routine that's easy to get used to. You can store cooked beans in the fridge for a day or so, and I've even frozen them successfully.

Lentils and split peas (dal to Indian cooks) don't need soaking, although Italian lentils are best when submerged for at least an hour. Soak beans for eight to 12 hours and chickpeas for 12 to 24 hours. I usually put pulses in to soak just before going to bed.

Cooking takes from 45 minutes to three hours, depending on the pulse. As a rough guide, you will need about three times the volume of water to beans, and you can enhance the flavour by adding celery, herbs, peppercorns or garlic cloves to the cooking water. Rinsing well reduces the windy effects – although the oligosaccharides that are the culprits can act as a prebiotic, feeding beneficial gut flora.

If your beans remain hard however long you cook them, it may be because you have extremely hard water, or because they're old. You could try adding a teaspoon of plain flour and a teaspoon of baking soda to the soaking water for every 200g/7oz of dried pulses to soften the skins, although nutritionists say that this destroys the vitamin thiamine.

A cornucopia of pulses

Black (turtle) beans: These are the *frijoles negros* of Central American and Cuban cookery, and the *moros* of Moros y Cristianos (black beans and rice). They are great in a chilli, and in black bean soup garnished with yogurt, onion and coriander.

Black-eyed beans: These are really peas, despite their kidney shape, and probably originated in western and central Africa. They are versatile and have a creamy texture. I use them in a veggie cottage pie, along with root vegetables and a handful of flat green lentils.

Borlotti beans: Beautiful beans mottled with purple or red on cream – although they go more of a brownish-pink when cooked – borlotti beans are a staple of Italian cookery and can be used fresh or dried. Try making your own baked beans by adding garlic, tomatoes, sage and olive oil, and cooking in the oven.

Broad beans: Also known as fava beans, these are often eaten fresh and even raw – serve young beans in their pods with pecorino cheese, so guests can pod their own. They are also great blanched, skinned and added to a seafood risotto or paella.

Cannellini beans: These small, white beans are another Italian favourite, especially in Tuscany. They have a delicate flavour and can be made into pastes or mashes as well as cooked whole. Mix with tuna and thin-sliced red onion with a dressing and herbs for a quick salad.

Split red lentils: Four-thousand-year-old lentil paste was discovered in a pharaoh's tomb in Thebes, and today these skinned, salmony red lentils are often called 'Egyptian'. They have an earthy, meaty flavour that's good in soups, and are used with ginger, garlic, onion, cumin and a touch of turmeric to make an Indian dal.

Chickpeas: Chickpeas are the main ingredient in hummus, falafels and the gram flour used in Indian cookery, and they crop up in curries, North African dishes with spinach, and Italian soups and pasta sauces. In fact, the chickpea is probably the most versatile pulse of all.

Puy lentils: Dark browny green in colour, these lentils can be cooked without soaking to make an accompaniment for salmon or sausages, or as a salad.

BREAD

The vast majority of commercial bread is made by a method designed for speed, mass production and long storage. It uses low-grade wheat, large amounts of yeast, enzymes, emulsifiers and processing aids. Connections have been drawn between the introduction of this standard method, called the Chorleywood Breadmaking Process, and the increase in conditions such as Crohn's and coeliac disease, and gluten intolerance. These claims have yet to be substantiated, but what's not in dispute is that many essential nutrients are missing from commercial bread when compared with organic versions made using traditional processes. The best bread of all is home-made.

RECIPE: *Baking your own bread*

✳ ✳ ✳ ✳ ✳ ✳ ✳ ✳ ✳ ✳ ✳ ✳ ✳ ✳ ✳

You can make bread by hand or with a dough hook or bread-making machine – these gadgets use electricity, but if they make home baking easier, that seems worthwhile. I used to feel a little intimidated by yeast cookery; it seemed somehow beyond me to get the dough to rise the way it should. However, fast-action yeast makes this all much easier, even if it isn't quite as purist as fresh yeast culture.

The main ingredients in home-made bread are strong flour (which has a high gluten content to make the dough stretchy), salt for flavour, yeast, warm water and sugar or another sweetener such as honey (for the yeast to feed on and create the bubbles that make dough rise), and butter, buttermilk, oil or yogurt, depending on the recipe (to give richness and a softer texture).

You can choose from a vast number of variations, from white loaves and wholemeal rolls to focaccia, seeded breads and pumpkin dough made with baking soda to give the lift instead of yeast.

Details will vary, but the basic method for yeast-risen bread can be broken down into four simple steps.

1. Prepare the yeast according to the recipe or packet instructions. Fresh or ordinary dried yeast is added to warm water and sugar and left until it begins to froth, but fast-action yeast is mixed directly into the flour, with the liquids added afterwards (see page 141).

2. Mix the dough, adding the yeast and liquid to the flour, and knead it.

3. Leave the dough to rise, covered with a tea towel, in a warm place, such as an airing cupboard, usually until it doubles in size. This can take as little as half an hour.

4. Shape and put in the tin for baking (some loaves need to be knocked back by punching and folding, then proved, or left for a final rising in the tin).

Cook's tip:

A number of chefs' cookery books include bread recipes, such as Giorgio Locatelli's Made in Italy *(the spelt loaf is simple and delicious).* Leiths Baking Bible *has an amazing range, and useful instructions, while if you like the idea of creating your own natural sourdough culture look at* Moro: The Cookbook *by Sam and Sam Clark.*

Kneading dough

Kneading ensures the yeast is well distributed through the dough, and helps to make the gluten from the grain soft and stretchy. It's worth doing for a full 10 minutes as the bread will rise more evenly and have a better texture.

Flour the work surface and your hands. Put the heel of one hand in the middle of the dough and push it down and away from you, so it stretches the mixture. Then pull the top end of the dough back over with your fingers, so you've folded it down. Give a quarter turn and repeat. Use alternate hands for each knead, or work with one for a while then swap over. Kneading is quite therapeutic, especially if you've been having a frustrating day.

My bread-making tips

♥ If you're a novice, try fast-action yeast. If I can make bread with it, I'm sure you can. Seasoned bakers may favour cultures of fresh yeast, but these are fragile and must be used quickly.

♥ For best results, mix fast-action yeast through about a third of the flour, add the liquid elements to make a batter, then mix in the rest of the flour. Usually, you will need to do just one kneading with fast-action yeast.

♥ A 7g mini-packet of fast-action yeast (about ¼oz) is the equivalent of about 20g (¾oz) fresh yeast.

♥ Don't have the water too hot, and don't add too much salt. Both of these will harm the yeast organisms. The water should be 37°C/98.5°F to 39°C/102°F – around blood temperature. If you don't have a thermometer, mix one part boiling water with two parts cold. Yeast needs moisture, warmth and sugars to produce the carbon dioxide that makes the dough rise, but will die off above 49°C/120°F.

- ♥ With wholegrain loaves you can substitute treacle, molasses or honey, or other natural sweeteners, for the sugar, to give different flavours.
- ♥ Some recipes call for buttermilk; if you can't lay your hands on any, try half full-fat yogurt and half semi-skimmed milk for a similar result.
- ♥ Always oil your bread tin to prevent disappointing bread-glued-to-tin incidents.
- ♥ Before you get the dough out of the airing cupboard (or wherever it's rising) make sure your oven has heated up to the temperature given in the recipe you're following. Make the transition to the oven as swift as possible, or your loaf may start to deflate.

Cook's tip:

To test if bread is done, remove it from the tin and tap the bottom – it should sound hollow. If the bread is still heavy and soft when squeezed (rather than resilient), put it back in the oven, without its tin, for another five minutes or so.

Choosing your bread flour

Strong white	The wheat flour used for bread has a relatively high protein content and is called 'strong' or 'hard'. It produces elastic gluten when moistened and kneaded. Choose organic unbleached flour where possible.
Wholemeal	This includes the bran and wheatgerm – both of which are removed in white flour – so retains most of the grain's B vitamins, minerals and vitamin E.

Spelt	An ancient precursor to wheat, spelt was brought to the UK by the Romans. It has a nutty flavour and its gluten is considered more digestible than modern wheat. Spelt flour is becoming more readily available.
Rye	Another widely used wheat alternative, rye flour has lower gluten content than wheat and needs more help to rise. It gives a distinctive flavour. For lighter loaves, mix rye with white flour.

JAMS AND OTHER PRESERVES

There's no way round this – many jams, marmalades and chutneys take time to prepare (all that peeling, chopping, seeding), cook (bubbling away for hours) and, sometimes, mature (chutney is best kept for a couple of months before opening).

On the other hand, some jams, such as raspberry or blackcurrant, are surprisingly quick and easy, and preserves are extremely gratifying to make. What could be more rewarding than going blackberrying on a late summer morning and then settling down to cook up your own bramble and apple jam after lunch, knowing that you'll soon be spreading it on buttered scones (for scone recipe, → page 154) for tea?

Preserves are not difficult and you don't need any special equipment – just a large saucepan or two, weighing scales, a wooden spoon and some empty jars.

Pectin is the magical ingredient that makes jams and jellies gel. Some fruits, such as strawberries and blackberries, have little pectin, while others, including apples, oranges, gooseberries and plums, have plenty. Often you can simply add a little pectin-rich fruit (such as apple to blackberries) or extra acid (some lemon juice with strawberries) to encourage your jam to set. Good-quality produce that is just ripe tends to set better than older fruit. Some seasoned jammers add green strawberries into the mix to improve the gelling. Why not gather the fruit at a pick-your-own farm (→ page 96)? You can use ordinary sugar, but specialist preserving sugar lessens the sugary scum that forms on the top (which otherwise you will need to skim off).

Store preserves in jam jars or kilner jars. If you're re-using old jam or pickle jars, wash them thoroughly and sterilize them, and make sure the lids have an intact plastic inner coating.

Cook's tip:

To sterilize jars, either run them through the dishwasher, if you have one, as part of a 60°C wash, or put them in the oven, set at 100°C/200°F/gas mark ½ for 10 minutes. If you're feeling energetic, you could always slow-bake some meringues while the oven's warm.

RECIPE: *My mother's blackberry and apple jam*

Well, my mother doesn't have the copyright on this recipe, but it's one of our favourites in her jamming repertoire. It makes about six 500g/1lb jars of jam.

Ingredients:

900g/2lb blackberries
150ml/¼ pint/5fl oz water
340g/12oz cooking apples
1 lemon
1.35kg/3lb sugar

Use two heavy-based non-aluminium pans. Place the blackberries and half the water in one, and the peeled, cored and chunkily sliced apples in the other with the rest of the water. Rub the cut lemon over the apples as you prepare them to help prevent browning. Simmer gently with the lids off until the apples become a soft pulp and the blackberries have softened but not disintegrated.

Meanwhile, put the sugar into an oven-proof bowl and your cleaned jam jars on a baking tray to sterilize them, and place both in the oven at 100°C/200°F/gas mark ½. Heating the sugar means it won't lower the fruit temperature so much when you add it, so you're less likely to overcook the jam – but if you forget, don't worry.

Use a potato masher to crush the apples slightly if necessary. Add the blackberries and a squeeze of lemon juice. Slowly add the sugar and stir until it's all dissolved. Turn up the heat and bring to a rapid boil.

As soon as the jam has reached the setting point (about 15 minutes) take it off the heat, skim off any frothy scum and allow to cool for about 10 minutes. Ladle the jam into the jars. I find a mug is useful for this in the absence of a jam funnel, but remember everything will be hot, so use oven gloves. Put the lids on the jars while still hot.

RECIPE: *Clementine marmalade*

The traditional Seville oranges don't properly come into season until January, but other citrus fruits are available in December, which means you can make marmalade as a Christmas gift. Buy organic fruit, so you don't have to worry about wax or pesticides on the skins. You will also need a piece of muslin about 30cm/12in square and a colander. These quantities make about five 500g/1lb jars.

Ingredients:

> *700g/1lb 9oz clementines (about 6 or 7)*
> *1 whole lemon, plus the juice of 1 lemon*
> *1 grapefruit*
> *2.5 litres/2¾ pints/88fl oz water*
> *1.25kg/2lb 13oz sugar*

Wash and then peel the clementines, finely shred the skin and tie it in the muslin. Place in a large, heavy-bottomed pan. Wash the lemon, chop off the ends and slice. Cut the peel and pith off the grapefruit and discard. Chop the flesh along with the clementines. Add to the pan (you may need more than one) with the lemon juice and water. Bring to the boil and simmer gently, with the lid off, for 30 minutes. Then take out the bag of shredded peel and continue to simmer for another hour and a half.

Put the peel aside in a bowl and use the muslin to line a colander. Drain the cooked fruit pulp through this into another saucepan. To extract the remainder of the juice, tie the muslin closed with string and hang it up (for example, from a mug hook) over a jug or bowl. Leave for an hour or two, or overnight.

Add the sugar and peel to the strained juice and warm over a low heat until the sugar has dissolved. Raise the heat and bring to a rolling boil. Make sure the pan contents come no more than halfway up, or you'll risk the marmalade boiling over. Skim off any scum that forms and test for a set. When ready, take the pan off the heat, do a final skim, then leave for about 15 minutes, so the peel is less likely to float to the surface. Put into jars, and add labels and decorations when cool.

A chutney for all seasons

Chutneys are a great way to use gluts of vegetables and fruit you've grown yourself, or to take advantage of neighbours' kind donations or local produce going cheap at the greengrocer's. The combinations are endless. Tomato with apple and courgette, and rhubarb with orange are just two examples. The list below may give you ideas for other seasonal chutneys. Dried fruits such as raisins, sultanas and dates add richness, and chillis and spices give punch and character.

Look for second-hand recipe books from the days when everyone made pickles and chutneys, or search for recipes online – and try out your own combinations and spicings.

Winter and spring

Lemon

Rhubarb

Summer

Red tomato

Apple

Gooseberry

Beetroot

Courgette

Aubergine

Autumn

Plum	Marrow
Damson	Squash and pumpkin
Bramley apple	Green tomato
Pear	

᷎ ᷎

MAKING THE MOST OF LEFTOVERS

In the UK we throw away 6.7 million tonnes of food a year, or about a third of what we buy. This isn't just peelings, either. One reason food is wasted is because these days we don't have the stock of fall-back recipes that were common knowledge during leaner times. We're not quite sure how to use the previous days' leftovers and the few stray vegetables that we didn't need for that recipe after all.

It helps to have a well-stocked store cupboard, with a range of staple ingredients, but there's also a knack to seeing whether what you've got in the fridge or vegetable basket can be adapted to make something you already know how to cook.

My method is to do an audit of what most urgently needs using. Then I think through the dishes I find easy to cook – would the ingredients go with pasta, make a frittata, or turn into a stir-fry? And what else do I need to get from the shops to make it work?

Potatoes
Cold cooked potatoes are, perhaps, the king of leftovers – they're so adaptable. Yesterday's cooked new spuds can be dressed to make

a salad – add some quartered hard-boiled eggs, green beans or cooked borlotti beans, salad leaves, tomatoes and olives to make a delicious veggie salad niçoise, or toss in some anchovies for extra interest.

Mash can be revived by placing it in an oven-proof dish, sprinkling with grated cheese and baking at 200°C/400°F/gas mark 6 – cover with foil if it's getting too brown on top. This method also works with cold risotto – especially for children, who won't mind that the rice has gone soft.

If you have a few potatoes in the vegetable basket and not much else, just bake them, and be creative with the filling. Sautéed leeks and leftover cream cheese or crème fraiche work well. Once the spuds are cooked through, slice a cross in the top, scoop out the insides and mix with your filling ingredients. Season to taste, scoop back in and continue cooking until the filling is crisp and lightly browned.

RECIPE: *Bubble and squeak*

✤ ✤ ✤ ✤ ✤ ✤ ✤ ✤ ✤ ✤ ✤ ✤ ✤ ✤

Ingredients:

Potatoes, cooked
Savoy cabbage or Brussels sprouts, cooked
Oil
Butter
Sea salt
Black pepper

Flour
Onions (optional)
Garlic (optional)

Mix roughly mashed cooked potatoes (floury ones are best, → page 175) with cooked savoy cabbage or sprouts. Heat some oil and maybe a knob of butter in a frying pan. When I was growing up, we cooked the whole mixture in the pan at once, until crusty and golden, seasoning with salt and black pepper to taste. Alternatively, you can form individual patties, dusted with a little flour.

Make sure your pan is hot enough before you add the mixture or it will take ages to crisp up. For variety, you could add onions fried until they're soft and golden, and crushed garlic.

Vegetables

Assorted veg box leftovers are candidates for soups, adding to casseroles and making into mashes. Sweet potatoes, swedes and carrots all make delicious mash. Spring onions and shredded, steamed savoy cabbage can pep up mashed potato. You can also use any stray, or old, vegetables to make stock, which can be kept frozen in handy amounts for two to three months.

Place roughly chopped vegetables, such as carrots, fennel stalks, celery (not too much or it will overpower the rest), leeks, onion and unpeeled garlic cloves, in a deep pan. Add a

few peppercorns and parsley stalks, with thyme or bay leaves if you want a stronger flavour, and cover with water. Bring to the boil and simmer, with the lid on, for about 20 minutes. Turn off the heat and leave to steep for 30 minutes to an hour, or until the stock has the required depth of flavour. Vegetable stock is useful for soups, paella and risottos.

Bread

Old-but-not-stale bread is good for toasting. Poached egg on toast and Welsh rarebits make great snacks or lunches. For Italian crostini and bruschetta, either toast the bread or, if you're cooking something in the oven, dry it there. Rub with a cut garlic clove and add a sprinkle of salt and olive oil, or a topping such as chopped fresh tomato with olive oil, basil and finely chopped olives. These go well with soup.

Dry white bread is the best for breadcrumbs (and summer puddings), although I do also make wholemeal crumbs. Use a food processor to crumb chunks of bread (or grate on a coarse grater) and store the crumbs in the freezer for when they're called for in a recipe (fishcakes, for example), or use straight away to make spaghetti aglio, olio, peperoncino (garlic, oil and chilli pasta). This is 'poor person's food', using fried breadcrumbs (pangrattato) in place of the more expensive Parmesan cheese. It's an inexact dish, so adjust the amounts to suit your larder and taste.

First make your pangrattato by heating olive oil in a frying pan and frying the breadcrumbs until they are crisp and golden brown. Remove and drain to remove excess oil – you could try brown paper bags instead of kitchen roll. While your pasta's cooking, finely chop a clove of garlic per serving and fry in olive oil until soft, along with crumbled dried red chilli to taste. Add the drained pasta and a handful of chopped flat-leaf parsley, season to taste with salt and black pepper, then sprinkle over the pangrattato.

Cook's tip:

For more ideas on using leftovers and keeping food at its best see www.lovefoodhatewaste.com.

COOKING WITH CHILDREN

There are all sorts of cookery tasks children can do and enjoy, even at a young age, which will hopefully set them up with the skills to cook for themselves later on. Mixing, adding ingredients, pouring, rolling, cutting out cookie shapes – all of these are possible even with toddlers. Simple preparation, such as podding broad beans and peas, can encourage children to try new foods. A fresh pea that you pop out of the pod yourself, after all, is as good as a Smartie.

Blackcurrants and redcurrants often come ready prepared these days, but as a child, de-stalking them was one of my special jobs. We used to run the tines of a fork down the stems, so they pulled off the fruit, then pick off the stalk-stubs that had stayed attached.

Sweet cookery is often a success with children, because there are plenty of stages they can help with before the final baking. Make sure the children's hands are washed thoroughly before you start, and it's a good idea for them to wear aprons. (You'll probably want one too, as much for protection against sticky hand prints as for your own spills.)

RECIPE: *Teatime scones*

✳ ✳ ✳ ✳ ✳ ✳ ✳ ✳ ✳ ✳ ✳ ✳ ✳ ✳ ✳

These quantities make about 14 scones with a 6cm/2in cutter.

Ingredients:

> *250g/9oz self-raising flour*
> *1 teaspoon baking powder*
> *½ teaspoon cream of tartar*
> *Pinch of sea salt*
> *40g/1¼oz unsalted butter*
> *1 tablespoon caster sugar (optional)*
> *2 heaped tablespoons sultanas or raisins*
> *1 egg*
> *120ml/¼ pint/4fl oz cold milk*

Set the oven to 200°C/400°F/gas mark 6 and line a baking sheet with baking parchment, or grease it with butter and then dust with flour, shaking off the excess. Sift the self-raising flour, baking powder, cream of tartar and salt into a large bowl. Add the butter in small pieces and rub it in using the tips of your fingers and lifting the flour up above the bowl – which brings more air into it. (I sometimes give Ethan his own bowl – if you do this, make sure to have a dustpan and brush ready for clearing up at the end.) When the mixture looks like fine breadcrumbs, stir in the caster sugar, if using, and then sultanas or raisins.

Beat the egg and milk together. Pour about three-quarters of this mixture into the scone mix and combine with a metal spoon or knife, adding more egg-and-milk until you get a soft dough (you shouldn't need all of it). Use your hands to shape the dough into a ball.

Roll lightly on a floured surface to about 2cm/¾in thick, then press out as many rounds as you can between you. Gently re-shape and roll the trimmings to cut more.

Brush the scone tops with the remains of the egg-and-milk mix and bake for 10–15 minutes until risen and golden brown on top – take them out when the sides are still springy to the touch, not baked hard. During this time, you can all clear up – I mean you can clear up, while the children play with the leftover scone dough.

RECIPE: *Pizza toppings*

✳ ✳ ✳ ✳ ✳ ✳ ✳ ✳ ✳ ✳ ✳ ✳ ✳ ✳ ✳

You can use half a home-made bread roll as a pizza base, or form separate rounds of bread dough (→ page 139). Alternatively, use circles of unsweetened scone mixture (→ above). Spread with a thin layer of tomato sauce (→ page 129), then let the children choose their own toppings and arrange them on the base. The following are popular options.

Grated cheddar (or mozzarella)

Torn slices of thin ham

Sweetcorn

Peas

Thinly sliced courgette

Steamed broccoli

Olives

Children often like to make a face on their pizzas, with olive eyes and a cherry tomato nose. A strip of red pepper for the mouth, and hair of ham or courgette finishes it off.

Parent's tip:

Save up wooden lolly sticks to make your own ice lollies. You don't need any fancy kit. Simply pour apple juice into shaped ice-cube trays and prop the sticks up in them. The natural sugars in the juice stop the improvised lollies going rock-hard.

How to be a green masterchef

Plan ahead where you can – it saves time, energy and effort.

If you're using the oven, try cooking something else at the same time, whether it's meringues, roasted vegetables or a crumble.

Save energy by putting lids on pans and not opening the oven door too often.

Cook one portion for now, and one for the freezer.

Whip up spicy pastes for days when you're in a rush – they keep well in the freezer.

Add more pulses to your diet – they're the 'forgotten food' and incredibly versatile once you get to know them.

Try baking your own bread.

Make jams and chutneys to preserve gluts of fruit and vegetables.

Become a leftovers connoisseur, and learn how to make something from almost nothing.

Get children involved as young green masterchefs.

6
GROWING
YOUR OWN

*E*ating our own home-produced potatoes was the unexpected highlight of our first year of growing our own. We'd only planted them to 'clean the soil' – which in non-gardening-speak means that because growing

potatoes involves a lot of digging, you can get rid of many pesky weeds at the same time – but the result was a revelation. The flavour and texture brought a whole new enjoyment to potato-eating, and they became the centrepiece of meals instead of just an accompaniment.

Of course, there are disappointments too when you grow your own fruit and vegetables – like the broad beans that gave a much-reduced crop because I didn't tackle the blackfly early enough. But offset against that were so many delights – raspberries eaten just picked, jewel-like alpine strawberries, all sorts of salad leaves, waist-high coriander, sweet beetroots, the prolific courgette plants kindly donated by a neighbour – and the broad-bean crop, while smaller than hoped for, was delicious.

From the monks who tended gardens around their monasteries, to the Michelin-starred restaurants with their own vegetable plots, a source of produce for the kitchen has been of prime importance to many an establishment.

For the green householder, growing your own cuts down on packaging and drastically reduces food miles – both in transporting produce to the shop and your own travel to the supermarket. In these days of food scares, it's a way of knowing you can trust what you put on your plate, and it can also help to keep food costs down, especially if you grow from seed (a packet of organic seed is around £1.50 and can last for more than a year).

Even if you have only a patio, balcony or windowsill, you can still grow something to enhance your eating pleasure. If you want to grow food on a larger scale, you could put your name down for an allotment (check with your local council for details).

GETTING STARTED

Much of this chapter is written with complete beginners in mind partly because I've started fairly recently myself, so can't claim to be an expert. Gardening is a huge subject and it can seem overwhelming when you're starting out. What I've realized, though, is that you don't need to be an instant expert. Most of us can get by with common sense and a bit of trial and error – you don't have to know it all to get a decent crop of leeks or blackcurrants.

- If you're not sure, start small. A few herbs in pots (→ page 170) and a tub of potatoes on the patio (→ page 173) will get you used to some of the principles of growing your own.
- In a larger garden plot or allotment, don't feel you have to cultivate it all straight away. You could prepare a limited area and concentrate on that first, then add to it the next season.
- Gardening does require time and effort, so only take on what you have the hours and energy for. That way you can enjoy your successes without feeling overwhelmed.

❧ If you know someone who's an expert (or willing to help with the physical work), try to enlist their help. For a head start, think about paying someone – or bartering or skills-swapping – for their assistance and expertise. We couldn't have done nearly as much as we have without our neighbour and gardening mentor, Tony Ashford.

❧ There's always another year in gardening – another chance to learn from mistakes (and successes), and another opportunity to try new varieties.

Kitchen gardener's tip:
Browse libraries and bookshops, new and second-hand. The Encyclopedia of Organic Gardening *(by the Henry Doubleday Research Association, now Garden Organic) covers all the key areas, or look for titles by Bob Flowerdew, Monty Don and Joy Larkcom. You can pick up the Royal Horticultural Society's* The Vegetable Garden Displayed *relatively cheaply; it was first published in 1941 to support the wartime 'Dig for Victory' campaign and remains recommended reading.*

Gardening organically

This means growing plants without the use of chemical fertilizers, pesticides, fungicides or weedkillers (although certain chemicals are permitted). The idea is to take the best from land-husbandry techniques that have been honed over the millennia during which humans have been agriculturalists, and supplementing them with modern findings, methods and products (such as biological pest controls).

What kind of kitchen garden?

You don't need a hundred-foot field of a garden to start growing your own. Yours could be one of the alternatives below.

- Pots and grow-bags on your balcony or roof terrace, making use of recycled containers such as old buckets, chimney pots, sinks, tin baths, old tyres and half-barrels.
- A square-foot garden (see www.squarefootgardening.com and articles at www.gardenorganic.org.uk) located in a corner of the patio that gets good sunlight. This type of garden is good for growing a range of crops intensively in a small space.
- A potager, where vegetables are mixed in with flowers in a cottage-garden style. This can attract beneficial insects to help pollination and keep down pests.
- A single vegetable bed you've decided to experiment with for a year.
- A formal arrangement of raised beds, with their sides made from timber planks (ensure the wood is untreated), reclaimed roof tiles or bricks. These are useful if bending down is a problem. They also tend to have better drainage, and the soil warms up more quickly in spring. If you add plenty of organic matter (such as manure) at the start they can also allow you to grow more intensively in your space.
- Some chilli plants and tomatoes in your conservatory.
- An allotment.

The soil

The soil is of paramount importance – it's what provides the nutrients that plants need, and determines how much air and moisture can get to their roots. An organic gardener aims to improve and replenish the soil largely by adding plant or animal-sourced matter, such as home-made compost and well-rotted manure, or by growing a crop that contributes to the soil when it's dug in, such as grazing rye or phacelia. These crops are known as 'green manures'.

Weeds

You might think organic gardeners would have a live-and-let-live approach to unwanted plant visitors, but in fact weeds compete with your beloved fruit and vegetables for water, nutrients and light. They can be removed by hand (by hoeing or weeding) or by spreading the area with a layer of mulch (→ page 180), which blocks out the light and so halts or slows weed growth.

Pests and diseases

If plants are healthy, they are better able to withstand insect and other attacks. This means planting them far enough apart, in good soil, and making sure they aren't stressed by lack of water (or too much). You can remove bugs by hand – nip out the tops of broad-bean plants, as I'll be doing promptly from now on if I spot the telltale stuck-together leaves – or use simple soap sprays and barriers. Biological methods include encouraging beneficial insects, such as ladybirds, or introducing natural predators, such as nematodes to control slugs. The aim is to achieve a healthy balance rather than a totally pest-free plot.

THE KITCHEN GARDENER'S YEAR

January

Place orders for seed

Turn compost heaps

Dig, and add soil improvers (if the weather allows and you haven't already done so)

Force rhubarb

Cut back autumn raspberries, and other fruit pruning

February

Plant hardy seeds, such as broad beans, outdoors

Sow seeds indoors

Chit seed potatoes by laying them in trays

Prune fruit trees, such as apples, and also redcurrants

Plant fruit bushes, such as raspberries and currants

March and April

Complete last-minute soil improvement

Sow many crops outdoors

Sow tender crops (ones that can't stand frost) indoors, including
tomatoes destined to go outside rather than in a greenhouse
Plant potatoes
Harden off (→ page 184) and then plant out frost-resistant
seedlings raised indoors
Plant asparagus crowns

May

Continue with spring sowing, including tender crops such
as courgettes and French and runner beans, although bear
in mind that many parts of the UK are still hit by late frosts in
May
Sow late-summer and autumn crops, such as sweetcorn (indoors)
and squashes, sprouts and cabbages (outdoors)

June to August

Water, particularly when plants are at crucial stages, such as
seedlings (→ page 236)
Sow tender crops and, later on, winter greens, such as corn salad
and chicory
Sow more of the fast-growing crops, such as salads, beetroots and
spring onions (this is known as successional sowing)
Transplant tender plants, and late-summer and autumn crops,
such as sweetcorn, outdoors
Plant strawberries
Begin the harvest
Prune blackcurrants and redcurrants straight after fruiting

September

Cut back summer raspberries

Take semi-ripe cuttings from woody herbs, such as sage and
rosemary

Continue harvesting

Plant autumn onion sets (miniature bulbs)

October to November

Sow green manure crops to overwinter

Sow crops to overwinter for harvest the next year, such as broad
beans, peas and garlic

Harvest cabbages, greens and root vegetables

Harvest late-season apples for storage

Clear plants that have finished producing

Order and plant fruit trees and bushes

December

Plan, prune, clear and dig

Force chicory

Your gardening tool kit

Try to keep tools clean and dry, so they last. Use a lightly oiled cloth (→ page 52) to wipe the blades of secateurs and pruners – the oil will protect them from rust. When you're starting out, see what you can borrow from neighbours, or look for second-hand but good-quality tools.

Spade

Fork

Trowel and hand fork

Cultivator: This looks like a strange fishing implement, with three prongs, but is very useful for opening up the soil and removing weed roots.

Rake: The kind with a flat head and rigid tines that you use to level the soil and rake it into finer particles.

Hoe: There are lots of different types. For removing young weeds, a Swiss oscillating hoe, with a sharp blade that you can push and pull through the soil, is efficient.

Wheelbarrow and/or trugs and buckets

Watering can: Try to avoid hose-watering from the mains when you can (→ page 236).

Gardening gloves

Canes, sticks and string: Save tree and shrub prunings for plant supports and to mark where you've sown seeds. Pea sticks are branching twigs that pea plants can wind themselves around. You can make a garden line, to mark straight rows for sowing, by cutting a long piece of string, tying each end to a cane, then winding the string around one of them (using your garden line, → page 182).

Deciding what to grow

- Choose the fruit and vegetables you like and use a lot, and those that are expensive or difficult to find in the shops. Soft fruit, for example, needs relatively little tending for the return – compare £2.99 for a single fruit punnet with £3.99 for an entire currant bush.

- Draw up a list. Look in books to see the range of vegetable and fruit crops, and check catalogues from seed suppliers and nurseries for varieties you like the sound of. Qualities such as disease-resistance can also be important.

- Plan so you'll be using your soil and harvesting crops all year round. Andi Clevely's *The Allotment Book* and others give handy tables of sowing and harvesting times, or invest in a wall-planner chart (www.organiccatalog.com). Get in a good selection of seed, so you'll always have something to plant, and start plants off indoors to get ahead (for sowing indoors, → page 183).

- To an extent, what you can grow will be determined by the space you have available, and if you have a greenhouse (but you can always be inventive on both counts). You may find that certain crops perform particularly well or badly in your soil and conditions, so check with neighbouring gardeners.

Kitchen gardener's tip:
Fruit and vegetables will do best in sunny, protected conditions (although they do need a flow of air, too, so don't cramp them in against high hedges). Watch how the sun moves around your garden at different times of day. Choose the spot where you'd most like to sunbathe, and site the vegetable plot there.

INDOOR HERBS

Small-space vegetable gardening is becoming increasingly popular, especially in urban areas. Even if you don't have anywhere outdoors, you can still fit some herbs in pots on a sunny windowsill – preferably a south-facing one that will get about six hours of light a day. For ease, and if you want just one or two, buy established plants from a garden centre or online from a site such as Jekka's Herb Farm (www.jekkasherbfarm.com). You'll need some pots (preferably re-used) a couple of sizes larger than the ones they're in, to give the plants space to grow and bush out a bit.

 Find some pieces of broken pottery (called 'crocks') and place one or two in the bottom of the pot, to cover the drainage holes. Put in some multipurpose potting compost, or a compost for houseplants (for notes on buying potting compost, → page 172). Water the plant well before repotting, then squeeze the container it's in gently to tip it out. Leaving the soil around its roots, place it in the new pot, add extra compost all round and firm it in. Water again, but don't leave it to stand in water.

You can also pot up the growing herbs available in supermarkets – carefully tease apart the seedling roots and choose the best-looking specimens.

For a larger crop – plenty of basil for pesto, for instance, or coriander for curries and pastes – sow seed indoors and then raise the plants in outdoor containers or in the vegetable garden.

Four herbs for the kitchen

Basil comes in a wide range of varieties, from sweet, to purple, to Thai. An annual herb (it lasts for one growing season), basil will keep going indoors into the autumn or longer. The seeds need warmth (about 18°C) to germinate. To harvest, nip off the top pair of leaves on each shoot, which will stimulate bushier growth.

Flat-leaf parsley is a biennial that's a great staple for the kitchen. The seed can be difficult to germinate, and take a month or more to come up; try soaking overnight before planting. To delay flowering in the second year, chop the plant back in the spring.

Chives are perennial, so should carry on producing for a few years. This herb likes a rest during the winter, so put the pot in a garage or shed for a couple of months when growth slows down.

Mint is another herb with a large choice of varieties, and is easy to grow from cuttings – if you leave a stem in water for long enough, it will probably start producing roots all by itself.

Kitchen gardener's tip:
Give herbs a good drink, but only when the soil is dry on top. To keep the air in a centrally heated home moist enough, stand the plants on a tray of pebbles filled with water to just below the pebbles' surface, or plant the pots in a windowbox, filling it up with potting compost. Give indoor herbs some fresh air by opening the window now and again. Use a seaweed-based liquid fertilizer as a weekly feed for container plants in the growing season. For other herb-growing tips, see www.gardenersclub.co.uk/growingherbs.asp.

Buying potting compost

What's sold as compost in the garden centre is different from the compost you make from garden and kitchen waste. Potting composts are used for container-grown plants and raising seedlings and cuttings, and have different recipes to tailor them for each purpose. Check that what you buy isn't peat-based – if a compost doesn't say it's peat free, it probably does contain peat.

I was initially attracted by John Innes composts, because they're loam-based (soil-based), but the traditional formulation does include peat, and there are also issues with where the soil may have come from (see www.johninnescompost.org). They are heavy, which is good for large plants, such as shrubs in containers, but not so good for pots you want to move around.

According to *Gardening Which?* (www.which.co.uk), peat-free composts still don't match up in performance, but since government targets mean manufacturers will need to go virtually peat free by 2010, there should soon be a much better choice. Also look out for options containing recycled peat, such as those from West Riding Organics (www.wrorganics.co.uk).

Making your own additions
Horticultural sharp sand (not builder's sand, although I've used spare from an old children's sandpit in our garden) can help to improve drainage, which is good for herbs. Vermiculite and perlite are often recommended for water retention, but they're produced from mined minerals and so are non-renewable. Think about using seaweed meal or fine, well-composted bark chips as an alternative.

Potatoes on your patio

As we discovered, home-grown potatoes are delicious, and you can grow them in containers as well as in the ground. Special potato planters have a sliding sleeve or doorway that allows you to remove your harvest gradually without disturbing the rest of the plant. To be even greener, you could re-use any good-sized container that's to hand, including a half-barrel, or even an old bath, or try a recycled plastic refuse sack. A container around 50cm/20in high and 35cm/14in wide will hold about three tubers, so if you're planting a tub for the patio, it's more economical to share a seed potato order with friends.

Chitting

Chitting potatoes means letting the shoots appear before you plant them. The idea is that they will mature earlier, although some people argue that potentially it means you'll get a smaller crop. For most potatoes, place them in a tray, or in egg boxes, with the rose – the end with the most buds – upwards. Keep in a light but cool place and wait for the shoots to grow. If you want large baking potatoes, take off all but two or three of the strongest shoots before planting.

Planting

Potatoes like the soil to be loose and well-worked, so if you're growing outside make sure the potato patch is well dug over – you could also use a cultivator (→ page 168). In a container, put a layer of crocks about 5cm/2in to 10cm/4in deep in the bottom, then a layer of potting compost up to 10cm/4in deep. Place the tubers on this and cover with 15cm/6in of compost – but leave a good amount of room at the top of the pot.

Earthing up

This means raking up soil over the plants or adding another layer of compost, which protects young leaves against frost and stops tubers going green and becoming inedible. You can either do two lots of earthing up – first when the plants are about 15cm/6in tall, and again when they've grown a good canopy of leaves – or else keep it to one go when they're a bit bigger (22cm/9in.). Certainly with the earlier earthing up, you're aiming to cover much of the plant.

Watering

Whether in the ground or in containers, potatoes need most water when they've just been planted, and when the tubers are forming (this is generally when the flower buds start to be visible). If the weather's dry, give them a really good dousing to the roots. In a container, they may also benefit from a feed with an organic liquid fertilizer.

Harvesting

Potatoes are divided into early, second early and maincrop varieties. Earlies are harvested roughly from June and maincrops from August onwards. As a guide, earlies are usually ready when the flowers are fully open, and maincrops when the foliage turns brown and the stems start to wither. In beds, dig your fork in a good distance from the plant – at least at the edge of the ridge – so you don't end up spearing your crop. With bottom-opening pots, you can remove the tubers as you need them.

Which potato variety for what?

Potatoes can be roughly divided into waxy types that hold their shape well for salads and thin slicing, and floury ones that are fluffier for baking and roasting; earlier potato varieties tend to be the smaller, waxier types and maincrops the bakers and mashers – but that doesn't always hold. Depending on your soil and weather conditions, the flavour and texture will vary. These are varieties that have done well for us or have been recommended by growers nearby. For notes on disease resistance as well as flavour, read the booklet *Alan Romans' Guide to Seed Potato Varieties*.

Mash: Edzell Blues, with a bluey purple skin, make the creamiest, easiest mash I've ever come across. Arran Victory are also good. With floury potatoes, you can always bake them before mashing, instead of boiling.

Chips and roasting: King Edward, Edzell Blue, Sharpe's Express.

Baking: Purple-skinned Arran Victory, Valor Red Duke of York (a slightly waxy summer potato, but if left to grow larger they bake well).

Small and waxy, for salads:
   Charlotte, Roseval, Pink Fir Apple, Ratte.

Larger and waxy: Charlotte.

Early potatoes are best eaten as soon as they've been lifted – so you probably won't want to grow too many, unless you can think of lots of potato dishes to make for the freezer. They can be left in the soil for a while, but may start to be attacked by hungry soil  creatures. Maincrop varieties can be stored, preferably in jute sacks and certainly not in plastic, in the dark at a temperature of 7°C to 10°C (don't let the frost get to them).

❋ **Kitchen gardener's tip:**
❋ *Tomatoes can do well on a patio, especially if you place them*
❋ *against a warm and sunny south-west-facing wall. Bush tomatoes*
❋ *are compact and grow well in containers, while traditional vines*
❋ *need stakes and string to tie them up. Grow pots of basil alongside*
❋ *your tomatoes and you'll have an Italian salad on your doorstep.*
❋ *For more ideas on container vegetables see www.selfsufficientish.*
❋ *com/container.htm.*

PREPARING YOUR PLOT

We were lucky with our garden – because it had been cultivated as a vegetable plot for years there wasn't a lot we needed to do to improve the soil. However, for many gardens this won't be the case, and this may mean it takes some time to get your plot to its best. That's no reason to be disheartened though – you can still raise delicious veg by sowing your seedlings in pots (→ page 183) and even adding potting compost to the planting holes if necessary.

Before you start, it's useful to know your soil's pH (acid, alkaline or neutral), as this will affect how well (or not) some plants will grow. Also note whether it's sandy and crumbly or clay-based and sticky. What you're aiming to achieve in the long term is something between the two textures – crumbly enough so it doesn't turn into a bog after rain, or set like concrete in drought, but not so free-draining that nutrients are washed straight out.

The first steps with a new plot are generally to clear weeds and dig over the ground. There are instructions for good digging technique and other gardening basics on the 'How To Be a Gardener' section of the BBC website, at www.bbc.co.uk/gardening, and there are tips for first-timers at www.selfsufficientish.com.

You will need to add soil improvers such as well-rotted compost, horse manure or bracken, recycled peat or compost from your local council (made from your garden waste collection). This helps the soil structure as well as adding nutrients. You can dig these in or spread over the surface as a mulch. For more about soil management, consult a reference book such as the *Encyclopedia of Organic Gardening*.

Ideally, we should all be recycling as much as we can from our own gardens – and kitchens – to feed our soil through effective composting. If that's not enough, use local sources for other improvers, and sustainable options such as organic chicken manure pellets. Neighbours may have spare compost they could donate.

Kitchen gardener's tip:

If you have a heavy clay soil, do your digging during the late autumn or winter and leave the soil in large clods. The frost will help both to kill off pests and diseases and also break up the soil – meaning less work for you.

What kind of composter do I need?

Medium to large garden, growing plenty of plants and your own veg
You'll probably want at least two large compost bins, so you can fill the next one as the first bin is maturing. Modular wooden composters are available from www.organiccatalog.com or try your local garden centre (from £85). Otherwise, simply pile the material in an old-fashioned unsupported heap, or construct your own composter for the cost of the materials – usually 10cm/4in by 10cm/4in untreated wooden posts and either wire netting or planks for the enclosure.

Small to medium garden with plenty of plants, or allotment
A single tower or similar recycled plastic compost bin will probably be big enough, especially if you compost autumn leaves separately in a wire-netting cylinder. Tower compost bins are widely available, including from DIY stores (costs vary, but subsidized bins from the council can be under £20).

Small or patio garden, with more kitchen waste than garden waste
Worm composting could be your answer – and you can even put a wormery on a balcony. The worms eat up the organic matter and turn it into extremely rich compost, plus liquid that's a great fertilizer. For tips and links see www.envocare.co.uk/wormeries.htm (cost about £90).

For cooked scraps in the garden
The Green Cone (www.greencone.com) will take pretty much everything from the kitchen, including meat, fish and bones, and convert it into water, carbon dioxide and a small amount of

leftover matter, or you could try the Green Johanna, from the same company. The water goes straight down into the soil beneath (cost from £70 – although check if your council is trialling them at a reduced price).

For cooked scraps in the kitchen

Bokashi is a mixture containing bran and effective micro-organisms (EMs) that ferment kitchen waste (don't add bones or paper). The process, developed in Japan, is pretty odourless, and the small, neat bins come with an airtight lid anyway, so it's a great way of clean composting in the kitchen. The results can go on the compost heap or straight in the soil, where they quickly break down (cost from around £60 at www.greengardener.co.uk).

Composting tips

- Include a mixture of ingredients. Have some 'greens', such as young weeds (avoid putting in seedheads), grass, peelings and teabags, 'browns' such as shredded card and paper, old plants and straw, plus crushed eggshells and wood ash.
- Newspapers and printed card are safe to put in as most inks are now vegetable-based, but it's better overall for the environment to send your papers and magazines for recycling.
- Woody trimmings take a long time to rot down – borrow a garden shredder or chop up tougher items with shears.
- Grass can form a sticky, smelly mat if left in layers, so mix it up with shredded paper.
- Don't put in dog or cat faeces, or bread, grains, dairy or meat products or most cooked foods, which can attract flies

and vermin. Onions and citrus fruits can make the compost too acid. Only add bags and wrappings labelled as 'compostable'.

🪴 Spread the roots of perennial weeds, such as dandelions and bindweed, in the sun to dry out before crumbling them into the heap. It's safest to leave out diseased plant matter.

🪴 To get your finished compost more quickly – and to kill off lingering seeds and diseases – try a hot heap. Gather enough material to fill the bin, make sure it's well chopped and mixed, and water it as you put it in if it's too dry. Cover with layers of cardboard or get a compost duvet (old carpet could contain hazardous chemicals). After a week or two turn the heap, remixing everything.

🪴 Even with a slower heap, turning the compost regularly will speed things up and allow you to see if you need to change the balance of greens and browns.

Mulches and no-dig gardening

Basically, a mulch is a layer that you put on top of the soil. It could be bark chippings, or a thick blanket of compost, or rotted manure, or cardboard, or a woven membrane, or crushed shells. It can help to retain moisture, suppress weeds and keep the soil warmer. If you are mulching, do it when the soil is moist and not too cold. Organic mulches, such as compost, also enrich the soil as worms and other creatures mix them with the earth.

No-dig gardening is largely based around using mulches. The idea is to leave the soil structure undisturbed, so instead of digging soil improvers in, you put them in a thick layer over the top. For more on this gardening philosophy see www.no-dig-vegetable garden.com and Charles Dowding's *Organic Gardening: The Natural No-Dig Way*.

WHERE TO FIND SEEDS AND PLANTS

Your local garden centre will probably have a decent selection of seeds and plants, including organic ranges from mainstream seed merchants, but look up plant nurseries in your area too, and online organic sources, such as www.organiccatalog.com, www.wigglywigglers.co.uk, www.suffolkherbs.com and www.tamarorganics. co.uk. If you're growing organically, it's not essential to buy organically raised seed, but check that it hasn't been treated with chemicals such as pesticides.

Heritage or heirloom varieties may have been cultivated successfully for centuries, before the advent of modern chemical methods, so can be especially good for the organic grower (try www.pennardplants.com). You could also swap with neighbours or through garden groups, and collect some of your own seed to use the next year. We let our coriander plants flower and form seedheads, which means we can also use the fragrant seeds for cooking.

Raising seedlings

Growing from seed is magical. How does that tiny, hard bead turn into a fully fledged, produce-bearing plant? There are two main ways to do it. The first option is sowing direct into the soil where the plants will be growing, or else into a nursery bed, where you start plants off before transferring them to their final location. The second is raising them in seed trays, pots or root trainers indoors on a windowsill, or in a greenhouse. This allows you to grow plants, such as basil and tomatoes, that need higher temperatures to germinate. It also means you can get ahead by raising seedlings before it would be warm enough outdoors, and begin growing a new crop before the old one has been harvested.

If you have a soil that is well-cultivated, you will probably want to use both methods. If your soil still has a way to go, or if slugs are a particular problem, then starting plants indoors has much to recommend it.

Sowing outdoors

When you sow into beds, rake the dug soil flat, then work the few centimetres (or inch) of the surface until it becomes fine and breadcrumby, removing any old bits of root, weed and stones. After an initial raking, tread the soil to compact it slightly, then rake again so you end up with a fine tilth.

Sowing in rows

The traditional method is to mark your rows with a garden line (→ page 168) according to the distance apart shown on the packet. Dig one cane in at the end of the row, unravel the string and push the second cane in at the other end, keeping the line taut. Draw a line along the row with a cane, or make a shallow drill with the corner of a hoe. With tiny seeds, such as carrots, sow as evenly as possible and when the seedlings come up, thin them out by carefully pulling up the less healthy-looking ones until you end up with the recommended spacing between plants (which is also shown on the packet).

With larger seeds, such as parsnips, sow two or three at a time the recommended distance apart and, when the seedlings come up, thin so that just one is left in each position (snip off the less successful seedlings with scissors). This is often referred to as station sowing. The advantage of rows is that it's easier to get rid of weeds, because you can tell where your seedlings are and hoe in between them.

Sowing in a grid

Here, instead of using traditional row spacings, you average the plant and row distances and mark out a rough grid of where you will sow the seeds. Then station sow a few seeds in each position. For example, with plants that usually need to be 10cm/4in apart in rows 20cm/8in away from each other, sow at 15cm/6in intervals. This type of spacing is useful for square-foot and other small-space gardening – but hoeing is more difficult. Whichever method you use, keep a record of what you've planted where.

Sowing indoors

You can sow seed indoors in seedling trays, individual pots or root trainers – either re-used, bought, swapped or improvised. A windowsill is a good place to germinate seeds, or try an airing cupboard (although you should make sure they are in the light as soon as they show above the soil).

A propagator is a tray with a clear plastic lid that has vents you can open to maintain a good airflow, and sometimes heating pads and automatic watering options. You can make your own (→ page 185), or simply secure a plastic bag over a pot to help keep the atmosphere sufficiently moist until the seeds have germinated and the first proper leaves appear.

Otherwise, all kinds of packaging can be re-used to raise seedlings, from toilet roll centres (good for plants with long roots, such as peas and beans) to egg cartons and tomato trays (some come with handy plastic lids to make a mini propagator), and you can even fold your own pots from newspaper. Sticks from children's ice lollies make good markers on which to write what you've planted.

Pricking out

This is the process of choosing the best seedlings and carefully removing them from the company of their siblings to pot up into a larger pot or plant outside (I find a bamboo barbecue stick helpful for removing them). If you use degradable pots (such as toilet roll centres), or modules where you plant a single seed in each space and push out the seedling when it's ready, this makes life easier.

Hardening off

Indoor-grown plants need some time to acclimatize to life outside, so leave them out for increasing periods during the day until they can take the wider temperature fluctuations outdoors.

Kitchen gardener's tip:
Stroke your seedlings. If you are growing seedlings indoors they can become tall and weedy. Stroking over them – ideally 10 or more times early in the day – can help them grow up sturdier. Also make sure they have enough light, but aren't in scorching direct sunlight.

MAKE: *Cardboard box propagator*

✳ ✳ ✳ ✳ ✳ ✳ ✳ ✳ ✳ ✳ ✳ ✳ ✳ ✳ ✳

You will need:

   1 cardboard box that will fit on a windowsill or other sunny surface

   A long ruler and pen

   Scissors and/or a craft knife and protective mat

   Kitchen foil

   Glue

   Plastic vegetable trays or a suitable size baking tray

   Clear plastic sheet, such as a large plastic bag or furniture covering

   Sellotape

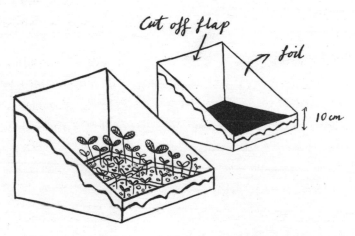

1. Mark a line about 10cm/4in up from the bottom of one long side of the box.

2. Cut the flap off the other long side, which will become the back, then draw diagonal lines across each short side from the top

corner to the line along the front. Cut along all these lines with the scissors or craft knife.

3. Spread glue over the inside of the box and carefully line it with foil, folding about 1cm/½in over each box edge.

4. Place the trays in the bottom to hold your pots.

5. Cut the plastic sheet so it can flap over as a 'roof' and secure at the back with Sellotape.

If you grow one thing . . . make it salad leaves

They're easy, they don't take up much room, and you can get packets of mixed varieties, such as Italian, oriental or spicy greens. Sow them outside (don't waste the thinnings, simply eat the baby leaves) or even raise them in a windowbox for easily pickable salad when you open the window.

Sow a second row – or box – a couple of weeks after the first, so that when your initial leaves are getting too old and strong, you'll have nice, young, fresh ones from batch number two. This is known as successional sowing. To harvest, simply tear or cut off a few leaves from each plant (preferably in the morning or evening, so they wilt less quickly) and they'll soon grow new ones.

PLANTS FOR FREE

Propagation, simply put, is about making new plants. As well as by sowing seed, this can be done by taking cuttings (from leaves, stems or roots), dividing plants into smaller clumps or plantlets, or 'laying', which means securing the stems to the ground where some plants will miraculously start producing roots. It's a great way of recycling your plants.

Taking cuttings can seem a little daunting at first, but it's often easier than you think. The winter before last I decided to use some loppings from our big rosemary bush to raise new plants by the house. All I did was dig a shallow trench, put in a little sand for drainage, and stuff in some sprigs of rosemary (with the lower leaves removed). It wasn't really the right time of year – it snowed, it rained, it frosted. A good few stems didn't make it, but I now have five established small bushes, all for no money and very little effort.

- Usually, cuttings are started off in a pot of compost, or other suitable container. When you're taking them, more is better – it'll increase your chances of success and make casualties less crucial. You can then choose the healthiest young plants.
- Look up the plant you want to take cuttings from for advice on the best way to do it, and to check what time of year to take them.
- You don't need to buy fancy hormone rooting powders, but try to give cuttings the right amount of moisture. They need good drainage so they don't get waterlogged (sharp sand can be useful, → page 172), and enough humidity so they don't dry out before they've rooted (put a plastic bag over the pot).

Kitchen gardener's tip:
Finding out the long- and short-range weather forecasts becomes more important when you're gardening. When planting or sowing, choosing a time when rain will come later or the following day means the plants will get a good watering in without you needing to add so much from the water butt or tap.

A SMORGASBORD OF PLANTING IDEAS

There are all kinds of ways you can be imaginative to enliven and make the most of what you have. In Cuba, for instance, people have become creative with producing food in every available space, even in containers up stairways.

Interplanting

Some crops take a long time to mature, while others come up quickly. Take advantage of these differing growth rates to plant an extra fast crop between two slower rows, such as radishes or baby salad leaves between parsnips or maincrop carrots.

Three-sisters bed

Based on a traditional Native American method, this needs fertile soil. Sweetcorn is planted at the spacing recommended on the seed packet, then a couple of climbing beans are sown at the base of each plant, so they can twine up them, and squashes are put in between to grow at ground level and help smother weeds.

Baby veg

If you want small vegetables, such as baby beetroots, plant them closer together, or in clusters.

Beans as sunshades and dens

With a collection of tall bamboo (or hazel) poles, all more or less the same length, you can make a bean screen. Push two of them into the ground so they lean towards each other and cross near the top. Tie them together where they cross and continue with another two poles. When you have a row, place one pole along the top V and secure for extra support. Plant two runner bean seeds at the base of each cane. For a children's den, arrange the canes in a circular tipi formation, leaving a gap for an entrance.

Strawberry pots

These are an attractive, space-saving way to grow strawberries. You'll need one plant for each little pocket or hole in the side, and three or so for the top. Plant in late summer or early autumn in a soil-less compost (which is lighter), choosing a sheltered position that gets plenty of sun. Keep the compost just moist. They'll need feeding during the growing season; while flowering and fruiting you could use a tomato fertilizer. Protect with straw during frosty nights.

Forest gardens

This type of gardening imitates the different levels of a forest, with fruit trees as the highest storey, bushes such as redcurrants in the middle, and herbs and perennial vegetables below, with some climbers and perhaps a few annual vegetables. It's a low-maintenance, productive approach that aims to work along with natural processes, and you don't need a lot of space to try it. See the Agroforestry Research Trust (www.agroforestry. co.uk) and Robert Hart's pioneering *Forest Gardens*.

Balcony peas

Plant climbing peas or beans in an old tin bath or other good-sized container, such as a wood-sided planter, and use the balcony railings to help them climb. Mix in some sweet peas for a waft of fragrance when you open the windows.

Crop rotation

Crop rotation helps to stop pests and diseases building up, and replenishes and makes the most of soil fertility. It's an important principle for organic growers, although I find working out the rotations baffling. It's a bit like a Rubik's cube – so if you have that turn of mind you may relish meticulously planning what to put where, and when. If you don't, a simple basic rule to remember is that most crops will do better if they aren't grown on the same spot year after year – especially potatoes and brassicas.

The principle of rotation dates from Roman times and was developed further during the Islamic Golden Age (in the ninth century). It really took off during the British agricultural revolution of the eighteenth century. Crops from the same family, or broader group, are deliberately moved around each year, aiming for a three to four-year gap before they return to the same position. It's important to know the plant family each vegetable comes from – cabbages, for example, are brassicas, while chard is related to beetroot, and tomatoes belong to the same family as potatoes so shouldn't be planted where you grew your spuds last year (like potatoes, they are prone to blight).

Organic gardening books will give you pointers for planning your crop rotation effectively, or try online articles from Garden Organic and the RHS, or log on to the forums at www.selfsufficientish.com.

TIPS FOR DEALING WITH WEEDS AND PESTS

- Clear out as many perennial weeds, such as dandelions and brambles, as you can before planting. These weeds will come up year after year if left, and bindweed and couch grass, for example, can regenerate from even a fragment of root.
- Annual weeds grow fast, seed and then die, so deal with them straight away. Hoe them as soon as they appear, or smother with a mulch. If you leave them, the next minute your plot will look like a jungle – I know this from experience. Some areas may need hand-weeding with a small fork, but hoeing is easier.
- Hoeing is most effective in dry weather, when the young weeds will quickly wilt, while hand-weeding is easiest when rain has softened the soil.
- Learn to love the weeds you can't contain. Harvest your nettles in the spring, and enjoy the fact you're raising caterpillar food. Chickweed can also be eaten, and children enjoy games with dandelions, buttercups and trumpet-shaped bindweed flowers (the rhyme round here goes something like: 'Polly had a dolly but her head popped off').
- Remove pests by hand where you can. Aphids – greenfly, blackfly and whitefly and other munchers can often be washed, sprayed or brushed off.
- Growing differently may bring a solution. If outdoor seedlings are being attacked by slugs, try starting them indoors (although if it's wet, they may still get munched up when you plant them out). If your area is prone to potato blight or tiny keel slugs,

grow early varieties, which mature before the time of year these problems take hold. Broad beans planted for an early start may be ahead of aphid attack.

- Encourage beneficial insects such as ladybirds and hoverflies, and make your garden bee-friendly (it will aid fruit tree pollination). Grow flowering plants around your vegetable plot – and even in it – to give a supply of nectar from spring to autumn, and think about overwinter homes (→ page 387).
- Fennel and dill attract hoverflies (their larvae eat aphids). Yellow flowers are a 'come over here' beacon to helpful insect predators, which is one reason marigolds are recommended. Some plants also produce deterrent chemicals – see www.herbsociety.co. uk/companion.htm and the National Vegetable Society companion planting page (www.nvsuk.org.uk).
- Remove plants when they have finished producing. Plant debris can harbour disease and attract less friendly garden creatures, such as snails and slugs.
- In theory an organic garden should settle down into a workable ecological balance after a few years, but if you have a persistent problem, look up organic methods of treating it.

Super berries

Blueberries have had good PR as a superfood, because of their phytonutrient content. However, blackberries, strawberries, blackcurrants and raspberries – all those gorgeous British summer fruits – also contain a group of flavonoids called anthocyanins and vitamin C, and are generally easier for most of us to grow, as blueberries need acidic soil.

Some varieties of strawberries fruit quite late in the year, extending the season when you'll be able to pick your own, and, if you're lucky, raspberries such as Autumn Bliss may continue producing right to the first frosts.

- You can buy bare-root bushes – which, as the name suggests, have been dug up from the nursery and had the soil removed – or plants raised in containers. Bare-root bushes are more economical, but they need to be planted out promptly and are usually available only between November and March.
- Use a local fruit nursery, if possible, and go to see the bushes or trees. Online, Deacon's on the Isle of Wight (www.deaconsnurseryfruits.co.uk) and Buckingham Nurseries (www.hedging.co .uk) are recommended mail-order sources.
- Plan to plant your fruit bushes in the winter months, before the growing season starts around March, but try to avoid periods when the ground may be frozen. If it is, you'll need to keep the bushes under cover and out of the ground for a while, and they may suffer, as one of my blackcurrants did.
- Prepare the plot well, following advice for the particular plant from a respected gardening source or book. Then your bushes or canes should last a good few years.

Kitchen gardener's tip:
If you love blueberries, you could try planting one in a container using an ericaceous compost – this is the kind that heathers and rhododendrons like, available from garden centres and online.

Planting an apple tree

There's something about an orchard, especially one with gnarled, mature trees. Apparently, our garden used to be filled with apple trees, and almost every plot around us still has at least one. We have a Bramley-type cooker that needed some careful pruning when we arrived, and we have added a quince tree, along with a Worcester Pearmain and an Ashmead's Kernel.

Fruit and nut trees add another level to a garden, and bring blossom in spring before their edible produce. But they take time before giving a decent crop. You'll also need to find out about the right rootstock to buy (depending on whether you want trained apple shapes such as cordons – good for a small garden – or else mini trees, or a full-size version at maturity), pruning and fertilization. To produce fruits, most apple trees need at least one other nearby that comes into flower at the same time, so insects can cross-pollinate them. Alternatively you could choose a self-fertile variety, or a 'family' tree with several varieties grafted on to one rootstock. There is plenty of advice to be found on all of this, online and in books such as the RHS's *Growing Fruit*. I reckon it's more than worth it.

What to do with your harvest

Something you may not be prepared for, when you begin growing your own, is the sheer bounty when a crop gets into its stride. One way round this is to plant small amounts to mature at different times; for example, leaving a couple of weeks between rows of broad beans. Otherwise, get your kitchen ready for full-scale production.

Early apples are best eaten as soon as they are ripe on the tree, and the same is generally true of early potatoes coming out of the ground (→ page 174). You can leave many other root crops in the soil and simply unearth them when needed. Later crops can be stored in a cool, dark place over the winter, with a good airflow. Check regularly, and quickly use up any that are deteriorating.

Vegetables such as beans and fruit such as apples can be sliced and frozen as soon as harvested. Open-freeze soft fruits such as raspberries (without washing) by laying them on a tray, then put in a box once frozen; or else make ice creams, sorbets and compotes.

Making jams and chutneys is a traditional autumn occupation (→ page 143), and you could also try pickling. Another idea is to swap any excess produce with fellow gardeners, or give it away to neighbours who have watered your plot when you were away.

Kitchen gardener's tip:

Enid Underwood, who kept a Bath allotment until she was 80, passed on this tip from her father. If you shell peas and trim vegetables while you're at the allotment (or in the garden), it lightens the load to carry home and you can put the pods and trimmings straight on the compost heap.

How to make your garden good enough to eat

Don't worry if you have a small space – there'll be something that you can grow in it.

You don't need to be an instant expert. It's OK to start small and have a few mishaps – every gardener does.

Herbs and salad leaves can be raised on a windowsill, and many other vegetables and fruit in containers.

Garden by organic principles, aiming to create nourishing soil and healthy plants that can withstand pest attacks.

Make your own garden compost to improve the soil and get rid of kitchen waste at the same time.

Buy peat-free potting compost for seedlings and containers.

Start your own seed collection – it's cheaper than buying plants and means you'll always have something to fill a gap.

Enjoy experimenting with different varieties and ideas such as strawberry pots and bean dens.

Keep on top of weeds, and help to control pests by growing plants that attract beneficial insects.

Get the recipe books ready and clear the freezer to make the most of your harvest.

7

WASTE
MANAGEMENT

Councils are getting very keen for us to recycle – *which is a good thing, given that UK households throw away almost 30 million tonnes of rubbish a year. The problem has been finding strategies to make sure*

we do it. Fortnightly rubbish collections have caused outrage, and pay-per-throw, where residents are charged for the amount being collected, could go the same way. But it really does make sense to recycle, and not just so that less waste goes into landfill. It also reduces raw material and energy consumption – a recycled aluminium can, for example, takes only 5 per cent of the energy needed to make one from raw bauxite ore.

When you start thinking along those lines – of saving resources, rather than simply limiting rubbish – it soon becomes obvious that recycling should really be the last resort, not the first. The recycler's mantra is reduce, re-use, repair, recycle. Take the example of what you could do to keep a sweetcorn tin out of the recycling box – it could be re-used as a desk tidy or to make a ladybird hotel (→ page 387). Better still, buy fresh cobs, rather than tinned sweetcorn, and compost the trimmings, or grow your own and cut the food miles to zero.

There's a danger that the recycling box could become the new rubbish bin, just sorted out a bit more, and maybe washed. Ideally, it should be a very final resting place, and not too full at that.

What's all this 'reduce, re-use, repair, recycle'?

When I first heard the word 'reduce' in this context, I thought it meant crushing your rubbish before you put it in the bin, but that was many years ago, and now I'm very keen on reducing. Here's what the mantra means in a nutshell:

Reduce: Cut down waste by reducing what you buy in the first place, and planning so you don't over-buy. Buy products that have less or no packaging, and swap, grow or make what you can.

Re-use: Find new ways to use what you've got, rather than simply binning things. Had a package in a padded envelope? Buy some sticky address labels and you can re-use it. Empty toilet roll bag? Re-use it as a bin liner. Re-use also includes swapping, donating and selling.

Repair: Fix things straight away rather than throwing them away or hoarding them in a cupboard – and if you can't fix it yourself, give it to someone who can.

Recycle: Separate items that can be collected by your council, or sent by other means to reprocessors, to be turned into something new (although some of what we send for recycling, such as saleable books and CDs, is actually being re-used).

HOW TO START REDUCING YOUR CONSUMPTION

We've become used to replacing things because we feel like it, not because they're worn out. There's also been a huge growth in disposable, single-use items. So what steps can we take to kick the consumer habit?

Get rid of the wipes

What's wrong with flannels to wipe mucky faces, and cloths to mop up spills? Figures from North America suggest that 83,000 tonnes of wipes and disposable cloths were used there in 2005. Scary.

Buy to last

Take the long view. Think about investing in a product for a good number of years. It may take extra research, it may cost more initially, but there'll usually be longer-term savings.

Be a late adopter

Some years back I seem to remember being rather impressed by minidisc players – but what iPod owner would bother with one of those now? Being late on the scene makes it more likely you'll avoid those technological dead-ends.

Procrastinate

If you wait long enough, you won't need a new winter skirt, because it'll be summer, and it's a good thing you didn't transform the spare room into a home cinema, because now it needs to be a nursery.

Buy re-usable

Many items, from razors to batteries, are available in re-usable versions, so go for them, and try to resist disposables, including plates and cutlery.

Buy second-hand

As long as it's in good condition, or you can fix it, so it won't end up on the scrap heap, second-hand is a good option, and often cheaper than new.

Borrow and hire

Toys, books, CDs and DVDs can be borrowed from libraries, drills and other tools from neighbours. Glasses and even fish kettles can be hired for special occasions from wine chains and supermarkets. If you feel bad about one-sided borrowing, give an appropriate gift – or help with a project – in return.

Buy what's needed, not just wanted

Whether it's a new car, a new coat or a new look for your home, do you really need it? Will it truly enhance your life, and the lives of those around you? And if so, is there a way to do it, or have it, that reduces its ecological stamp – such as choosing something salvaged or recycled?

Ethical buyer's tip:

When you do need to buy something new, you can check the ethical and environmental ratings of the companies behind the products through Ethical Consumer *magazine and its buyers' guides (www.ethicalconsumer.org.uk; you will need to subscribe for online Ethiscore information).*

The Zero Waste ideal

In the UK, Bath and North East Somerset council has pioneered Zero Waste challenge weeks. The idea is to put nothing into your rubbish bin for seven days, so you buy and use only things that are recyclable or compostable. Bury St Edmunds council in Suffolk now runs a similar scheme, and St Arvans in Monmouthshire is aiming to became a Zero Waste village. It's actually very difficult to achieve a completely empty bin (unless you take pretty radical steps), but Zero Waste – like zero accidents – is a target to aim for.

The Zero Waste Trust in New Zealand (www.zerowaste.co.nz) has led the way globally. Its vision is to revolutionize the whole way we think about rubbish. Instead of products becoming 'waste' at the end of their life, we should see their components as resources waiting to be used again. The Trust advocates improving the way we design and manufacture products so it's easier to reclaim their useful elements when they no longer work in their original form. It's a philosophy based on a 'cradle to cradle' approach, rather than 'cradle to grave'.

Going for Zero Waste in your weekly bin

We've been trying for a while in our home to cut back on rubbish and have trimmed back quite a bit, but there are still items that inevitably end up in your landfill bin. Here are some of the culprits you may find lurking, even if you're trying hard, and a few ideas for dealing with them. (For a guide to recycling things you didn't think could be recycled, → pages 211–14).

Problem 1: Plastic packaging This includes food packets, make-up containers and all those bits of expanded polystyrene.
Possible solutions: Buy more loose goods. Opt for second-hand furniture and appliances, which won't come with all that

packaging. Look out for low-packaging beauty brands, such as Stella McCartney's Care (www.stellamccartneycare.com), Nude (www.nudeskincare.com) and Aveda (www.aveda.com). Make a pact to re-use as much as you can, such as tomato packaging for plant drip trays and empty moisturizer or bath salts tubs to store home-made play dough (→ page 380) or small bits and pieces.

Problem 2: Cooked kitchen waste This is an issue if your council doesn't do a food waste collection. Cooked foods, meat, fish, dairy and grains can attract vermin, so aren't a great idea on the compost.

Possible solutions: Get a bokashi bin or a Green Cone (→ pages 179 and 178) – or a pet pig (only joking). Save and use leftover food (→ page 149).

Problem 3: Multiple materials Packets and goods that combine materials – from Tetra Paks and coffee packets to toys – are difficult to recycle, but not necessarily impossible.

Possible solutions: Buy more goods loose or in bulk, and make your own soups and juices. See www.tetrapakrecycling.com for collection points. Give well-washed toys to charity shops or friends' children, and repair broken ones if possible – you can take broken-beyond-fixing electronic toys to council recycling centres. Try using your local toy library for more variety.

Problem 4: Items that are broken or don't work any more This includes plates and glasses, lightbulbs and computer printers.

Possible solutions: Chipped plates are still usable; if the edge is sharp, rub it down with a little fine sandpaper. Glue broken crockery or use pieces as crocks for pot plants, or raw materials for making mosaics. Check if electricals and electronics really are beyond repair, or try Freecycling them (→ page 207) – friends put a non-working vacuum cleaner on Freecycle, and someone was very happy to take it to fix at home. Broken glass and broken lightbulbs need to be wrapped carefully – then should go in the bin. (For how to dispose of a broken CFL safely, → page 79.)

Problem 5: Magazine wrappers These seem to have become ubiquitous for newspapers, subscriptions and junk mail.

Possible solutions: Cut your newspaper consumption and read the news online – or else visit the library, or have a leisurely brunch at a local café that stocks the papers. Drop your subscription, and/or complain (some publications are moving to degradable bags). Instead of ripping them apart, cut the end off wrappers so you can use them as liners for small bins. (For cutting down on junk mail, → page 342.)

Waste watcher's tip:

Instead of disposable coffee cups, either use your own mug or, if you need something with a lid for your journey, invest in a vacuum-insulated cup such as those produced by Avantro (www.avantro.com) and Sigg (www.mysigg.com), among others. However, ceramics and steel take a great deal of energy to produce – so make sure you're going to use it for years, not months.

RE-USING

Imagination – that's the key to re-use. Many things we bring into our homes can be used over again, either by making them replay their original role, or by giving them a new function that perhaps no one else has thought of. Innovative designers are making furniture out of old washing-machine drums and shopping trolleys, but you could be more modest. I once had a coffee table that was a wooden packing pallet.

I enjoy the challenge of re-using. However, it does mean we have heaps of 'one-day-that-might-be-useful' objects around the house, mainly in (re-used) brown card boxes. So you might need an old-fashioned box room, or spare corner of the garage, to fit everything in. Although, as it all piles up, that's another incentive not to bring so much of it home in the first place.

Waste watcher's tip:
Re-using goods (where they basically stay in their current form) takes less energy and resources than recycling (where they're processed back into the raw materials before being turned into something new).

Ten re-uses for plastic pots

You'll have your own ideas for all the second uses you can make of tomato boxes/last year's birthday cards/pieces of ribbon/sweet wrappers, but one of the things we have hanging around is yogurt pots (→ page 214). Luckily, they can be quite useful. Plastic pots, whether they originally contained yogurt, cottage cheese, fromage frais or anything else, can be pressed into service as some of the following. Before using pots for food or drink, check they have recycling code 2, 4 or 5, as these are regarded as the safest.

1. Vases for cut herbs

2. Storage tubs for small toys or screws and bolts

3. Scoops for emptying water when drains are blocked

4. Paint containers for children's craft time

5. Planters for orchids, whose roots need light (the smaller ones are good for raising seedlings)

6. Children's bathtime toys

7. Ice-cream or sorbet cups for garden parties (children's size yogurt pots are very handy)

8. Greywater (→ page 240) collectors for garden watering

9. Holders for pens or crayons

10. Measuring scoops for wild birdseed bought in large sacks

Selling and donating

If something's in good condition, but you really don't want it any more, there are many ways in which you could find it a new home.

- ♥ Auctions: If it's something that you'd think of taking on *Antiques Roadshow*, find out rough values by checking with Miller's antiques guides; for local auctioneers, visit www.ukauctionguides.co.uk.
- ♥ eBay and other online auction sites.
- ♥ Charity shops: Check first that they will accept what you're offering.
- ♥ Schools and hospitals: Either of these may welcome donations of materials for craft projects or school gardens, or well-cared-for toys.
- ♥ A card in a local shop window: Try advertising locally, either in a shop or the classified pages of the local newspaper.
- ♥ Offering it on your local Freecycle (→ page 205).

Freecycling

The Freecycle network is a grassroots, non-profit organization started by Deron Beal in Tucson, Arizona in 2003 (see www.freecycle.org), which now has millions of members worldwide. Freecycle's slogan is 'Changing the world one gift at a time'. It provides a local forum where you can offer unwanted items – rather like a web-based, money-free classified section. You can also put in requests, but the etiquette is to be a giver first.

I joined our local group because we had a bike shed and a worm composter that were surplus to requirements. As well as finding new homes for those, I came away with some lovely dried garden flowers as eco wedding confetti. It's great for anything for which you don't want (or couldn't get) any financial return. Being local, it cuts down on 'furniture miles', and you can stipulate if you'd prefer the item to go to a charity, school or other project.

REPAIRING

Cheap goods mean we're more likely to abandon broken objects than try to fix them, but being able to do a good repair job is a worthwhile skill. Clothes (→ Chapter 11), ceramics, appliances and even plastic items can often be given a new lease of life – and if you have children, they may demand that you attempt to put their favourite toy back to how it used to be.

Make use of glue

Many repairs can be made successfully just with glue – or, more accurately, adhesive, since originally 'glue' meant the hard, gelatinous substance that comes from boiling up animal collagen.

First, you'll need to work out what type of glue you need – fabric glue, cyanoacrylate (such as Super Glue, for non-porous materials), ceramic glue, wood glue, or simple paper glue. If you have no idea what to use, try www.thistothat.com, which recommends adhesives for sticking different surfaces. Also read the label carefully to make sure the glue will do what you want it to. Check manufacturers' websites for more details.

Next, you'll need a place to work and a place to keep the object safe while it dries, or 'cures'. Make sure you've got good light to work by, and some tweezers if you're dealing with small objects. Follow the instructions on the tube, but here are some general tips:

♥ Choose the least toxic glue option you can, and keep the room well ventilated.
♥ Make sure the surfaces are clean, especially with ceramic or glass. You can do this on a mug that's lost its handle, for example, by lightly sanding the broken ends with glasspaper.
♥ After you've applied the glue and fixed the pieces together, wipe away the excess with a clean cloth – you may need to use acetone (nail varnish remover) for some types of adhesive. Clean your hands thoroughly before any glue dries on them.
♥ Masking tape can be useful to hold a bond together – but make sure you don't end up with the tape permanently stuck on.
♥ With crockery, make sure the bonded area won't come into contact with food or drink, in case chemicals leach from the adhesive.

If you think an appliance is broken . . .

Unfortunately, lots of gadgets and appliances are difficult, if not impossible, to repair these days. Simple electrics and mechanics have given way to complex electronics and sealed units. However, there are ways you can at least troubleshoot what's gone wrong, and work out whether it's something that's easily remedied (the limescale that meant water couldn't get through my dishwasher's spray arms, for example), or if you'll need a professional.

♥ If it's not immediately obvious what the problem is, find the instruction booklet – if you still have it. If not, don't worry – go to the manufacturer's website, or else Google the make and model to see if someone has posted helpful tips.

♥ Try a general appliance troubleshooting site, such as www. howstuffworks.com (which is American, so bear that in mind with matters such as voltages), or use a forum such as those on www.ukwhitegoods.co.uk and www.screwfix.com.

♥ If you need a professional, try to get a recommendation. Otherwise, go to the relevant trade association, such as the White Goods Trade Association (www.whitegoodstradeassociation. org).

RECYCLING

Your local council will probably be bombarding you with lists of what you can and can't put out for recycling, and when. These days they take everything from fridges and car batteries to garden waste, so check on your council website to see what you can bring to the depots as well as put in your recycling box.

If you're not sure where to recycle (perhaps you're renting a holiday cottage), try the postcode finder at www.recyclenow.com. The www.wasteonline.org.uk site has information on re-using and recycling all kinds of different goods.

Look out for charities, such as Oxfam, who are happy to take mobile phones, inkjet cartridges and PDAs, which they can sell or recycle in return for funds. Fonebak (www.fonebak.com) operates phone recycling schemes for retailers and charities, while schools can raise cash by collecting mobiles and printer cartridges for Recycool (www.recycool.org).

Waste watcher's tip:

Wash out tins and bottles – and remove lids – to ease the recycling process, then squash them to save space and therefore energy in transport. (Check with your council that it doesn't need bottles left intact for its system.) I have trouble squashing tins by hand (or foot), but you can get can-crushers from eco shops such as www.naturalcollection.com.

Recycling puzzlers

What can you do with the items your council doesn't take, and the things you're not sure about?

Building materials
Councils may let you take a small amount of debris from DIY enterprises, including soil and rubble, to the local depot. Re-use bricks, stone and timber, or sell them, or donate to neighbours, charity projects or through Freecycle. For larger quantities, contact a skip-hire or disposal company that recycles a high proportion of building waste, or try a Hippobag (www.hippowaste.co.uk).

CDs and DVDs
If your CDs aren't in good enough condition to sell or give away, and you have too many for coasters or garden bird-scarers, try specialist recyclers such as www.recyclingcds.com,

www.keymood.co.uk (Ross-on-Wye, also takes VHS cassettes), www.plasticwaste.co.uk (Manchester), www.polymerrecycling.co.uk (Wirral) and www.thelaundry.biz (London). Libraries may be glad of the cases as replacements.

CFLs, or energy-saving lightbulbs

 Councils offer a recycling service for energy-efficient bulbs, and IKEA operates a takeback scheme. (CFL safety, → page 79.)

Computers

For working computers, try local schools, charity and community organizations, and through Freecycle.

Otherwise, www.wasteonline.org.uk has a good information sheet on computer recyclers and refurbishers that supply both local and international projects (some also take printers and other peripherals). The Data Protection Act requires computer recyclers to destroy permanently all data on hard drives, but if you're passing on a computer, make sure to wipe everything.

Drink cartons

Find out if your council collects these by checking the interactive map at www.tetrapakrecycling.co.uk. Otherwise, post them to the Tetra Pak recycling centre (you can download address labels).

Furniture and carpets

Some community and charitable organizations re-use and recondition furniture, for example the SOFA Project (www.sofaproject.org.uk). The Furniture Reuse Network has a map search (www.frn.org.uk) to find other local groups. Old carpets are not recommended for mulching allotment plots because they may contain hazardous chemicals that could leach into the soil.

Metals

The industrial boom in China has meant that many resources, from fencing timber to copper, are in shorter supply in the UK, so pushing prices up. Contact a local scrap metal merchant and recycler – members of the British Metals Recycling Association are listed at www.recyclemetals.org. Your council should have a metals section at its depot.

Paints

Most paints are categorized as hazardous waste and can be disposed of at council depots. If you have usable paint, donate it to a community project, such as those supported by Community RePaint (www.communityrepaint.org.uk).

Plastic carrier bags

Some councils collect these, or else you could take them back – after many re-uses – to recycling points at supermarkets.

Shoes

Give shoes in reasonable condition (secured in pairs) to charity shops, for sale in the UK or export to developing countries, or take shoes in any state to council depots or charity shoe banks. Worn-out ones can be recycled, for example to make children's playground and sports surfaces. Check if shoe companies and retailers offer a takeback scheme, such as the one run by children's store One Small Step One Giant Leap (www.onesmallsteponegiantleap.com). For Nike Reuse-A-Shoe drop-off locations (they take any brand of trainers) see www.letmeplay.com/reuseashoe.

Spectacles
You can take glasses in good condition to many opticians, who collect them for Vision Aid Overseas (www.vao.org.uk).

WEEE
The European Waste Electrical and Electronic Equipment (WEEE) Directive means that producers and retailers of products from toasters to toys may offer a takeback service, and must at least tell you where you can take WEEE locally, or arrange collection. There's more information at www.environment-agency. gov.uk/weee. You can also take electricals and electronics to council depots. But only take this route if you've exhausted the possibilities for re-use and repair.

Yogurt pots and other plastics
Sadly, there's not much of a market for recycling yogurt pots, margarine tubs or other rigid plastics – despite the recycling symbols you'll see on some of them. For information on plastics recycling, see the industry body, www.recoup.org, and → page 218 for a guide to what the recycling numbers mean.

Waste watcher's tip:
To find out more about how packaging is evolving to make it lighter, more effective and efficient, and more easily recyclable, see the retail section of the WRAP website, www.wrap.org.uk.

Organizing your recycling

Recycling has spawned a whole new category of kitchen equipment – the recycling sorter. I simply stack things in the council's green box, which is fine if you have a utility room or other space to keep things out of the way, but not knowing where to put your recycling may be an obstacle that stops you from doing it.

You'll find stacking crates, jute carriers and re-usable woven plastic bags at eco stores and household shops, even including Heal's. Try to opt for something sustainable rather than encouraging more new plastic to be brought into the world.

Kitchen caddies and compost crocks with carbon filters will reduce the odour from food scraps – although I just use a pedal bin that we didn't need elsewhere. For other kitchen composting options, → page 179.

While plastic carrier bags are still around to re-use, the sleek Binvention (www.sproutdesign.co.uk), made of a single sheet of aluminium from which you hang the bags, is probably the chicest recycling sorting option.

For a home-made option, try dyeing old pillowcases as re-usable separators. I'm thinking of repurposing the tote that came with a copy of *Marie Claire* years ago, and trying to find others in charity shops.

You could involve children in painting cardboard boxes, or decorating any other suitable storage containers you have.

Buying recycled

The recycling ideal is to create a closed loop, so that instead of constantly taking more raw materials (especially oil or metal ores, which can't be renewed) we make new products from the remains of old ones. So as well as recycling, try to buy recycled where you can.

From paper to horse bedding, kitchen worktops to computers, more products than you may think are made from recycled material. Find out about specialist producers at www.recycledproducts.org.uk.

In supermarkets and other shops, look for the percentage of recycled content in products such as bin liners and toilet paper, and go especially for those that contain 'post-consumer waste' – which is the stuff you and I put in our recycling bins.

❖ **Waste watcher's tip:**
❖ *Composting is an extremely useful way of recycling food scraps. If*
❖ *you compost your wet waste, such as peelings, coffee grounds and*
❖ *teabags, it means they won't be mouldering in your general*
❖ *rubbish bin. (→ page 179.)*

IS ALL PLASTIC BAD?

It's easy to demonize plastic – it's made from fast-disappearing resources (oil and natural gas), it takes squillions of years to degrade (well, a million years for a Styrofoam cup or plastic bottle) and it chokes wildlife. Plastic doesn't get a good press, but not all plastic is equal – there are more than 10,000 types – and not all plastic is necessarily evil. Plastics are invaluable in the world of medicine – as in heart replacement valves – and new medical polymers are being developed all the time. There is also a climate change argument in their favour, as it takes less energy to make and transport a thin plastic carrier than a paper equivalent.

However, most plastic ends up in landfill. Even if it's one of the new biodegradable types, it won't degrade efficiently here, because landfill sites are deliberately designed that way – to help stop hazardous chemicals leaching out, and cut down production of the powerful greenhouse gas methane. Plastics are recyclable, but when oil is cheap it isn't economic to do so and in recent years some reprocessing has stopped. For more information, see the plastics details at www.wasteonline.org.uk.

The world now uses about 100 million tonnes of plastics a year, compared with 5 million tonnes in the 1950s. Some people are choosing to live plastic free, but for most of us that can be a tough challenge, because plastics pop up in all kinds of products, including cosmetics, paints, the labels on fruit and the insides of tins and jar lids. (For dedication and inspiration, see blogs such as www.fakeplasticfish.com and http://plasticfree.blogspot.com.)

So what's the answer? I believe it's a question of really thinking about how we all use plastic, where it truly is the best choice of material and where it's unnecessary, and making sure plastic is recycled, rather than used once, to reduce the amount manufactured.

Rethinking plastic

♥ Whether it's toys or leather-free bags, buy plastic to last, not to throw away – try to get away from thinking about plastic as cheap and therefore disposable. Use alternatives where possible, such as wooden toys.

♥ Choose recycled over new, virgin plastic products.

♥ Don't be so gloomy about high oil prices – it could make recycling a wider range of plastics a viable option again.

Health effects and codes

Plastics can release fumes into the air (often referred to as off-gassing) and chemicals into foods or liquids stored in them (something called leaching). The lingering smell of a new car is an example of off-gassing. There are safety restrictions on the plastics used in food packaging, and safety levels set for the chemicals that may leach from them. However, research studies often produce conflicting results.

The following codes were designed so recyclers could differentiate between plastics – although currently only a small fraction of those that could be recycled are collected. However, they can also help us as consumers to identify which plastics are deemed safest for health and the environment, and which we might want to be more careful with.

The list of products under each plastic is intended as a general guide only, since different brands may use different plastics. Check the bottom of containers for the embossed code or ask the manufacturer if you are unsure.

Polyethylene terephthalate (PETE)

Collected by many councils. Bottles made from this plastic are meant for one use only, so to be safe, don't refill and re-use them for drinking. Do not store food in used ready-meal containers. However, they are not known to leach any suspected carcinogens or hormone disrupters.

Used for: Water and soft drink bottles, medicine bottles, ready-meal containers.

 ### High-density polyethylene (HDPE)
Collected by many councils. Regarded as a safer option for food storage, although bear in mind that chemicals from plastics may leach more easily into fatty foods, such as milk.

Used for: Many containers, including milk, laundry detergent and shampoo, and some toys.

Polyvinyl chloride (PVC)
Hard PVC is generally inert, but soft PVC needs a plasticizer to make it flexible. Certain phthalate plasticizers have been a big concern, especially in products for children, and some have been banned or restricted. A number of toy manufacturers and retailers, including Mattel and IKEA, have signed a pledge to phase out the PVC in their products. Manufacture and disposal of PVC can create dioxins.

Used for: Some mineral water, squash, cooking oil and shampoo bottles, pipes and tubing, shower curtains, seat covers, some food trays and clingfilms, wipeable fabric coatings.

Low-density polyethylene (LDPE)
Regarded as a safer option for food storage.

Used for: Some carrier bags and food bags, bin liners.

Polypropylene

PP Regarded as a safer option for food storage since it is not known to leach any chemical nasties, but it is hazardous during manufacture.

Used for: Storage containers such as Tupperware, yogurt and margarine tubs, straws, disposable nappies, document wallets.

6 Polystyrene

PS Mainly used as foam or expanded into little bobbles. Hazardous benzene is used in its production, while styrene is a suspected carcinogen. A major source of marine pollution, and not easily recycled because of its low scrap value.

Used for: Disposable drinking cups, meat trays and takeaway trays, Styrofoam insulation, packaging, CD cases.

Other

OTHER This covers combinations of the above and less common plastics. Old and cracked polycarbonate can leach small quantities of bisphenol A, a chemical that has raised health concerns, and the amount increases if alkaline cleaners are used (washing soda is strongly alkaline), or with heat. However, this code also includes bioplastics.

Used for: polycarbonate (hard, clear plastic containers, including baby bottles), melamine (picnic and children's plates), compostable bioplastics (bags, bottles).

How to trim your waste

Love what you have and buy only what you need – and look forward to extravagances as the treats they are.

Try buying second-hand, or swapping, borrowing or hiring to lay your hands on what you're after.

Spot crafty ways to reduce packaging – such as buying larger packets, spying out brands that go light on packaging, and seeing if health-food shops and stalls do refills for brands such as Ecover.

Don't just throw away – before you put anything in the bin, see if you can devise a creative or practical way to re-use it.

Join your local Freecycle.

Make a vow to find out exactly what your council will recycle, and then put it all out on the right day.

Use the recycling depot, but try to be organized so you do as much in one trip as possible.

Get to know your plastics and try to stop thinking of them as disposable.

Close the circle by finding out what recycled products you can use in your household.

8

THE WATER CYCLE

During the 'spring drought' of 2007, when it hardly rained for six weeks or more, I became almost obsessive about saving water in our house. Perhaps it was over-compensation for the fact that we had just sown some new grass in our garden. The seed was a hardy microclover mix that doesn't need much maintenance once established, but while the little green needles of new leaf were spiking up I had to soak it thoroughly every few days.

Indoors, our house became like a laboratory. I had rows of used yogurt pots lined up on the kitchen worktop, filled with all the water that would otherwise have gone down the sink plughole. It was scary how many yogurt pots there were, just from washing up, washing hands, cooking vegetables . . . I re-used as much as I could, then, for health and safety reasons, had to consign the rest to the sewerage system.

Maybe it's just as well that this unseasonable warm, dry spell was closely followed by the fabled 'rubbish wet summer', so I could relax a bit.

WHERE DOES ALL THE WATER GO?

In the developing world, people may survive on 5 litres of water a day – which is the minimum for drinking, cooking, washing and cleaning. In contrast, in Britain we tend to use between 120 litres and 220 litres per person in the home, and about another 100 litres from our share of industrial and commercial water consumption. Rising population, more houses being built and increased water use – plus the potential effects of drought periods – are putting pressure on UK reserves.

The Centre for Alternative Technology reckons that trying to cut back to 80 litres per person per day is a realistic target in an ordinary home with modern appliances. The two biggest water guzzlers in an average household are the toilet (35 per cent of home water use) and bath (15 per cent) – although our local water company, Wessex Water, reckons that over the summer months half of customer water demand is for dousing the garden.

Only a tenth of the water supplied to our homes is actually used for drinking – yet all of it is of drinkable quality. Doesn't that sound mad?

Water manager's tip:
Saving water saves energy. If you're using less hot water, it will cut water-heating bills. And since water is pumped to our houses, we also reduce the energy used by the water companies. On the other side of the equation, using less energy saves water, because a lot is consumed by electricity generation.

Your 'water footprint'

As with energy, it's useful to know how much you're using. Installing a water meter is the most accurate option, but (and this is a big but) under the current system it will only really make sense financially if you have a small household and make sure you are – or become – a fairly low water user. For details and conditions, check your water company's website. A number of water companies, plus the BBC News website (search at http://news.bbc.co.uk), have online calculators – although note that there are many variables, and calculators are always based on a set of assumptions.

Leaks from supply pipes

Nearly a quarter of expensively filtered and cleaned drinking-standard water is lost through leaking and cracked pipes. The water companies have been dragging their feet about doing more to reduce leakages in their networks, but 27 per cent of the losses are due to the supply pipe that goes from the property boundary to your house or flat itself.

It's a confusing system, but the current regulation is that this pipe is the customer's responsibility – so it's down to us to do something about it (although changes may be on the way, see www.environment-agency.gov.uk).

Signs of a leak can be damp spots along paths, or areas of lawn that are particularly green. Water companies will cover the cost of repairing pipes to the edge of your property, but you will need to pay a reputable plumber for anything inside your boundary.

TAP WATER AND FILTERING

In our household we drink tap water pretty much all the time, mostly from a carbon-filter jug to improve the taste. In the past 15 years or so the quality of British tap water has improved markedly. The Centre for Alternative Technology describes UK mains water as excellent, and it gets the thumbs-up from Friends of the Earth, too.

The general advice is to stop buying mineral water in bottles (which isn't very environmentally friendly) and stick to your tap. Water from the tap is better regulated anyway: there are limits on contaminants, from pesticides to lead, plus a catch-all stipulation that the water must be 'wholesome' – in other words, it mustn't be a danger to health.

For details of your local water supply, see your water company's website. For more general information, try the Environment Agency (www.environment-agency.gov.uk), Drinking Water Inspectorate (www.dwi.gov.uk) and independent information body the Foundation for Water Research (www.fwr.org).

If you are particularly concerned about water additives, you may want to look into one of the various types of water filter available.

At present, chlorine is the best way of killing off bugs in the water, but it leaves an unpleasant taste. This can be largely removed by a jug-style carbon filter, but it is advisable to keep the water in the fridge because the chlorine's bug-defeating qualities will have been removed. A heated debate is currently raging about adding fluoride to tap water. See the National Pure Water Association (www.npwa.freeserve.co.uk) and British Fluoridation Society (www.bfsweb.org) for opposing views. Your local water company or health authority can tell you if your water has added fluoride.

Much research has yet to be completed in the area of hormone disrupters (endocrine modulators) and prescription drugs finding their way into tap water, so it's hard to know how worried we should be. Only top-of-the-range filters can deal with these kinds of chemicals.

Water manager's tip:
Used mineral water bottles aren't the best thing for carrying water with you. They're hard to clean effectively and there are concerns that chemicals may leach from some types of plastic. Stainless steel, aluminium and friendlier plastic options from Klean Kanteen (www.kleankanteen.com), Sigg (www.mysigg.com) and Nalgene (www.nalgene-outdoor.com) are available from camping outlets.

HARD WATER

Hard water is the enemy of appliances. The limescale (mainly calcium carbonate – in other words, rock) that forms from it furs pipes, crusts around nozzles and, if things get really bad, can make your heating elements pack up. It can also reduce the efficiency of hot water heaters, because it insulates the water from the heating element.

Dishwasher salt and water softening agents in washing detergents are designed to combat some of this effect. For more

about hard water and appliances see
www.washerhelp.co.uk/limescale. html.

Water manager's tip:
To descale a kettle, cover the element with half water and half white distilled vinegar and boil. Pour out (perhaps save for later use to clean windows, or for washing up), then boil again with fresh water and a couple of teaspoons of baking soda (to help remove the vinegar odour). Boil a last time with plain water.

Magnetic water softening

I've been using a Magno Ball in my washing machine and dishwasher, and (in my very subjective study) it does seem to help things come out softer and cleaner. Like similar devices, it's a magnet buffered by a rubbery coat. Water flows through it and is conditioned by the magnetic field so the limescale crystals don't build up on surfaces. (For those with a technical turn of mind, Professor Martin Chaplin explains some of the science at www.lsbu.ac.uk/water/descal.html.)

It can help you reduce detergent use safely in your washing machine, but I have a note of caution – don't be tempted to use it in place of dishwasher salt. After an experiment along these lines I had to keep unclogging the nozzles on the dishwasher's arms by picking off the bits and treating with lemon juice – not one of my finer eco moments.

❀ **Water manager's tip:**
❀
❀ *You can buy magnetic descalers to go in kettles and toilet cisterns –*
❀
❀ *as long as your cistern isn't boxed in and inaccessible. Try online eco*
❀
❀ *shops, such as www.spiritofnature.co.uk.*

REDUCE AND RE-USE

The 'reduce, re-use, repair, recycle' slogan gets shortened in the case of water. What we want to do is cut down how much comes out of the tap in the first place, and then make the best use of it we can by re-using what's called 'greywater' (→ page 240).

When we do send water down the plughole, it makes sense to ensure it's in as reasonable a state as possible. Did you know, for example, that every litre of non-ecological washing powder can take 20,000 litres of water to treat it before it can go back into our water system safely? If you're re-using water on plants, it's especially important to check what you've put in that water in the first place.

Toilet tips

The most efficient dual-flush toilets can use as little as 2.5 litres of water for the regular flush and 4 litres for the maxi one – compared with 9 litres or more for an old-fashioned cistern. Although they are more expensive (£150 to £250) they can earn back the extra on water bills if you have a meter.

♥ Flush only when necessary and don't put lots of extra paper, such as tissues, down the toilet because they could cause a blockage.

- ♥ A variable flush works with handle flushes, so you can control the amount of water you use for each flush. See www.interflush.co.uk and www.peterton.co.uk. They cost about £20.
- ♥ If that isn't an option, a toilet hippo can save 3 litres per flush, although it is only suitable if you have a large cistern with an old-style siphon rather than a valve. Contact your water company or see www.hippo-the-watersaver.co.uk. To make your own version, fill a 2 litre (or less for a smaller cistern) plastic drink bottle with water.
- ♥ Don't flush twice. If water-saving devices are causing you to double-flush, they're not worth it.
- ♥ Check if your valve is leaking. Valve-system cisterns have a tendency to leak, dripping up to 30 litres of water a day into the pan. To check, put on a pair of rubber gloves and dry the back of the toilet pan, just below the rim. If you can't see a telltale drip, hold a piece of toilet paper there for half a minute to see if it stays dry.

Bathing

The average bath is estimated to use 80 litres, so a daily bathe accounts for a very large volume of water. In my view, we've become sucked into a cleanliness culture that encourages us, if anything, to over-wash. As a child, in the 1960s and 1970s, it was the norm to have a daily wash and just one bath a week – and no one talks of those decades as being particularly smelly. Showering or bathing too frequently can strip the natural oils from your skin and scalp and, especially with chlorine in water, it isn't good for conditions such as eczema.

- ♥ Try to keep showers to three minutes, especially if you're addicted to a daily deluge. Power showers are as water wasteful as baths, so use these less often.
- ♥ Run shallower baths and keep an eye on the water while it's running, so you don't end up with a horrendously hot bath that you have to fill up with cold to make it comfortable (or vice versa).
- ♥ Take a step back in time and get yourself some lovely, fluffy flannels. Daily (or twice-daily) washing at the basin was good enough for most of the twentieth century, and it's quicker too.
- ♥ If bathtime is your me-time (from experience I know this can be especially the case for new mothers), think about alternative activities, such as curling up with a good book, having a manicure or massage, or doing something creative that you enjoy.

Washing the dishes

Dishwashers or washing-up by hand? Which is the most water and energy-efficient? It's a subject of heated debate – and it depends on your dishwasher and your washing-up technique. The most efficient dishwashers can now use less than 10 litres of water for a full load.

Since I would find it hard to give up our dishwasher, I'm probably not the most objective commentator on this one. These suggestions are about getting the best from both methods.

Dishwasher good practice

- ♥ Only run your dishwasher when it's full.
- ♥ Make sure you have the water-hardness setting correct and don't run out of dishwasher salt.
- ♥ Find the quickest, lowest-temperature setting that works for most of your dishes – you can always clean stubborn food remains by hand.
- ♥ With most dishwashers there is no need to rinse plates before you put them in, but scrape off scraps.
- ♥ Choose eco dishwasher tablets and rinse aids, which don't contain phosphates or environmentally unfriendly polymers, or use lemon vinegar as a rinse instead (for recipe, → page 36).
- ♥ Clear out your filter regularly. Occasionally, run a short empty wash with a cup of white vinegar to get rid of limescale and slimy grease build-up.

Water manager's tip:
When buying new dishwashers and washing machines, check their water efficiency at www.waterwise.org.uk and look for the Waterwise Marque.

Washing-up good practice

- ♥ Always use the plug and/or a washing-up bowl. A saucepan or bowl you're washing up is a good alternative, and means you'll probably use even less water.
- ♥ Wait until there's a good amount to wash.

- ♥ When running the water, don't waste the cool while you're waiting for the hot to come through – use it to fill pans that need a soak, or for non-greasy washing-up, or for watering.
- ♥ Instead of starting out with a big bowl of sudsy water, just put a little washing-up liquid on your brush or scouring pad. When an item has been cleaned, rinse it with hot water into the waiting washing-up bowl. Carry on like this and when you have enough hot water, swap to rinsing with cold – which saves energy.
- ♥ Sprinkle stubborn, baked-on residue in roasting tins and baking trays with baking soda, then dampen with a little water and leave overnight.
- ♥ A sink drainer will help to stop debris going down the plughole.

Plugs and bowls – the forgotten heroes

Water is so taken for granted in the UK that we often leave the tap running with no thought. I still catch myself doing it sometimes. Toothbrushing for two minutes morning and night accounts for about 9 litres for each person per day, for example. One way to start realizing just how much unused water goes down the sink is to put the plug in before you start to run water. As the basin fills up, you'll soon see how much is there and (hopefully) be prompted to turn off the tap.

If you have dirty hands from gardening or DIY, wash them in a small basin of water and change this a couple of times, rather than doing it under a constantly running tap. If you have trouble remembering to turn off while doing your teeth, fill a small glass (aka a tooth mug) with water before you start and use that for swilling instead. Use a bucket for car-cleaning and a bowl for washing vegetables.

A leaking tap

A tap leaking at one drop per second wastes 10,000 litres of water a year. Most drips can be stopped by renewing the washer, although sometimes the metal seating on which the tap valve rests is damaged (you can get repair kits for this). Taps that are dripping around the spindle – the part you twist – or the base of a swivel spout or shower diverter require different treatment (you'll need a new gland or O-ring). If you have ceramic disc taps, the discs may have become scratched and need replacing.

If you're tackling the job yourself, you'll need an adjustable spanner, or set of open spanners, and possibly a pipe wrench; a piece of old cloth (to pad the jaws of the wrench); a set of screwdrivers; an old screwdriver for prising; the sink or basin plug (so you don't lose any vital parts down the drain); and a towel (to put in the basin and cushion it in case you drop anything heavy). Take the old tap part, or be able to quote the model of tap, when you go to buy the new part. You'll also need to know where the valves or stopcock are (so you can turn off the water supply).

Detailed instructions for mending a leaking tap can be found in DIY books, such as *Reader's Digest Complete DIY Manual*, and demos can be viewed online – try VideoJug (www.videojug.com) or www.leakingtaps.co.uk, which is run by a London plumber).

Although changing a washer, at least, is a fairly simple job, if you lack confidence or don't have the right equipment, you may prefer to ask someone with the correct tools to come and sort your tap out for you.

The garden

Our garden is in a state of transformation, as we create a formal-ish kitchen garden with raised beds, alongside areas for play, flowers and relaxation. The idea is to make it suit its surroundings and not need too much added water.

There are many ways to save water in the garden, from improving your soil's water-retentive properties if it's sandy (water easily runs through sandy soil) and choosing the right plants for drier areas, to watering and maintaining your garden wisely. See the Garden Organic website (www.gardenorganic.org.uk) and Royal Horticultural Society (www.rhs.org.uk) for advice.

♥ Use a trigger spray hose attachment, not a sprinkler. If you have a sprinkler, you are required to be on a metered water supply.
♥ Even better, ditch the hose completely. On many allotments you have to make do with a watering can. In fact, after the seedlings have become established, even vegetables and fruit often need watering at key times only. Check in your favourite gardening book – it will save you effort as well as water.
♥ Water the roots, not the leaves. Giving plants a good soaking every few days (or less for established plants) is better than a daily dribble because it encourages roots to grow more deeply. Watering at cooler times of day – in the morning and evening – reduces loss from evaporation (morning is best if you have a slug problem). For large gardens, you can get irrigation kits that snake around plant bases, including some that will work from a raised water butt (see www.organiccatalog.com and www.homebase.co.uk).

- ♥ Group containers together. It will help retain humidity. Try adding a water-retentive medium, such as seaweed meal. Placing pebbles on top of the soil in containers with trees or climbers will help roots stay cool and reduce water loss.
- ♥ Don't cut lawns too short in hot weather. Also, do it less frequently.
- ♥ Get weeding in the spring. Weeds will take the water that you'd really like to be going to your produce or favourite specimens.
- ♥ Don't leave wide expanses of soil. Water will evaporate more quickly from them. You could mulch or put in ground-cover plants, both of which can also help to suppress weeds. (For more about mulches, → page 180.)

RAINWATER HARVESTING

Installing a water butt is the easiest and cheapest way to make use of rainwater for jobs such as watering the garden and washing the car. You can easily divert water from gutters and from shed roofs. I also leave gardening trugs and buckets in the open, especially during summer downpours, to collect all the water I can for our container plants.

The main problem with making the most of free water is long-term storage. We get most rain from autumn to spring, but need most in the summer. For our kitchen garden we're thinking of investing in an extra-large butt, perhaps even an underground one. But before going for an option like this, check that your actual water use, and the amount you can collect, will make it worthwhile.

Type of water butt	Approximate cost	Details
Standard plastic	£40	Capacity around 200 litres. Usually made with a proportion of recycled plastic. A diverter fits on your guttering downpipe to fill up the butt and let water through to the drain when it's full. Widely available.
Mini butts	£25	Smaller, 100-litre capacity.
Wall-mounted	£60 and upwards	These slimline butts are less conspicuous, and could be an option for a flat with a roof terrace, where load-bearing would be an issue. See www.crocus.co.uk and www.greenbuildingstore.co.uk.
Oak barrels	£100	A traditional barrel converted into a brass-tapped water collector, from www. suffolkbarrel.co.uk.
Wooden drum	£200	Much larger capacity, around 600 litres. Can be a garden feature. Collects rainwater with the lid off, or through a downpipe diverter. No need to drain in winter. See www. organiccatalog.com.

XL size butts	£700 and upwards	Tanks of 1,500 litres and more for the garden can be partially or fully buried. They use a low-power pump and filter. See B&Q at www.diy.com and www.rainharvesting.co.uk.
Wheelie bin converter	£12	Turns any wheelie bin or other plastic container into a water butt that will fit Hozelock connections, from www.cat.org.uk/shopping.

Water manager's tip:

For a cheaper butt, especially for larger sizes, think about a re-used juice storage tank. Old orange juice containers, with a capacity of 1,500 litres, can be around £150 from www.dvfuels.co.uk in North Wales, who will fit taps.

Indoor use

In theory, we could use rainwater for all our household needs apart from drinking and cooking. The problem is all the storage and peripherals, such as pumps and electronic monitors, that you need. It can make sense for new buildings, but if you are thinking of converting an old property, bear in mind that prices can be £2,000 or more. According to the Centre for Alternative Technology, it is not always financially or environmentally beneficial.

See the free CAT Information Service at www.cat.org.uk/information.

WHAT IS GREYWATER?

Greywater is used-but-not-necessarily-dirty water. In the home, generally it's everything except the toilet. So that means shower, bath and washing-up water (as long as it isn't scummy), water used for cooking, the drippings from the teapot and even the outflow from the washing machine. You can buy gadgets that will make greywater re-use easier.

Note that you shouldn't use greywater on vegetables, fruit or herbs that you will be eating, and rotate watering so that anything in it – such as detergent – does not build up in the plants. This is especially important for container plants. Greywater isn't really suitable for seedlings, either.

Untreated greywater from baths and showers contains some micro-organisms, which means it should be used as soon as possible to be on the safe side.

♥ As long as you haven't put oils in it, bath water can be re-used for hand-washing or soaking laundry.

♥ During dry spells, I stand a bucket next to me when I shower, to collect water for plants.

♥ In the summer of 2006, drought-beating siphons became popular. These fit in the bath and have a filter; they work as long as the collection point is below the level of the source. See www.droughtbuster.co.uk and green shops.

♥ If a separate pipe from your bath and/or shower runs outside, and is accessible, you can put in a permanent greywater diverter, such as those from www.watertwo.co.uk, for less than £30.

♥ You could also try attaching your washing-machine outlet pipe to a hose, to use rinsing water for the garden.

Be nice to your drains

Three-quarters of drain blockages are caused by disposable items. Solidified cooking fat is another big blocker. I'm sure you wouldn't dream of putting any of the following down your drainage system, but just in case you need reminding, here are some of the things to avoid. While sewage undergoes stringent filtration and treatment these days, small amounts of some chemicals still get through into waterways.

Cooking oil (or any other oil)

Food debris and grease from pans (scrape these into the bin or kitchen waste collector)

Sanitary products

Baby wipes or nappy liners (even ones labelled flushable)

Cotton wool

Coffee grounds (they belong on the compost)

Paint

Pharmaceuticals of any kind

Caustic chemicals

Strong solvents

HOW TO UNBLOCK A SINK

I've got over the 'ugh' factor when it comes to unblocking sinks and drains, mainly because I've had to do it a few times since we moved into our house. This step-by-step guide details how to tackle increasingly stubborn blocks. Most can be fixed without the need for a plumber, and all these solutions mean you can avoid buying dangerous, corrosive chemical unblockers. Once the block is cleared and you've put everything back together, go to Step 7.

Warning!

Do not launch into any of these methods if you have already tried a chemical unblocker.

Step 1: Can you clear it from the plughole?

Most clogs are caused by grease, hair, soap and other debris. Tweezers and/or a bamboo kebab skewer are helpful tools for clearing them.

Step 2: Get out the plunger

Place the plunger over the plughole, fill the basin with water to above the sucker cup and close the overflow with a cloth. Push down and up on the handle about 10 times, keeping a good seal. After the final plunge, lift off with some force. Repeat as many times as it takes.

Step 3: Fizz off

For a minor blockage – when the water still runs away slowly – pour down half a cup of baking soda, then half a cup of white vinegar. Put the plug in the sink and cover the overflow. Leave for a couple of minutes for the mixture to get fizzing, then pour down about 250ml/½ pint/9fl oz of boiling water. (For more about baking soda and vinegar, → pages 23–34.)

Step 4: Removing the trap

Your sink will have either a U-bend or bottle trap. Before you start, empty the sink and place a large bucket underneath it. With luck, your trap will be easy to undo by hand, but you may need a pipe wrench (cover the jaws with a cloth to protect the basin fittings). Make sure you know how everything fits back together, and that there is still something supporting the weight of the basin. The clog may come out into the bucket, but if not, read on.

Step 5: Send down the snake

A plumber's snake – aka plumber's auger or corkscrew cable – is a flexible cable on a crank that will go round the bends in pipes. You should be able to find one in a hardware shop, or improvise by bending an old wire coat hanger or length of gardening wire. Wind out the snake down the open drainage pipe, like a fishing line, then corkscrew it around to break up any mats of debris. If that doesn't fix it, try the overnight treatment.

Step 6: The overnight treatment

You could use washing soda or an enzyme cleaner. First, screw everything back together and check for leaks. For the first option, wearing rubber gloves, pour a cup of washing soda and 200ml/⅓ pint/7fl oz of warm water down the drain and leave overnight. (Don't use a strong solution like this too often, or it could damage your pipes.) In the morning, try the plunger again.

'Natural' drain cleaners use enzymes to digest the organic matter in the blockage. Follow the instructions for the product you have bought.

If neither of these works, it's time to get in that plumber.

Step 7: Clearing up

Wash through with plenty of fast-running water. To help remove any remaining grease, pour down one cup of baking soda followed by 1 litre of boiling water. Repeat this treatment any time you think your drain is getting grimy. It will also help to deodorize the drain.

How to manage your water wisely

Work out your 'water footprint' and think about getting a water meter.

Forget about bottles of mineral water and drink water from the tap instead.

Don't flush the loo so often.

Explore alternatives to a long, hot soak in the bath to pamper yourself.

Wash more, shower less.

Brush up on your dishwasher tactics and washing-up technique, so you're being as water-efficient as possible.

Remember to use the plug and washing-up bowl – don't leave taps running.

Don't use a sprinkler in the garden, and preferably not a hose – unless they're fed by harvested rainwater.

Get a water butt (or several) that suits your garden water needs.

Think up five new ways to re-use greywater before breakfast.

Be nice to your drains – use baking soda and plungers, not corrosive chemicals.

9

LAUNDRY LORE

W hen a group of children were invited by a TV programme to experience the daily life of Britain during the Second World War, they were appalled to be hand-washing their pants with a

washboard and a tub of water. Even in the twentieth century, doing the laundry was a process that could take days, from the initial soaking and boiling to the drying, folding and ironing. The Victorians set aside Monday as wash-day (hence 'Blue Monday'), so that everything could be ready for church the following Sunday, but prior to that, washes were considered so onerous that they might be attempted only every few weeks.

In the twenty-first century, clothes have to be worn for about five minutes before they are tossed into that wondrous labour-saver, the automatic washing machine. But do you really need to do all those washes? Or use all that powder? Cutting down on your washing, and using lower temperatures, saves water, electricity, the various powders and liquids that go into the machine, and wear and tear on your mechanical laundry slave itself. The especially good news for the green householder is that ironing is banned (almost).

You don't need to wash it if . . .

. . . it doesn't smell. Deodorant scents and slight cooking odours can often be dispelled by airing in a well-ventilated room, or on a hanger tied to the washing line. Towels last longer if you hang them to dry between uses.

. . . there's no visible dirt. Skirts, jumpers, jackets and trousers need cleaning much less than underwear and T-shirts.

. . . you can wear it for a dirty job. There's no point using nice, freshly laundered clothes for gardening and cleaning.

THE GREEN WASHING RULES

Ideally, we would all follow the green washing rules, but in reality you may need to bend them a bit, and that's not a completely terrible thing to do.

- Wash clothes less.
- Wash at 30° (check that your machine does a proper wash at 30°C, not just a delicates wash, or if you can manually override the wash temperature).
- Use a washing agent that's as biodegradable as it's possible to buy.
- Reduce the amount of washing agent (although → page 249).
- Choose large sizes of detergent or other washing agents and softeners, preferably in recycled and recyclable packaging.

The green rules are useful principles, but for the good of your washing, and your washing machine, there are times when you may want to do a hotter wash, or be a bit less than emerald green on the type of washing agents you use.

I've been doing a lot of experimenting to discover what really works, and the conclusion I've reached is that laundry isn't a one-size-fits-all question. It's a matter of finding what's best for you and your household.

GETTING THE MOST FROM YOUR WASHING MACHINE

Washing machines are becoming more energy-efficient, and better at conserving water, but still, every year, 500 billion litres of water are pumped through UK washing machines, and £800 million worth of electricity is used to run our average of five washes a week. We can help to reduce these huge amounts and use our washing machines more effectively. These tips have been put together with help from Andy Trigg, a washing-machine engineer and white-goods specialist with 30 years' experience, who runs the Washerhelp site (www.washerhelp.co.uk). (For more on choosing new appliances, energy and eco labels, → page 71.)

Wait until you can wash a full load. If you live on your own, consider putting different items in the same wash, such as dark towels with dark clothes, and doing more hand-washing.

Make sure your water is sufficiently softened. Modern detergents include a softener, which is one reason why larger doses are recommended for hard-water areas. (For more on water softening, and how limescale can damage your machine, → pages 228–229.)

Don't overload. Clothes won't wash so well if you do. You should have space to wiggle your hand about in the top of the drum. The maximum load given for your machine is for cottons; the weight limit is much lower for other fabrics, especially woollens, so check the instruction book.

Don't underload, either. As well as the environmental implications, underloading can make clothes bunch on one side of the drum, putting it out of balance and affecting the spin.

Check and wipe out the drum. Make sure there's nothing from a previous wash, and that children – your own or visitors' – haven't put things such as flowers (many can stain) or other objects in there. Leave the door open between washes to help prevent mould. Now and again, wipe the drum, seal and door using a cloth moistened with white distilled vinegar.

Clean the powder drawer and filter. This will help your wash to come out fresh, and stop your machine's drainage pipes becoming clogged. For really stubborn slime, mix a tablespoon of washing soda in a cup of water.

Doing a cleansing wash

Washing-machine engineers and manufacturers recommend that with today's lower washing temperatures you should do a regular higher-temperature wash to clean out greasy residues and undissolved washing powder, and kill off bacteria and black mould. It may not sound that green, but it can be worth doing to extend the life of your washing machine.

Set your machine to 60°C and use a washing detergent with a bleaching agent – or add oxygen laundry bleach (sodium percarbonate is best). In place of fabric conditioner, pour in half a cup of vinegar, which is a de-greaser and disinfectant, and can help to zap limescale. I usually pop in a few cleaning cloths to make full use of the wash, although the usual recommendation is to run it empty.

Washing at low temperatures

Making 30°C your default wash temperature will mean big savings on energy and carbon dioxide emissions (about 1.6 billion kilowatt hours compared with washing at 40°C, if we all did it). More sophisticated powders – both conventional and ecological brands – are designed to give high performance at low temperatures. They usually contain enzymes to help break down proteins and fats.

At first, I couldn't quite believe that a temperature of 30°C would get a general wash clean, even though I put jeans in at 30°C to retain their colour. Now I do most of my washes at 30°C, with occasional higher-temperature loads of towels, bedding and tea towels – soaps and detergents have antibacterial qualities, but in a low-temperature wash tea towels can sometimes come out not as clean as you'd like them to be, especially if you don't use any kind of bleaching agent.

The not-so-good news

To get good results from a low-temperature wash you may need to do some pre-treatments or pre-soaking – especially if you've opted for an eco powder without bleaches or enzymes. Underarms, food marks and ground-in dirt are the main culprits – but treating them doesn't take long when you know how (→ page 257). A bio powder (such as Ecover's bio tablets) does give improved overall results for more heavily soiled loads.

> **Launderer's tip:**
> *If you're washing at low temperatures and are disappointed with the results, try some of the other tactics in this chapter instead of simply turning up the temperature or adding more powder. Softening the water more, for instance, could deliver a better wash, or adding a percarbonate laundry bleach to whites and colourfast fabrics.*

Are eco washing powders and liquids better?

The short answer is yes for reducing environmental pollution and for those with sensitivities, but the jury's out for cleaning power and climate change. Here are some of the factors to consider:

- Studies by independent consumer tester *Which?* indicate that results achieved with the best of the current eco cleaners don't match up to those obtained with big-brand detergents. However, other research has found that ecological non-bio powders can give results as good as the market leader. It depends whether you want the absolute best cleaning there is, or are happy to make do with something more modest for the environmental benefits.

⌂ The washing agents – called surfactants – used by eco brands, such as Ecover (www.ecover.com), Bio-D (www.biodegradable.biz) and Clear Spring (www.faithinnature.co.uk), are plant-based, which makes them more sustainable, and means their production generates fewer harmful byproducts than conventional detergents. These companies also try to follow ethical and environmentally friendly production practices.

⌂ Conventional laundry cleaners may include optical brighteners, silicones (to reduce foaming) and synthetic perfumes. Research by Ecover has found that many ingredients in these cleaners biodegrade poorly, or not at all, under normal, natural conditions.

Reducing powder amounts

This has several advantages.

♥ All detergents place a burden on aquatic life, if they get into waterways, so you could be reducing your impact.
♥ You'll save cash and reduce packaging waste.
♥ Putting in too much powder means it may not be rinsed out properly, aggravating sensitive skins and leaving detergent residues (with the dirt attached) in your clothes.

However, be careful not to reduce powder by too much – not putting in enough makes the cleaning less effective, and could mean you're not protecting your washing machine sufficiently from limescale.

Start by checking the recommended amount on the packet and then reducing it slightly, and use an extra water softener, such as a Magno Ball (→ page 229), which will make your detergent work more efficiently in harder water areas.

Launderer's tip:
Add a couple of tablespoons of baking soda to your powder or liquid, or in place of fabric conditioner. It will act as a deodorizer and water softener, but using too much can leave white streaks. The baking soda works as a washing booster in the powder drawer by neutralizing some of the compounds in water that can interfere with detergent action, so it can be helpful if you're cutting back on powder.

Zero-detergent washing

Eco washing balls and soap nuts are available online, and probably from your local hardware shop. Both are economical if you use them for a lot of washes. The verdicts are from my own tests, and what I've heard from other users.

High-tech option: eco washing balls
These look like small planets, and contain minerals that ionize water, so that the water itself can lift dirt without a detergent. There's no residue, so you can cut out the rinse cycle, saving on water and energy, and the cleaning is extra gentle. The original Ecoballs®

(www.ecozone.co.uk) will do around 1,000 washes, while cheaper versions last for around 100 washes. Check that copycat washing balls do not contain sodium lauryl sulphate, a harsh surfactant that has been linked to skin irritation.

Eco washing balls work fine with lightly soiled loads, but you'll need pre-treatments and stain removers for food spills and make-up marks. You can't use fabric conditioners with them, or mineral-based water softener powders or tablets, but you could try lavender water in the rinse.

Low-tech option: soap nuts

These are the shells of the Indian soap nut, and you put them into the washing-machine drum in a fabric bag. They are gentle and can be added to the compost when they're spent. Add a water-softening agent or Magno Ball to protect your machine.

The nuts themselves don't smell pleasant, but the wash comes out with a light soapy fragrance. They are effective on dirt but, predictably, not so fantastic for food marks, and are good for sensitive skins.

Launderer's tip:

Check if detergent is being properly rinsed out by sluicing an item from a wash in a basin of water and seeing how many bubbles it makes. When Ethan was a baby he had some eczema, so I got worried about washing powder irritating it. The research I discovered suggested that it wasn't the type of washing powder that mattered so much as how good the rinsing was. Today's washing machines nearly all rate poorly in Which? tests of rinse efficiency – partly because of the demand to reduce the amount of water they use.

Which washing option is best for you?

Sensitivities: Try an ecological brand, and make sure you're not using too much detergent, especially in soft-water areas. Experiment with eco washing balls or soap nuts.

Climate change quick fix: If climate change is what you care about most, but you don't have time for pre-treatments, perhaps it's worth looking at a concentrated low-temperature big-brand cleaner; or use an eco option for lightly soiled washes and keep the big guns for when there are serious spills and stains.

No genetically modified organisms (GMOs): Enzymes are usually produced by genetically modified micro-organisms – even those in Ecover's bio washing powder and tablets (although it is looking at other options). If this is a worry, go non-bio.

Reducing landfill and greenhouse gas emissions from transport: Buy the most concentrated option you can, and in large and/or refill packs. Choose recycled, and recyclable, packaging (bottles are easier to recycle than plastic tubs). Consider multi-use eco washing balls.

SPECIAL TREATMENT

One way to prolong the useful life of clothes is to treat stains before washing. But make sure you're not too rough or the cure could end up causing more damage than the original problem, especially on old or delicate fabrics.

♥ Tackle spills and mess fast, before they have time to dry –
although some solids, such as mud, are easier to remove by
brushing off when they've dried.

♥ For liquids, soak up what you can with a clean towel or cloth.
If there are blobs of whatever's been spilt, scrape them off.

♥ Check the fabric type and care instructions – a delicate silk or
synthetic fibre might not respond well to some treatments.
Some materials will have to go to the dry-cleaner, and
upholstery and carpets also need a different approach to avoid
soaking with water (→ page 48).

♥ Deal with the stain well away from anything else that might get on
the garment (in other words, not over a full sink of washing-up).

♥ If treated quickly, many marks will come out with a little water
and detergent, and then you can pop the item in the next wash.

♥ Use cool water – ice-cold and hot can both set some kinds of
stains. Don't use bar soap or soap flakes unless you know the
stain you're dealing with – soap will make vegetable-based
(tannin) stains, such as tea, coffee, fruit juices and wine, much
harder to remove.

Pre-treatments

Although ideally stains should be treated individually, as soon as
they happen, in reality – and especially with children's clothes –
they often don't get dealt with until just before washing. If that's
the case, here's a range of strategies you could put into action
(→ tip on page 32 for books with spray and soak recipes to make
up and bottle).

Hard-wearing fabrics

For clothes that can take tough love, arm yourself with some washing-up liquid, an old scrubbing brush and a general eco stain remover. This is the drill I usually follow. Lightly brush off any dried-on remains. Moisten the stain with a little cool water and try the brush again. Dab the stain with a drop of washing-up liquid and work in with your fingers. If no luck, try again with the brush. Finally, resort to a stain remover.

More delicate materials

For finer fabrics, forget the brush. Instead, add a drop or two of glycerine to the mark and work this in with some detergent. Rinse out before washing. (For more about glycerine, → page 37.)

Underarms

Neutralize odours and help to remove stains by soaking affected areas in a solution of two tablespoons of baking soda in 400ml/ ¾ pint/14fl oz of water for about an hour (sometimes less). Alternatively – and this is especially for silks – add half a cup of white vinegar to half a cup of warm water. Note that vinegar can change the colour of some dyes.

Grime

If you don't want to scrub too hard with washing-up liquid, you could spritz grimy parts with white vinegar instead and then pop in the washer. A vinegar spray works well for urine stains on children's pants.

Friendlier bleaching

Sometimes bleaching is the only option – especially when you've already washed an item and found that the marks haven't magically disappeared.

Household hypochlorite bleach is definitely too strong for clothes – it can create holes and weaken fabrics as well as killing colour. Sodium percarbonate and other oxygen bleaching agents (including hydrogen peroxide) are safe for coloured fabrics, but don't soak clothes for too long and don't use them if the care label says not to bleach. Never mix oxygen bleaches with other stain removers or minerals – always rinse in between. Avoid using any bleaching agent, including lemon juice, on silks or wool (although you should be able to get away with a weak vinegar solution).

Before modern bleaches were developed, one recommendation from household manuals was to employ the whitening properties of May dew, laying garments on the grass for several days. For mild bleaching, you could try these home-made solutions:

Lemon juice and sunlight: Good for white and natural cotton. Use the lemon juice as a spot treatment on stains (→ page 264), then hang in the sun. Launder as usual afterwards.

White distilled vinegar: Mix a cup of vinegar in a bowl of water as a pre-soak. Add more if there's no effect, but don't repeat too often because, like all bleaches, it could start to degrade the fabric.

Launderer's tip:

To sweeten the smell of laundry baskets, put in a lavender bag or two (→ page 300). This can also help to deter clothes moths – an increasing problem as we opt for more natural fibres. Regularly shake out the bottom of your laundry basket to remove the dust and fluff that attract moths.

Sorting your washes

Washing at lower temperatures means there's less chance of colours running, but it's still worth sorting your wash to help keep colours rich, and white and light tones bright. Also, different fabrics require different treatment – you can't just throw everything in a 30°C wash that's designed for cottons. Check the care labels and if you're not sure what they mean, look them up at www.care-labelling.co.uk.

Type of cloth	Washing notes
Towels	Wash a batch of towels together – a single towel in with delicate garments can unbalance the load. To kill off bacteria, wash on a 60°C cycle every few washes and/or use a powder that includes bleach, or add an oxygen laundry bleach. Fabric conditioner coats towelling fibres and makes them less absorbent.

Tea towels and kitchen cloths	Where necessary, wash at 60°C to disinfect and/or use a conventional powder or laundry bleach. Iron cotton or linen cloths after the wash to kill any lingering bacteria.
Bedding	If you have an allergy, or infestation, use a 60°C wash occasionally as lower temperatures won't kill bed bugs and dust mites.
Dark-coloured clothes	Use a washing agent without bleaches or optical brighteners. Hang out of direct sunlight to avoid sun-bleaching.
Light colours	Even at low temperatures, group these separately to keep colours clear. Blues can go in with the dark wash.
Wool	Use the wool cycle, as woollens need low temperatures for both wash and rinse, and a different machine action. Use a specialist wool and silk liquid (most detergents are too alkaline). Avoid biological powders and stain removers, because the enzymes can attack wool fibres. Some loose-knit wools keep their shape better in a machine than when washed by hand.
Silk	Some silks will stand a delicates wash. Use a specialist wool and silk liquid. Avoid biological powders and stain removers.
Synthetics and other delicates	Protect delicate items by washing them in a pillowcase. Non-colourfast items are best treated separately by hand, using a non-bio washing agent.

Checking for colourfastness

♥ Wet a small patch of the garment on a seam or other inconspicuous area. Place an old piece of white cloth over it and press briefly with an iron. If the dye stains the cloth, the item isn't colourfast – hand-wash it on its own in cold water and don't soak. Reds, pinks and oranges, as well as blue denim, are the usual culprits.

♥ If you do get a colour run that affects other garments, wash them again immediately and add a dose of a percarbonate laundry bleach. Alternatively, try a mild dye remover, but check that it's suitable for the fabrics and won't strip out any colour you want to keep.

Do you really need fabric conditioner?

Fabric conditioner coats fibres and reduces static in synthetics. For other materials it acts as a detangler, rather like hair conditioner, but it reduces absorbency, which is why it isn't recommended for towels. It's also bad news for some high-tech fabrics.

The strong scents in conventional fabric conditioners come from synthetic fragrances. If the label says 'parfum', it could mean a multitude of different chemicals – and at least some of them are known to trigger allergic reactions.

Drying your clothes outside will give a naturally fresh fragrance, even in many cities – or you could try . . .

⌔ adding water with a couple of drops of lavender or other essential oil to the fabric conditioner compartment
⌔ making a fragranced vinegar, which will also help to keep clothes soft by aiding rinsing, since vinegar helps to remove detergent residues. (For a lemon vinegar recipe, → page 36.)

⌷ using lavender, rose or another flower water that's normally sold for ironing or cooking – although not if it's coloured. Middle Eastern grocers are a good source for rosewater, especially if you want to buy in bulk. (For ideas on softening clothes, → page 254.)

Hand-washing tips

Many washing machines have very good hand-wash cycles these days, but doing it yourself clocks up even more eco brownie points. You could even re-use greywater from a baby's bath, or paddling pool.

♥ Wool, cashmere and silk are all hand-washable, despite dry-clean-only care labels, and will often wear better when hand-washed. Watch out for elastic ruching (which can stretch or degrade) and inserts or trimmings in different fabrics (which might behave differently from the main fabric, and spoil the shape).

♥ Use an eco hand-wash liquid suitable for wool and silk – definitely not your usual machine detergent – or else try liquid castile soap, such as Dr Bronner's (www.drbronner.com), or soap-nut liquid. Wool and silk are affected by alkaline washing agents, so definitely *don't* use washing soda with them.

♥ Start with the lightest colours first, and dunk bright colours separately in case they aren't colourfast.

♥ Never wring hand-washed clothes, especially wool. Instead, squeeze gently.

- ♥ With most fabrics cold rinsing water works fine, but for wool the rinse water should be the same temperature as the wash. For silks, add a tablespoon of white vinegar to re-acidify them.
- ♥ Most delicates can be drip-dried over a bath. For silks and wools, or anything you're afraid might go out of shape, a great tip that I've only recently discovered is to lay them flat on a towel, roll it up and squeeze gently before arranging them to dry on another towel (for wool) or a hanger (for silk). Carefully pull woollens back into shape and dry slowly, well away from radiators.

Launderer's tip:

If woollens shrink slightly, or other clothes lose their shape, the problem can sometimes literally be ironed out, by reshaping and pressing with a warm iron and using a dampened clean tea towel or pillowcase to protect the fabric. Ironing relaxes wool fibres.

Dry-cleaning

Some types of tailoring – especially if there's padding in a jacket – and some fabrics do need dry-cleaning. To reduce the need for this, air clothes after wear and spot-clean marks carefully (→ page 264).

Check the system your dry-cleaner uses, and when you bring clothes home make sure to air them outside, or in a well-ventilated room. The traditional dry-cleaning solvent, perchlorethylene, or perc, is a pollutant. However, it is likely to be phased out as regulations and consumers demand greener alternatives.

- GreenEarth (www.greenearth.com) uses a silicone-based solvent that appears to be safer and is better for the environment as well as your clothes, but that doesn't mean it's ideal and questions have been raised about its health effects. It's fairly widely available in the UK.
- Liquid carbon dioxide harnesses the 'soda water effect' to bubble dirt out of clothes, and employs gas that is a byproduct of existing industries. The carbon dioxide is non-toxic, and it uses less energy than traditional cleaning, but the detergents may contain some volatile organic compounds (VOCs). It's currently available in North America and Europe, and will probably reach Britain soon.
- Professional wet-cleaning uses water in a controlled way, and is suitable for many fabrics. This is probably the most eco-friendly option all round, so ask your dry-cleaner about it.

Spot treatment

This method is especially useful for dry-clean-only fabrics, such as silk, for upholstery and carpets, or for anything you don't want to soak in the basin or treat too roughly. If you can, test the treatment (→ page 48) on an inconspicuous area first, such as a seam – just to make sure it doesn't have a horrible effect. Many stains will respond to the armoury of kitchen chemicals and household minerals on pages 256–257, but a few will always prove stubborn. The final result might not be perfect every time, but that's partly because some stains require long, multiple treatments to remove them – whatever you're using.

- ♥ Work on the inside of the fabric if possible, to push the stain out, and so that any scuffing or discolouration from over-vigorous treatment is less likely to show.
- ♥ Place the stained area over a pad of non-coloured fabric. This will absorb the spill. As it does, move the garment to a clean piece of fabric.
- ♥ Carefully dab on the treatment with a clean, non-coloured cloth – scrubbing can spread the stain and damage fibres. With carpet, it can damage the pile.
- ♥ Start from a little outside the stained area and work inwards – this will lessen the chance of leaving a coloured ring.
- ♥ You may need to reapply the treatment several times. If you're trying different treatments, always flush with clean water in between, and don't load up several chemicals on top of each other.

Tactics for common stains

If you look online, you'll find hundreds of wildly different suggestions for dealing with particular stains. I can't say I've tried every one – or even every natural one – but the table below shows those I've found most helpful. You'll probably have your own favourites and additions.

If all else fails, after a number of tries, rinse it all out and soak robust fabrics in a solution of percarbonate bleach before laundering. You can also use a percarbonate bleach solution as a last resort for carpet stains – but make sure to try it first on a hidden area, in case it affects the dye. If the mark still won't go, try to have a calm moment, and accept that the stain may never quite come out – just fade with time.

Stain type (surface)	Treatment	Comments
Apple, banana peach	*For a new stain:* Rinse or sponge with cool water. *For an older stain:* Soak in a solution of 1 cup/150g/1½ oz washing soda and 500ml/1 pint/ 18fl oz water before laundering, or dab on a solution of baking soda for more delicate fabrics.	These are stealth stains – they look innocuous at first, but set to a nasty brown. Try to rinse them out when they're still fresh.
Bird droppings	Scrape off as much as you can, then rinse or sponge with cool water. Dab remaining marks with lemon juice and leave for an hour. Rinse, and if stains persist try a solution of 1 cup/ 150g/1½oz washing soda in 500ml/ 1 pint/18fl oz water.	A tricky one, because it depends what the birds have been eating. Make sure to rinse thoroughly in between treatments. Percarbonate bleach may be your only answer.

Blackberry, blackcurrant, raspberry, redcurrant	*For a new stain:* Stretch cotton or other heat-friendly fabrics over a bowl and pour through a stream of boiling water from about 20cm/ 8in above. *For an older stain:* Work in a little glycerine, then flush with coolwater. You could try bleaching the remainder with lemon juice or percarbonate.	The boiling water method goes against the usual advice of using cool water on fruit and sugar stains – but it works! Also useful for wine, tea and coffee. For carpet, pour on soda water, blotting with a towel, and reapply as necessary.
Blood	Soak in cool water until the stain is out, then launder. A little salt added to the water may help.	Don't use soap or hot water as they could set the stain.
Chocolate (and coffee)	Soak or dab with a little milk, then wash out with washing-up detergent. If there's any stain left, spray or dab with a little vinegar, leave, then rinse out.	Don't use soap or hot water as they could set the stain (but → above for the boiling water method).

Crayon	Rub with a little baking soda and washing-up detergent on a damp cloth – but be gentle. For more delicate fabrics try working in a little glycerine, then launder.	On walls, try heating the crayon with a hairdryer then wiping off with a microfibre cloth, but go very gently.
Egg	Scrape off as much as possible, then soak in a bowl of cool salted water.	Don't soak in hot water as it could set the stain.
Glue	Try softening the glue by soaking in warmed vinegar for a few minutes.	There are many types of glue, so you may need to look online for ideas about removing the sort you've used.
Grass	*For a new stain:* Soak or dab with white vinegar or lemon juice. *For an older stain:* Work in a little glycerine then rinse. Try the vinegar treatment on any remaining stain.	

Ink – washable	*For a new stain:* Flush or sponge with cold water and blot up as much as possible. A little detergent may help. *For an older stain:* Work in a small amount of glycerine, then rinse well and try detergent.	The traditional method is to soak in milk, but this isn't suitable for upholstery or carpets.
Ink – ballpoint	Conventionally this is treated with an alcohol such as methylated spirits. You could try vodka, or else glycerine.	
Lipstick	Work in a little glycerine then wash out the grease with a solution of 1 cup/ 150g/1½oz washing soda in 500ml/1 pint/18fl oz water. For bad stains on robust fabrics try a scrub of baking soda and detergent.	

Mould and mildew	Try soaking in sour milk before rinsing and laundering, or bleach stains by soaking in percarbonate laundry bleach.	Very difficult to remove.
Oil, grease and dressings	Shake cornflour over the mark, then brush off when it has absorbed the oil. Treat any remainder with neat washing-up liquid, then launder. You could try working in a little glycerine as a pre-wash treatment.	The absorption technique is useful for non-washable fabrics and for carpets.
Pollen	Don't rub pollen – blow it off or lift away with sticky tape.	
Red wine	Pour over soda water or white wine. Blot, then pour on again as needed. Or try the absorption technique with cornflour or cornmeal.	Salt could make any remaining stain harder to remove.

Tomato pasta/pizza sauce	*For a new stain:* Work in some neat washing-up liquid, rinse and then soak in 1 cup/ 150g/1½oz washing soda to 500ml/1 pint/18fl oz warm water. *For an older stain:* Moisten with glycerine, then soak in washing soda solution.	This is a tricky one because it's a combination stain – there's oil as well as pigment. Try these methods for curry as well.

Launderer's tip:

For more stain removal tactics see Natural Stain Remover *by Angela Martin and* Better Basics for the Home *by Annie Berthold-Bond.*

DRYING

For me, there's nothing like the fresh scent of line-dried washing, and sunlight has antibacterial properties. I like a single line – or you can string a couple across a narrow garden – but rotary versions are more compact for large washes and small spaces. You can also buy outdoor lines on metal arms that fold against a wall, or freestanding multi-line structures. Try to avoid locating your line under trees – bird droppings are one of the real annoyances of drying outside.

Make sure garments are turned inside out to protect the right side from sun-bleaching, dust and suicidal insects, and pull gently into shape so they're as close as you can get to how they should look when dry. Holding the bottom corners and flicking sharply can help to flatten clothes and household linen. As far as possible, peg by waistbands, hems and seams to avoid peg marks. Don't line-dry jumpers or fabrics that could stretch.

Indoor drying

In bad weather, or if you have no outside space, airers (aka drying racks) come into their own. You can buy them in various shapes and it's useful to have a few, to cope with large washes. Note that untreated wood can leave marks.

We all need to do an emergency drying operation now and again, but try not to get into the habit of cranking up your heating to dry clothes quickly. Hanging washing direct on a radiator increases energy consumption, and can create condensation. Ideally, dry washing in an unheated room with the window open, and keep the door closed so heat isn't drawn in from elsewhere in the house – although in winter this may not be practical. There's a balance to be had between energy-saving and ending up with your clothes still damp after several days.

Soft clothes without a tumble dryer

A friend with a young baby asked me about keeping clothes and towels soft if you line-dry. It is possible – some tips are listed below – and as an incentive, remember that drying just one load a week without the tumble will save 78kg/172lb of carbon dioxide emissions a year. Just think what you can save by putting all of them on the line or airer.

Don't wash towels or clothes too often. Over time, repeated washing makes fibres stiffer – as well as causing dyes to fade.

Use extra water softener, especially if your water is very hard. Softer water means less build-up of limescale on your clothes. Try a Magno Ball in the drum (→ page 229).

Use less detergent. Detergent residues can leave clothes sticky and hard.

Don't dry your washing on the radiator. Avoid that cardboard feel . . .

Bring your line drying in at dusk. For the softest clothes, you don't want to desiccate them, so if your washing has gone stiff – easily done on a hot, sunny day – leave it out until the dew is just falling. If it feels a little damp still, air indoors overnight.

Give them a good rub. Even if towels and clothes are less than fluffy after drying, they soon soften up when you use them. If you're concerned for the delicate skin of babies, rub the fabric together in your hands – you'll notice it soften.

Buy organic cotton. Anecdotal evidence (and my own experience) suggests this is usually softer than other cottons. The reason, apparently, is that the fibres aren't broken down by the chemicals used in conventional farming and processing.

Give up ironing now!

It's the most disliked household chore and, as a green householder, you don't have to do it! I actively enjoy finding ways to smooth clothes without ironing, and have honed these tips over the years. They should help reduce the amount of ironing you have to do.

- ♥ Lower spin speeds crease clothes less (although they will add to drying time), so in good drying weather you could reduce the spin rpm.
- ♥ An eco fabric conditioner may help creases fall out more easily.
- ♥ Take clothes out of the machine as soon as possible and hang to dry straightaway.
- ♥ Be a perfectionist about pulling garments into shape, and dry shirts on hangers. Do up buttons and pull seams so they're straight, not puckered. To open out mangled sleeves, push one hand down the sleeve from the shoulder; then, holding the cuff with the other hand, pull it back up with the fingers opened wide.
- ♥ Dry on the line – the breeze can help blow out wrinkles.

♥ Hang or neatly fold your dry washing straightaway. (I occasionally forget and leave clothes in an 'I'll hang them up in a minute' pile – undoing all my careful reshaping.) Bed linen can lose creases through the ironing effect of being neatly stacked.

♥ Change your style – live with the odd crumple (unless you're going for a job interview, of course) and choose more casual clothes and T-shirt fabrics that will do without the iron.

If you really must iron . . .

⌗ Follow the advice above so you're not dealing with a creased bundle. Even if you have a steam iron, many fabrics are easier to flatten when not-quite-dry. For silks, do it while the garment is still damp, and/or iron through a damp cloth.

⌗ Do your ironing in batches to save electricity. You could choose a favourite TV or radio programme and aim to iron your way through it.

⌗ Start with the coolest-setting clothes first. You may find that some will do on a lower temperature – such as ironing cotton on the wool setting – especially if you use steam or iron them while still damp.

⌗ If your steam iron's instructions stipulate distilled or filtered water, use that. Descale your steam iron regularly – check the instructions or use vinegar.

How to launder with environmental delicacy

Don't over-wash clothes, and only do full loads in your machine.

Make a 30°C wash your default setting.

Use hotter washes thoughtfully – for kitchen cloths, to deep-cleanse bed linen and towels and to maintain your machine.

Use as biodegradable a washing agent as possible.

If you do need something stronger, try pre-soaks and natural stain removal treatments – or keep a bio powder for hard-worn clothes.

Experiment with reducing detergent amounts, but make sure you soften water sufficiently.

Vow to wash small numbers of delicates by hand, and air and spot-treat dry-clean-only garments so they need a full clean less often.

Think twice about fabric conditioner.

Try out natural stain removal tactics to prolong the life of clothes.

Dry clothes on the line or airers.

Just say no to ironing!

10

CLOTHES THAT WILL LAST

Being thrifty with clothes doesn't mean buying rubbish or looking dowdy. Wearing a vintage gown or jacket, you can feel fantastic, and enjoy a quality of fabric and finish that are well nigh impossible to come

by in most modern fashion. If you nurture your favourite wardrobe items – whether that's coloured T-shirts or a pair of boots – they'll give you fine service for many years.

We've become used to cheap imports and constantly changing 'must-haves' in the shops. Clothes can be a pleasure as well as a necessity, but there's a cost to 'cheap chic'. Usually it's paid by the workers growing crops such as cotton, who are exposed to pesticides; the communities whose water is contaminated by dyes; and the child labourers and others who suffer exploitation and dangerous conditions in under-regulated garment factories. Now the facts are becoming much better publicized, changes are beginning on the high street.

Thrifty wardrobe tip:

In the UK, the campaigning organization Labour Behind the Label reports on companies that are good employers, and those paying poverty wages. See www.cleanupfashion.co.uk.

THE LIFETIME WARDROBE

There's no tactful way to say this – most of us own, and buy, too many clothes. Between 2001 and 2005, annual spending on women's clothing in Britain rose by 5 per cent to £24 billion (yes, billion), and in the 10 years from 1997 to 2007, women doubled the number of garments they bought. We've somehow got used to purchasing almost a whole new wardrobe each season – and then we're encouraged to de-clutter and get rid of everything we don't wear, taking the rejects to the charity shop to assuage our guilt. At its worst, it's a kind of binge-purge cycle.

The concept of a lifetime wardrobe runs counter to this. The idea is hardly new – it's just that we've forgotten it. Developing a lifetime wardrobe means choosing clothes that will last – in terms of both fabric and style – and then looking after them. So it's more to do with creating a personal look that gradually evolves over the years as you do, than with grabbing the latest trends, whether they truly flatter you or not. It also means keeping faith with momentarily out-of-favour clothes that you still like, knowing that you'll pick them up again one day and love putting them on once more. And it means having just enough clothes to fit each occasion, rather than buying yet another pair of black trousers when you already have two.

What your lifetime wardrobe might contain

Of course, this will depend on your work and life, as well as your style, but here's an idea of what a woman's collection might look like. New items can be added as old ones wear out or are handed on. I've realized that, in fact, I currently own more clothes than this, but it's meant to be a guide, not something you'll be marked on like an exam.

Outerwear

A good winter coat – not too heavy, given warmer winters, but enough to keep out a biting wind.

An all-weathers jacket, preferably with a hood; or else a raincoat.

A smart jacket to wear as a spring top layer, but also under a coat when it's colder.

Trousers, skirts and knitwear

Jeans – I wear jeans a lot, so I like to have two wearable pairs at all times, plus an older pair that I don't mind getting dirty in the garden.

Trousers – a smart pair, a wear-all-the-time pair and a light summer pair.

Skirts – a warm one for winter, one for spring and autumn and a light one for heatwaves, plus one for smart occasions (or substitute more trousers if you don't wear skirts much).

Suits – one or two if you really need them for your job, but separates will be more flexible in your wardrobe.

Cardigans (or hoodies, or light jackets, depending on your style) – a light one for summer evenings and a wool one for winter at least. I have quite a few cardigans because I get cold easily and like to layer them so I don't have to turn the heating up.

Jumpers – a chunky knit for instant cosy warmth and a couple of thinner ones for layering.

Tops and dresses

Enough shirts and/or jersey tops to get you through a winter week (so you don't need interim washes).

Enough blouses, T-shirts and fluttery tops to get you through a summer week.

A dress or two – I don't wear dresses much, but it's nice to have at least one you love for summertime lazing.

Undergarments

A few pairs of thick tights (they last longer).

Socks and underwear to get you through a full week.

Camisoles and strappy tops – which can double as vests in the winter, and be worn for yoga classes.

Shoes and accessories

A pair of smart shoes, a pair of loafing shoes, a pair that will survive the rain.

Sandals that don't kill your feet.

Smart boots.

Walking boots – also good for when you're digging the vegetable patch.

Wellies – you can pull them on over anything for instant waterproofing.

A tote big enough to carry shopping.

A handbag for smarter occasions.

Thrifty wardrobe tip:

Instead of spending a fortune on the latest fashion bag, hire one from an online 'bag library', such as www.fashionhire.co.uk or www.handbaghirehq.co.uk.

Capsule wardrobe for men

Clive appears to survive happily with a collection of T-shirts and several pairs of jeans in various states of frayedness, plus some short-sleeved summer shirts and a couple of well-chosen jumpers. But then, he does work from home. Asked for more serious consideration, he suggested these tips to keep a rounded but svelte male wardrobe.

- A smart winter coat is probably only necessary if you have a job that requires you to wear a suit, otherwise you'll get more mileage from a warm waterproof jacket.
- Two suits will keep you prepared for most occasions, if you're not wearing them every day: a light one for summer weddings and parties, and a darker one for interviews, important meetings and funerals. Add at least one white formal shirt and a couple of ties, so you don't have to rush out and buy something you hate at the last moment.
- A messenger bag is handy for everyday use, so you can keep your smart satchel for meetings.
- Invest in thick, warm socks for winter walking and gardening. Alpaca is soft, breathable and insulates well (although it isn't cheap), and you can get British alpaca from www.toftalpacashop.co.uk.

PRUNING, NOT UPROOTING

To keep it at its best, the lifetime wardrobe does need occasional pruning and nurturing. Try not to feel guilty about what you have already. OK, so perhaps you made a few rash purchases, but don't be too hasty in letting go of half your wardrobe – I was on the verge of getting rid of a camel-coloured zip jacket that I now rely on as a wardrobe staple – and don't leave yourself so short that you immediately have to go out shopping again to fill the gaps.

Clothing reallocation

The number of clothes sent to charity is increasing – especially new, cheap clothes with the tags still on – but think before you donate. Many of these clothes could be rescued and resuscitated for your own wardrobe, saving the resources and energy of manufacturing new ones, and the transport costs and emissions of trips to the shops.

Used to be lovely but it's got a tear/lost a button/moth holes
All of these are potentially fixable or can be camouflaged.
(→ Chapter 11.)

I still like it but it's out of fashion
Can you accessorize it back into fashion, by adding a belt to a cardigan or dress, for instance? Or combine it with other clothes in a different way, such as layering? Can you defy fashion and wear it anyway? Or transform it into something more à la mode (→ Chapter 11)? Alternatively, you could store it away in the almost certain knowledge that, in a few short years, it'll be the height of desirability, and you can feel a little bit smug when everyone asks where you got it.

I still like it but it doesn't fit any more
This is a tricky one – do you hold on to it to see if you'll ever be that size again, or not? If you swap or give away a well-loved

garment to a friend, at least you'll see someone else getting good use out of it. If it's too big, you could see if a tailor can alter it without too much bother.

Cast-offs I'm not embarrassed to show my mates
Try holding a swap party with friends (called 'swishing'), sell it on eBay or through a clothing exchange, or set up a stall at a local clothes sale. Otherwise, donate it to charity.

Definitely past its best
If it's still in reasonable condition, try it with a local charity shop. If they don't rate it, they will probably pass it on to a textile recycling company, which may send usable but not quite peak condition clothes to developing countries. Perhaps it would be good for a children's dressing-up box, or to wear while decorating or doing other dirty jobs around the home.

Beyond rejuvenation
Cannibalize for trims, buttons and patching fabric, and cut up the rest for dusters. If the fabric's not suitable, check with local charities if they can sell it on to a textile recycling company, or take it to your council's recycling depot. Unwearable clothes may be turned into industrial wipes, or their fibres may be rewoven into new clothes or used for mattress packing.

❖ **Thrifty wardrobe tip:**
❖ *Swapping is a great alternative to selling. Try sites such as*
❖ *www.whatsmineisyours.com, or the swishing party events organized*
❖ *by Futerra (www.futerra.co.uk), Swap-a-Rama Razzmatazz*

(www.myspace.com/swaparamarazzmatazz) and Renideo in
Scotland (www.renideo.co.uk), or hold your own swishing party (see
www.swishing.org).

SHOPPING LESS

Some people vow to 'not shop' as a challenge; as a statement; as a
moral position. For me, it happened initially because I'd just given
birth. Not that I gave up shopping completely. In fact, despite
hand-me-downs and trying out re-usable nappies, we did rather a lot
of shopping for Ethan in that first year. But I didn't have much time
to shop for myself, and we didn't have a lot of spare cash, either.

In Ethan's first couple of years I bought a handful of new
clothes – and some seasons went by without a single purchase.
I did try buying cheap, but because I wore all my clothes so much,
the less well-made ones fell apart, or the fabric went limp or
irreversibly bobbly. It was the slightly more expensive
'investment' buys and long-lost favourites from my storage
suitcase that brought me through.

I still buy less than I used to, and shopping plays a
much-reduced role in my life. For some jobs, though, especially
office-based ones, a wardrobe of smart, new-looking clothes is a
necessity. There are, however, more interesting ways of acquiring
clothes than trekking down the standard high street.

Ethical acquisition

If 'reduce, re-use, repair, recycle' is the mantra for cutting the
household waste that goes out, perhaps we need a similar slogan

for vetting what comes in. How about 'rehomed, re-used, remodelled, ethical'?

This is a shorthand for saying that it's best to opt for swapping items – preferably as close to home as possible – through friends, Freecycle (→ page 205), or a swap site (so they're rehomed). Alternatively, buy from local second-hand sources, such as jumble sales and charity shops, or through online shops, such as eBay or specialist vintage outlets (re-used), or choose clothes that have been refashioned (remodelled) from old fabrics, such as those from Traid (Textile Recycling for Aid and International Development, see www.traid.org.uk). If you want to buy something new, choose organic, sustainable and fairtrade sources (ethical) where you can.

The balance will be different for everyone, but it'll give you a glow if you try at least one of the RRREs when you're looking for something different to wear.

Before you go shopping . . .

Even if you're not doing a sort-through, at least open all your cupboards to make sure you haven't forgotten about a pair of sandals lurking there. In the same way as making a list is useful for food shopping, it can be invaluable to note down what you really need, and in what colours, before you go out or log on. If you're particularly into list-making (as I am) you could even split your wish-list into priorities.

Having said that, some of the clothes I wear most are the ones that I loved at first sight. So following your heart can sometimes lead you in the right direction, too.

Buying vintage

I used to buy a lot of vintage clothes from market stalls and shops. These days, as well as independent shops, there are online stores, many run by individuals, plus Oxfam Originals, the Notting Hill Housing Trust and some Topshop outlets. For high fashion, try Rellik near Portobello Road (www.relliklondon.co.uk) and Beyond Retro (www.beyondretro.com). Listings of vintage sales can be viewed on www.whatsmineisyours.com.

Second-hand buying and care tips

- Before you buy, check if there are any missing buttons, tears or stains and decide if you can get them fixed, or if they don't matter (→ Chapter 11). Old stains are unlikely to come out.
- Garments that are a little too large can often be adapted by a good tailor, who could also replace broken zips. It's worthwhile

trying to get the work done straight away – I've had things lying around for ages unworn because they're waiting to be altered.

- Older fabrics are often more delicate. Check what the garment is made from and ask for cleaning advice in the shop. Also try online forums such as www.thefedoralounge.com. Dry-cleaning isn't necessarily better for antique fabrics.
- Air clothes thoroughly to dispel odours. Try dunking washable fabrics in lukewarm water with a tablespoon of baking soda. White vinegar is better for wool and silk, but check for colourfastness first (→ page 261). For more delicate items, shake some baking soda into a box, wrap the clothing in acid-free tissue paper, put it in the box and leave for a few days.

Thrifty wardrobe tip:

You can buy recycled tissue paper for ordinary storage, but for clothing make sure it's the acid-free kind. Look at The Green Stationery Company (www.greenstat.co.uk) and Recycled Paper Supplies (www.rps.gn.apc.org).

Buying new

Ethical clothing – fairtrade and sustainable, organic, recycled or remodelled using vintage fabrics – is becoming ever easier to find.

On the high street
There's People Tree in Topshop and Selfridges (www.peopletree. co.uk), while Marks & Spencer has made a big commitment to using fairtrade cotton, setting standards for reducing chemical use and pollution by its suppliers, and even selling recycled synthetic trousers. Gap has launched a range of organic babywear and

Product (Red) lines, donating a percentage of profits to fight AIDS in Africa (see www.joinred.com for details and other brands involved), and you can find organic or fairtrade cotton from H&M to Sainsbury's. Expect to see more of this – and ask for organic and fairtrade options in your favourite shops if you don't.

Online
The number and range of online eco stores is growing all the time, so the following suggestions are just a few points of departure to start you exploring. Try boutiques such as Adili (www.adili.com) and The Natural Store (www.thenaturalstore.co.uk), and general eco stores such as Natural Collection (www.naturalcollection.com).

You can buy direct from a whole range of smaller suppliers, from cotton basics by Gossypium (www.gossypium.co.uk) to hemp and silk lingerie from Enamore (www.enamore.co.uk) and remade clothes from Junky Styling (www.junkystyling.co.uk). On The Soil Association's Organic Directory website (http://www.whyorganic.org/involved_organicDirectory.asp) you can search for local outlets by area. Other directories include www.ethicaldirectory.co.uk and www.alotoforganics.co.uk.

FABRICS AND FIBRES

Natural fibres aren't necessarily green fibres. Pesticides, chemicals used in making material from the raw components, dyes, and the large number of chemical surface treatments that are standard practice today all add to their chemical load. They can also take large amounts of water and energy to produce. With organic materials, many of the ethical and chemical issues have been addressed.

Hemp	As eco-friendly as it gets. Doesn't need pesticides or herbicides, has a wide range of uses (including making paper and biofuel), is strong, long-lasting and warm. Combined with cotton or silk, it produces a durable fabric without losing the softness. The fabric industry isn't technically set up to make hemp cloth, so it may be a while before it becomes widely available.
Linen	Woven from fibres of the flax plant. Even non-organic flax requires far fewer pesticides than cotton. Most linen is now produced in China. Eco linens, made with low-impact dyes, are available.
Bamboo	Renewable, grows fast without pesticides, non-GM. Bamboo makes a soft fabric that launders well and is naturally antibacterial – what's not to like about it? In general, it is a greener option, but the majority of bamboo fabric is made in a similar way to rayon, using some pretty caustic chemicals. Look for Soil Association or similar accreditation.
Cotton	It may be a regrowable fibre, but cotton uses 25 per cent of the world's pesticides and 20,000 people die each year from accidental poisoning, according to the World Health Organization. Many farmers suffer starvation levels of poverty. Organic cotton involves far fewer chemicals, and in the longer term could help farmers trade their way out of poverty.
Recovered fibres	Some companies recover cotton sweepings, which are usually left as waste from manufacture, and mulch them back into a cotton-wool-like state that can be re-spun.

Wool	Long-lasting, resilient, warm and absorbs moisture well (good for sports clothes). Conventionally reared sheep are likely to have been dipped in hazardous organophosphates for pest control. Making wool from fleece is water- and energy-intensive – more so than cotton or polyester. But with organic wool, welfare and environmental standards are much higher, and no harsh chemicals are used in production.
Silk	In theory, silk is a sustainable material, but a major issue is the ethics. The moths are usually killed before they break a hole in their silky cocoon, to keep the long strands intact. For 'peace silk', they are allowed to emerge, and a different process is used for spinning the yarn.
Fleece	Synthetic. In 1993, Patagonia (www.patagonia. com) started making its fleeces from waste plastic bottles. It takes about 25 two-litre bottles to make a fleece, saving 80 per cent of the energy used for a virgin fleece. The company also recycles old, worn-out fleeces from any source.
Tencel (generic name: lyocell)	A man-made fibre produced from natural materials. It's a more eco-friendly version of rayon or viscose, made from wood grown in sustainably managed forests. Strong chemicals may be used in the dyeing or treatment of the finished material, so check for this.

Thrifty wardrobe tip:

For frank exposés of fibre manufacture and more on what to choose, see the Organic Clothing Blog from Lotus Organics at http://organicclothing.blogs.com.

What about synthetics?

There are arguments for and against synthetic fibres. Most of them, including nylon and polyester, are products of the petrochemical chain, and energy-intensive to make. However, they don't use as much energy and water in the dyeing process as most natural fibres, and they don't take land, water or pesticides to grow.

Call me a 'light green', but some synthetic fibres may have a role, especially if they can be sustainably recycled. After all, nylon fibre can now be retrieved from synthetic carpets. One problem is that often the more attractive synthetics are marked as dry-clean-only and may be damaged by washing.

Thrifty wardrobe tip:

For news, ideas and fun reading, see blogs such as www. stylewillsaveus.com and www.hippyshopper.com.

Do you want to know where your jeans come from?

A billion pairs of jeans are made each year. Denim has been transformed from workers' wear to a fashion fabric. These days it is so treated with enzymes, pumice and sandpaper in specialized denim laundries that it can wear out quicker than other originally more fragile materials. But eco awareness and denim purism (yes, there are denim-heads out there who have whole forums devoted to the minutiae of finishes) are making traditional denim look increasingly attractive.

The cotton

Before the late nineteenth century all cotton was organic, which means that the first jeans, from the 1850s, were also organic. Now an increasing number of brands, from Ascension (www. ascensionclothing.co.uk) to Loomstate (www.loomstate.org), are insisting on organic cotton for their jeans, and even Levi's has an Eco jean.

The dye

About 50,000 tonnes of dye are discharged into waterways each year, along with huge amounts of salt (used to help fix dyes so they don't run). The dyes can contain heavy metals and compounds that become carcinogenic in the aquatic environment. So-called Azo dyes are particularly notorious. Traditional indigo, as used for the original blue jeans, is a plant dye. The jeans come out of the dyeing vat yellow, then change to indigo as the dye oxidizes in the air.

The washing

What washing? In contrast to the enzyme treatments and bleaches used on most jeans, Howies (www.howies.co.uk) has turned to rubberized washing balls to help remove just enough of the indigo so it doesn't stain your hands or shoes. Then there's 'dry' or 'raw' denim, which has a slight sheen and hasn't been washed at all.

Ethical shopping guide

New names are popping up all the time, so the outlets listed here are merely to get you thinking along ethical lines.

Working week

Fairtrade underwear from M&S

Skirts and jackets from a designer clothing exchange, or by ClothWorks at www.thenaturalstore.co.uk, or merino wool by Karen Cole (www.karencole.co.uk)

Trousers and shirts from www.peopletree.co.uk and high fashion from Noir (at www.fashion-conscience.com)

Dresses from vintage stores or by Stewart + Brown (at www.adili.com)

Bag swapped with a friend, or from eBay

Weekend lounging

Underwear (and jeans) from www.howies.co.uk, and hipster shorts from www.terramar.co.uk

Jeans from vintage stores or by Kuyichi and Del Forte (at www.adili.com), or deluxe handmade jeans from www.sharkahchakra.com

- Organic and ethically produced knitwear from www.keepandshare.co.uk – or dig around at charity shops and local jumble sales
- T-shirts from a vintage shop, or by Katharine Hamnett (www.katharinehamnett.com), or Edun (www.edun.com)
- Trainers by Veja (from www.adili.com)
- Bags, belts and alpaca hats from www.pachacuti.co.uk

Night out

- From dresses and sparkly tops to strappy sandals and bags – try swishing (→ page 284), designer clothing exchanges and local clothing sales (items are usually in good condition)
- Student shows, with new designers who have an ethical edge
- Organic chiffon and hemp silk from Ciel (at www.equaclothing.com)
- For a special occasion, a vintage kimono from www.thenaturalstore.co.uk
- Jewellery from vintage market stalls or Made (from www.adili.com)

Boys

- T-shirts and hoodies by THTC and Tonic (from www.thenaturalstore.co.uk)
- Jeans by Howies, Nudie, Edun, and a growing number of ethical brands – or go vintage
- A bespoke suit (which will, at least, last a long time)
- British-made workwear styles from Old Town and Tin House (www.old-town.co.uk)
- No Sweat baseball boots and lo-tops from www.earthandwear.co.uk, or Simple Shoes (www.simpleshoes.com)

A greener linen cupboard

When you're buying new bedding or towels, try to make them organic cotton or bamboo, and unbleached for minimum environmental impact. You can get organic cotton bed linen in the high street (at Habitat, for example). Old sheets can often be patched if there's only a small hole (→ page 320), or else they're good for undersheets to help protect mattresses, or for making Halloween ghost costumes, lavender bags (→ page 300) or a cotton lining for home-sewn clothes or bags. Past-their-best towels are invaluable for mopping up spills, or can be cut down to make face cloths.

New, commercially bought curtains and blinds may be treated with fire retardants that could contain hazardous chemicals. High-quality, second-hand curtains are available from The Curtain Exchange shops (www.thecurtainexchange.net), or you could make your own (or have them made) with vintage or eco-friendly fabrics.

Making your own

I remember as a child browsing through Vogue pattern books with my mother, and the ritual of pinning the fluttery paper on to the material, then cutting it out with pinking shears. We even did some dressmaking at school.

Home-made clothes, once a staple of most people's wardrobes, have for some years been on the seriously endangered list – although sewing machine sales suggest they are becoming more popular again. By making your own you can get a more accurate fit and choose the fabric you want in the style you want, as well as saving money. (For sewing basics, → Chapter 11.) If the idea of sewing makes you come over all fingers and thumbs, consider paying a seamstress or tailor to do it for you.

Sustainable sewing fabrics

I asked Jenny Ambrose, founder of eco fashion label Enamore (www.enamore.co.uk), for advice on sourcing organic cottons and other greener materials for sewing projects.

 Vintage fabrics are probably the easiest. Try antiques fairs, car-boot sales, eBay and collectors, plus there's always someone who's clearing out their granny's attic.

 Buying organic cotton and sustainable fabrics, such as hemp, can be expensive if you are ordering in small quantities, but try www. hempfabric.co.uk, www.thehempshop.co.uk (for undyed materials) and www.greenfibres.com.

 US website www.nearscanaturals.com has coloured and printed fabrics (although many aren't cheap) and sewing 'notions' such as lace. The company regularly ships worldwide, but bear in mind that measurements are in yards and inches, and you'll need to add in the cost of customs and shipping.

CARING FOR YOUR WARDROBE

Looking after your clothes and accessories makes good green sense. Protecting them means less washing, and following care instructions – and mending as soon as you spot a rip or hole – will cut your clothing footprint and help them to last. (For more about mending, → Chapter 11.)

- ⊞ Get yourself an apron – and then ensure you wear it to protect your clothes while cooking. Aprons used to be worn most of the time in the home, and for many other jobs.
- ⊞ Change out of work or special-occasion clothes when you get home, then air them, so you'll need to wash them less often.
- ⊞ Tumble dryers can make clothes wear more quickly, because of the repeated abrasion. (Yet another reason not to use them.)
- ⊞ You can carefully remove the 'pills' from woollens with a small pair of scissors. Don't pull them because this will damage the fibres even more.

Storing clothes

Clothes, like food, should be kept somewhere cool and dark, not too hot and not too cold, and definitely not dirty. Unless clothes rails are properly covered, dust may settle on them and colours fade. A nice clean, dark wardrobe is your best bet.

Try not to cram clothes together on the rail – they hang better with some breathing space. Jumpers, and anything else that might stretch, are best folded. Open up the doors occasionally to give everything a good airing. Shake clothes out and move them around – this may encourage you to look beyond your usual staple favourites.

Packing away seasonal clothes

I like the ritual of unpacking my spring-summer and autumn-winter wardrobe. There's comfort in the never-ending cycle of time and the promise of a whole new season. Often I'll rediscover

clothes I've forgotten (and some I'd sooner forget). I find a
suitcase works well enough – although sometimes it means taking
everything out when I need it for a holiday. Everything should
be clean before you pack it.

For special-occasion clothes that you hardly ever wear, it's worth
wrapping them in acid-free tissue paper and finding a more
permanent place to keep them. Make sure your storage area is dry –
and that all the clothes are fully dry before you put them away. I also
like to throw in the little packs of silicone gel that come in some
packaging to absorb excess moisture. Some people recommend
plastic bags for airtight sealing, but they don't allow clothes to
breathe.

Moth defence

Moth holes usually show up after washing, but if you spot them
when a garment has come out of the wardrobe, wash it again.
A neat trick is to put small items (such as non-washable delicates
and soft toys) in a plastic bag and give them a blast in the freezer
for a few days to kill off any remaining eggs.

Moth repellants are usually made from scented plants that the
insects don't much care for, including lavender, bay leaves, cloves
and rosemary. You can buy sachets for drawers, wardrobes and
laundry baskets, or you could try cedar-wood balls. When these
lose their scent, buff lightly with sandpaper, or add a drop or two
of cedar-wood oil.

Regular vacuuming of areas where dust and fluff accumulate
will take away what for a clothes moth looks like attractive bedding
and foodstuffs. Don't use traditional moth balls that contain

naphthalene or paradichlorobenzene, because these are toxic to both pets and humans.

MAKE: *Lavender bag*

✳ ✳ ✳ ✳ ✳ ✳ ✳ ✳ ✳ ✳ ✳ ✳ ✳ ✳ ✳

Pick the lavender when the flowers are young. You can either strip the flowers straight off the stems, or cut the stalks and hang in a cool, dark place to dry.

You will need:

A magazine page, newspaper or other re-used paper, and a pen
Pins
Dressmaker's scissors
Vintage fabric, such as an old tablecloth or serviettes, or dress fabric
Needle and thread
Ribbon, lace or other decorations
Lavender

1. Draw the shape of your lavender sachet on the paper – perhaps a simple square, or a heart. For a bag that you'll pull closed with a ribbon, draw a rectangle.

2. Fold the material in half, right side in, and make sure any pattern is aligned. Pin on your paper shape and cut out (you could make several at once).

3. Pin the fabric pieces together, right sides facing, and tack all round, leaving a small space – or the top edge – open. Sew up the seams with backstitch (→ see page 311), then press.

4. For an open-topped bag either trim the top edge with pinking shears (which leave a zigzag shape), or turn under and sew a hem.

5. Turn the bag right way out and press again (→ Chapter 11 for basic sewing and pressing).

6. Fill the bag with lavender and either sew it up with over-and-over stitch (→ page 311), or close tightly with ribbon. If you like, add lace to the edgings.

Thrifty wardrobe tip:
You could also make lavender bags from a pair of colourful socks (try children's socks) that have lost their heels and/or toes. With a sewing machine, run a couple of rows of zigzag stitch across where the leg part meets the foot. Push in some lavender, then sew two more zigzag rows further up the leg section. Now chop off the unwanted bits of sock. Ideal for sock drawers (of course).

Shoe care and cleaning

Leather is a contentious issue – not only for vegetarians and those concerned for animal welfare, but because tanneries use some unpleasant chemicals. Alternatives include vegetable-tanned and dyed leather from makers such as Terra Plana (www.terraplana. com) which also collaborates in the recycled clothes label Worn Again. Other options include canvas shoes with latex soles, raffia shoes, and the gorgeous-but-expensive handmade creations of

Beyond Skin (www.beyondskin.co.uk). And as far as shoes are concerned, plastic might not be the devilish option it's usually regarded as.

- Don't dry wet shoes near a radiator. Instead, pad into shape with newspaper or other absorbent paper from your recycling box and leave somewhere airy.
- Take shoes to be re-heeled and re-soled before your socks are making contact with the pavement.
- Keep a selection of shoeboxes to store out-of-season footwear.
- If salty marks from snowy winter days won't wipe off with a damp cloth, dip the cloth in a little vinegar. This will also remove surface polish, so you'll need to re-polish afterwards.
- Wearing the same shoes every day is bad for your shoes and potentially bad for your foot health. Shoes absorb a lot of moisture from your feet and need time to dry properly – and high heels or shoes that don't fit properly can bring problems from corns to shortened Achilles tendons and displaced toe joints.

Leather

Shoe cream is best for softer leathers while polish is good for harder wear and more shine. Choose a cream or polish in the correct colour, or a neutral for shoes in light or unusual colours. You'll also need an old cloth to put on the polish – part of a retired tea towel will be just fine – and a shoe brush (dark or light).

Spread newspaper on the floor or table and wear an apron, or lay an old towel over your lap. Brush off any dried mud, or wipe it off with a slightly damp cloth. Hold the shoe by placing your hand inside it – that way you're less likely to get polish all over your fingers. Use the cloth to take a wipe of shoe cream or polish. If the polish is cold and hard, rub the surface in circles with the cloth to soften it a little. Apply it to the shoe in a thin, even layer. Then polish with the shoe brush using a to-and-fro action (not round and round). This removes any excess polish and gives a light sheen. Repeat with shoe two. For more of a shine, buff up with a duster.

Suede
Brush lightly with a soft suede brush – never one that's been near polish. Some tougher marks can be removed with a wire brush but prevention is better than cure, so treat as soon after buying as possible with a non-aerosol silicone spray in a well ventilated space.

Patent leather and plastic
Wipe with a soft, lint-free cloth, or a damp cloth, to remove mud and marks. Patent leather can get dry and crack over time; you could always try the old remedy of rubbing on some petroleum jelly and leaving it to sink in.

Low-sheen leather
Keep this supple, without adding shine, by wiping over with a cloth dipped in a half-and-half mix of light vegetable oil and white distilled vinegar.

Fading and mishaps

♥ Hide scuffs and faded areas by rubbing on a little renovating polish of the correct colour before polishing the whole shoe. For unusual colours, try an oil pastel from an art shop, and then polish with neutral shoe cream.

- ♥ Use felt-tipped pens to conceal marks and dents on high heels. On patent leather, use a dab of nail varnish.
- ♥ On leather-covered stilettos and other high heels, you may find you get little raised scales where the heel has, annoyingly, been swallowed up by a hole in the pavement. Camouflage these by gluing torn pieces back down and then polishing with a matching colour. Sometimes the warmed handle of a metal spoon will help iron out the puckers.

How to be thrifty *and* gorgeous

Shop less and try to buy only what you need (and just occasionally what you can't live without).

Get to know what really suits you to reduce wardrobe mistakes and develop a lifetime wardrobe.

Cast an eye over wardrobe discards – can you revive them or use them for something else?

Resist purging so much that you leave gaps you need to fill by shopping.

For new additions, try swaps, vintage, jumble, charity and remodelled rather than simply heading to the high street.

For cheap clothes, try second-hand as an alternative to ultra-low-price new.

Get to know the ethical and organic sources – they're especially good for basics, but you can now also fill a business or fashion wardrobe with them.

Take care of clothes and shoes to help them last longer.

11

MAKE
DO AND
MEND

As I sit down to write this chapter I have just spent the past 45 minutes mending a blouse, a top and a skirt. It's not something that I do particularly often, but for 15 minutes each it's revived three garments

that would otherwise have been discarded or left to hang around uselessly in the back of the wardrobe. I have to admit that one of the mends was needed as a result of my over-enthusiasm. Before I knew that enzymes are the enemy of silk, I'd been rather too vigorous in my trials of stain pre-treatment techniques, and a silk jersey top was the eventual casualty.

Mending and embroidery used to be one of the main 'woman's jobs' around the home; girls were taught stitching from a young age, and many would be experts by adulthood. Seeing the intricate needlework in Bath's Fashion Museum is astounding; I'm fairly neat with a needle, but it puts my handiwork very definitely to shame. This detailed work was done by professionals, but even for amateurs stitching was an expected skill, not something out of the ordinary. It would be on a par, perhaps, with knowing how to send and organize email today.

There are still people who love to do needlecraft, but give most of us a pincushion, thread and fabric and suggest we make something, and you might as well ask us to reconstruct the space shuttle. However, even in the ultra-modern world, knowing how to wield a needle and thread can be a useful thrifty skill – and curiously satisfying.

WHY MEND CLOTHES?

You may feel you don't have enough time in your day (or week, or lifetime) to mend clothes, or revive them by re-dyeing or remodelling, but there are some very good reasons to do it.

- You won't have to say goodbye to old favourites quite so soon.
- In less time than it takes to get to the shops you'll have a newly expanded wardrobe.
- You will make big reductions in your clothing footprint.
- You can give old, languishing items a new fashion twist to bring them up to date.
- You can mend and transform charity-shop and second-hand sale purchases cheaply.

If you really find that sewing isn't for you, try to find a local seamstress or tailor. Ask friends and neighbours for recommendations; look for cards in local shops and then ask to see samples of their work; or ask the fashion stores who they use for their alterations. Some jobs, such as re-lining, or altering tailored clothes, need to be done by an experienced professional.

What you can do to bring clothes back to life

What you decide to do with your ailing clothes will depend on how much you care about the item, and its condition. Before you start hacking a blouse to bits it's worth considering the most effective route from what it is now, to what you'd like it to be.

Mending: This covers putting right minor accidents, and wear and tear, including re-sewing hems, buttons and buttonholes, repairing seams and closing small tears and moth holes. Patching is a slightly more radical mend because it's visible – but you could make a feature of it with appliqué (→ page 322).

Reviving: Smallish, cosmetic interventions such as re-dyeing black clothes to make them look as though you bought them this season (a handy tip picked up from a friend). Adding edgings, braid, ribbons and appliqué, and changing buttons, also come into this category.

Remodelling: Altering the length of skirts, changing the shape of a top or neckline, chopping sleeves or legs – anything that means your garment is a different shape from before. Also dyeing to change colour.

Transforming: This is where you're saving items from being turned into rags, for example by felting wool, and making curtains or tablecloths from dyed sheets. If it all goes wrong, you can always use the results as cleaning cloths.

> ***Needlecrafter's tip:***
> *Don't throw away wrecked tights – they're useful for soft stuffing.*
> *And if you find some long-out-of-date rice or lentils lurking in the*
> *cupboard, they could be repurposed for filling fabric doorstops and*
> *beanbag toys (→ caterpillar draught excluder, page 64).*

SEWING FOR BEGINNERS

I'm assuming almost zero knowledge about needlework, so if you're not a total novice, please bear with me (or skip this section).

Sewing isn't rocket science, but you do need to concentrate when you're new to it, and good light is essential. John Lewis is a great place to find sewing basics; otherwise, look for haberdashery shops (sadly, a fast-dying breed in town centres, but see the wondrous www.bedecked.co.uk), craft outlets and sewing notions stalls at markets.

Useful stitches and how to do them

First find some scrap material to practise on. Then cut a length of thread – from about your elbow to the tips of your fingers is good to start with – in a colour that contrasts with the fabric (it'll be easier to see what you're doing). Thread one end through the eye of the needle and pull until you have one long piece and a trailing end of about a finger-length.

Now I'm going to suggest you tie a knot. This isn't strictly good needlework practice, because it can leave a little bobble, but it can be useful in situations where small securing stitches might be too visible. Take the end of the longer piece of thread, hold it next to the needle and wind it three or four times fairly closely around the needle tip. Then slide the proto-knot down the needle and down the length of the thread with your finger and thumb and pull tight just before the bottom.

Your sewing kit

If you have a lovely raffia sewing box, that's great, but I just use one of the rather nice card-with-a-cord-handle bags you get from some clothes shops.

Needles: It's useful to have several sizes. Thin, sharp needles are good for silks and finer cottons; thick, blunt darning needles, which have large eyes, are what you need if you're using thickish wool.

Thread: I've gradually accumulated reels of different colours over time, and can often find something good enough to suit whatever I need to mend or stitch. When you're buying thread, don't rely on your memory – take a cloth sample along and try to match it in daylight.

Pins: I often use safety pins for jobs such as taking up trousers – they mean you're less likely to do yourself an injury – but for larger projects, dressmaker's pins are much quicker.

Scissors: Small ones for cutting thread and sharp, larger ones for slicing through fabric (try to get proper dressmaker's scissors).

Seam unpicker: Easier than scissors or a pin for un-making seams and undoing mistakes, but go gently so you don't damage the fabric.

Tape measure and straight ruler

Thimble: Very handy for stopping the eye end of the needle digging into your finger when working with thick material.

Running stitch
Push the needle and thread up through the material until knot meets fabric – but not so hard that the knot pulls right through.

If it does, try making it bigger by doing a few more winds round the needle. Now push the needle in and out of the fabric, making the stitches and the spaces between them all the same length. You can do several stitches at a time, and in fact this makes it easier to keep in a straight line.

Backstitch

This is what you use to hand-stitch a seam. With the needle and thread pulled up through the fabric, make a stitch behind where the thread comes through. Then bring the needle back up the same distance in front of the stitch. Complete the second stitch by going backwards again; if you can, push the needle down through the hole made by the first stitch, to give a continuous line. Try to keep going straight and with stitches the same size – which can be a challenge.

Over-and-over stitch

This stitch is useful for drawing two edges together, or to sew on appliqué shapes. Fold one edge of your material over and crease with your fingernail (on a real project, you'd press the fold neatly). Pull the needle and thread through from the back of the fabric to the front, a few millimetres in from the fold. Repeat, pushing the needle through from back to front a little further along. Keep all the distances regular and you should start to see a pattern of diagonal stitches over the top of the fold.

Blanket stitch

A feature in itself, blanket stitch is used for sewing on patches and appliqué shapes, and can also be used for buttonholes. Pull the needle and thread through from the back of the fabric, about a centimetre down from an edge. Push the needle back in from the front, about a centimetre along, but before you pull it tight pass the needle through the long thread loop. After a few stitches you should see a pattern of vertical stitches up to the edge of the fabric, with a chain of thread running along the top.

Needlecrafter's tip:

You'll find instructions and diagrams for other stitches on the Embroiderers' Guild website, at www.embroiderersguild.com/stitch. Try www.videojug.com for online demonstrations, or look for local sewing classes, such as those run by HobbyCraft stores (www. hobbycraft.co.uk). Browse second-hand shops for sewing manuals.

MAKE: *Needle book*

✳ ✳ ✳ ✳ ✳ ✳ ✳ ✳ ✳ ✳ ✳ ✳ ✳ ✳

A simple-but-useful first needlework project for yourself or to try with children. We made needle books at my junior school and I still have mine, complete with my name stitched crookedly on the front in pale pink embroidery silk.

You will need:

> *Newspaper or other thin scrap paper to make your template*
> *Felt-tipped pen*
> *Ruler*
> *1 piece of coarse-but-colourful fabric (such as a loose upholstery weave) about 25cm/10in by 15cm/6in*
> *1 piece of felt about 25cm/10in by 15cm/6in*

Pins

Sharp scissors

Ordinary thread in a colour that will show up

1 slender needle and 1 larger needle (for wool)

Tapestry wool, embroidery silk or other chunky thread

Appliqué or embroidered designs for decoration

An iron and a cloth (a piece of old pillowcase will do)

1. Choose the shape of your needle book. A clamshell design works well, or you could make it a simple rectangle. The case will open out like a book, so will need a straight edge along one side.

2. Draw one half of your template shape on the newspaper using a ruler for the straight edge. Fold your cover material in half, in line with the weave, and pin on the template so that the straight edge is lined up along the fold. Cut out the template and fabric – but leave the folded edge intact – then cut out the felt in the same way.

3. Decorate the cover by drawing and then embroidering your initials, or sewing on ready-embroidered shapes or appliqué (→ page 322). Make sure you don't pucker the fabric; press lightly on the wrong side, protecting the decoration with a cloth.

4. Line up the felt on the wrong side of the fabric and pin the two materials together. Tack in place with ordinary thread, about 1.5cm/5½in inside the edge, using long running stitches. Sew the raw edges of the materials together with blanket stitch all the way round, using colourful wool or embroidery silk and securing with a couple of small over-and-over stitches. Fold the case in half

again and crease along the spine. Open out and sew along the creased line of the spine with running stitch – in the same colour or a different one. Press the case closed.

Sewing machines

I've concentrated on hand-sewing in this chapter, because it's more instant and you don't need to invest in a large piece of machinery. But for some jobs, and for making your own clothes from scratch, a machine saves so much time that it's practically essential.

The first sewing machine I used was an ancient Singer where you turned the wheel with your right hand, leaving only your left to guide the material. If you can unearth a treadle machine, which you power with your feet, that would be pretty much the ideal green solution. I've borrowed a friend's machine for some of the projects in this book, such as the caterpillar draught excluder (→ page 64). You could always try requesting one on Freecycle (→ page 205), or finding one through friends or relatives.

Needlecrafter's tip:
On a sewing machine, it's essential to set the correct thread tension and stitch length – which will differ for each material. In general, you need shorter stitches and tighter tension for finer fabrics, but even if your machine has an auto tension facility, the only real test is to try out the settings on a scrap of the actual material. Replace sewing machine needles frequently for the best results.

MENDING

Stitching hems

The easiest hem to mend by hand is, in fact, the type where you can't see the stitching – the kind round most skirt and trouser bottoms. You just need to use a simple hemming stitch in a matching colour.

If you're only mending a short stretch of hem use a pin or safety pin to keep the fabric in position. If more has come down, pin back accurately and then tack the fabric layers together in a contrasting colour. To do this, sew with a long running stitch about half a centimetre in from where you'll be hemming.

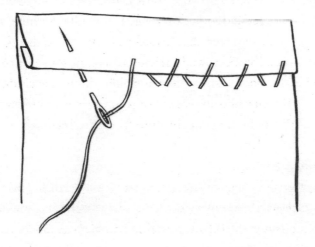

Now you can start hemming. Rather than a knot, use a couple of small stitches on the inside of the hem to secure the thread. Now pick up a couple of threads from the outer fabric, push the needle a few millimetres diagonally under the hem and pull through.

Repeat the process so you get a series of Vs along the hem edge. Check on the right side of the fabric to make sure the stitches aren't showing too much, or pulling on the fabric. It's better to unpick a few dud stitches than be unhappy at the end and have to start again.

Top-stitched hems

This is where you can see the line of stitching on the outside of the garment. You'll need a sewing machine, or – if you're very neat and it's a short section – you could try hand-sewing with backstitch. For jeans, use a sewing machine and special denim needle, with thick top-stitching thread – or go to a professional.

Jersey materials, such as T-shirts

If you are using a sewing machine, it needs to be one that does stretch, or overlocking, stitches, because jersey can curl up when sewn on an ordinary machine. If you are hemming by hand, simply sew as normal and don't worry about the raw edge, or else use the rolled hemming technique described below. Keep the stitches fairly loose, to allow for the elasticity of the fabric.

Rolled hems

These are used for silk scarves and other delicate fabrics. Re-roll the hem (roll and hold with your fingers as you stitch along) and use over-and-over stitch in a matching colour.

Sewing on buttons

If you don't already have a special place for those spare buttons that come with new clothes, allocate one now – although in a place where it won't show, you can get away with a button that's reasonably similar and of the same size. If you don't have a matching button for a jacket, or a decorative cardigan button, you might think of replacing the whole set – maybe even buy some vintage buttons and use the opportunity to bring new life to the garment.

If new buttons are a little smaller than the originals, you can always put in a couple of stitches to reduce the size of the buttonholes. If a cardie has stretched, larger buttons can help it stay done up.

Button-sewing hints

- Check carefully where to sew the button back on. If you can't see any telltale pieces of thread, or holes, put on the garment, do up the buttons and mark where the missing one should go with a small safety pin.
- When sewing on buttons, I tend to use the thread doubled, with a knot at the end, because it's quicker.
- Make sure to sew the new button on at the same tension (that is, with the same stitch length) as the others. You may need to keep pulling on the button to adjust the length; with buttons that stand proud, wind the thread around under the button several times.

Fixing buttonholes

You can re-edge a buttonhole with a closely spaced blanket stitch, or look up how to do the slightly more convoluted buttonhole stitch (there's a helpful comparison and diagrams at www.heritageshoppe. com). If the buttonhole has completely unravelled, it can be helpful to put tiny running stitches round it, near the edge, to keep everything in place while you work.

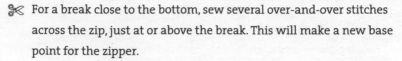

Broken zips

- ✂ For a break close to the bottom, sew several over-and-over stitches across the zip, just at or above the break. This will make a new base point for the zipper.
- ✂ If teeth are missing some distance from the bottom, you may need to take out the zip and reconsider. Could you fix the opening with poppers, or hooks and eyes?
- ✂ If you really want to replace the zip, you may need a professional – unless you're good with a sewing machine and zipper foot.

Repairing a seam

If the fabric is intact, and it's just the thread that's gone, you can easily mend most garments either with a sewing machine or by hand. If you're hand-sewing, use backstitch and try to make the stitches as close to the size of the originals as possible (in other words, very small). More importantly, keep in a straight line and press the seam open when you've finished.

As with hems, jersey can be more of a problem. Either do a loose backstitch, or I sometimes find that two lines of running stitch – so that the second line fills the gaps in the first – gives a more elastic result.

If the fabric is torn around the seam, you'll probably need some more drastic treatment. With a small tear the easiest remedy is to iron a piece of adhesive-backed patching fabric – available from haberdashers – on to the reverse to act as reinforcement. These patching fabrics come in everything from denim to finer materials. With a larger tear, or where patching would be too obvious, you might need to do some remodelling, such as changing the line of the seam to avoid the torn area, or making the garment into something else so you can cut away the damaged part.

Dealing with moth holes

I reckon this is one of the most worthwhile fixes, and surprisingly easy on jersey materials and finer knits – as long as your cardigan or jumper isn't looking like a lace doily. Try to mend your moth holes before the garment next goes in the wash, or the fabric may start to unravel.

- Find ordinary thread the same colour as your garment – it's easier and finer to work with than trying to match wool. Embroidery silk can be good for subtle tones and fabrics such as cashmere, or try the manufacturer to see if they can supply mending yarn (sometimes you will get a small amount in the little bag that also contains spare buttons).
- With a fine needle, and no knot, catch up a thread right at the edge of the hole. Leave a trailing end as you pull the needle through. Go round the perimeter of the hole, catching up stray stitches from the knit. Work on the wrong side of the fabric, but check frequently to make sure the stitches are not too conspicuous on the topside.

✂ Gently pull the hole closed, making sure that all the stray ends come through to the wrong side. Secure with a couple of stitches and snip off the trailing end.

✂ If the repair is unsightly, use a patch, appliqué or a ready-made embroidered decoration (→ page 321) to disguise it.

How to sew a patch

Patches can be in the same fabric (such as when patching sheets), or be made into a feature. When patching, make sure the fabric is large enough to cover not only the hole but any worn areas, then allow another 2cm/¾in as a margin. Squares and rectangles are easiest to work with if you're doing a utilitarian patch rather than a decorative one.

For a patch on top of the fabric, press under a hem of about 1cm/½in (or less) all the way round the patch, then pin and tack it in place on the right side of the fabric, with the grain going the same way as the sheet or garment. sew all round the edge with an over-and-over stitch, or use zigzag stitch on a sewing machine. To help protect the remaining fabric, you may want to cut out the hole neatly in the same shape as the patch , but a few centimetres or an inch smaller, then fold under the edge by about 1cm/½in, snipping a small diagonal into the corners, and sew in the with over-and-over stitch. Alternatively, you can patch from the inside of the garment and neaten the edge of the tear by sewing around it. Again, the stitching can either be a feature, or you could do tiny stitches to hem under the torn fabric for a more subtle mend.

REVIVING

Try revival techniques to make cast-offs more desirable again. Plus you get to spend magpie hours ogling shiny beads and pretty ribbons.

A treasury of revival techniques

Edgings and braids: I love ric-rac braid – you can get vintage versions from www.donnaflower.com, or there's the famous VV Rouleaux (www.vvrouleaux.com). Sew it a short distance in from the hem of a top or blouse, or under an edge for a scalloped effect. Other lovely braids are available, in daisy patterns for example, and also crocheted edgings.

Buttons: Replace plain originals with buttons in decorative patterns or contrasting colours (black on pastels, or the opposite hue on the colour wheel) for a more dramatic effect. Raid relatives' sewing boxes or try eBay, which has everything from antique enamel to novelty hotdog shapes.

Ribbon: This can be effective worn as a decorative belt for a dress or cardigan, or you could sew it around the neck of a fine-knit jumper (velvet works especially well). Cardigans can be transformed with ribbon edging along the neck and front – the problem is the buttonholes. To get round this, use poppers or hooks and eyes as fastenings instead.

Ready-made decorations: You can find all sorts of birds, butterflies and flowers in ribbon and beading, or the kind of embroidered badges that were popular in the 1970s – great for quick cover-ups on moth holes and stains.

Appliqué

In appliqué, pieces of material or embroidery are sewn on to another fabric to create designs. You can use appliqués as decoration and to disguise holes, with shapes such as leaves, butterflies, flowers or abstract circles. Non-fray fabrics, such as felt, work particularly well, because you can cut complex shapes without needing to turn under a hem. For shapes in finer fabrics, such as silks and organzas, try ironing them on to a thin fusible interfacing, such as Vilene; or layer a translucent material on top of a more robust one with a double-sided iron-on webbing, such as Bondaweb.

If you are using fabrics that fray, either turn under a hem or sew on with zigzag stitch on a sewing machine, or a close blanket stitch by hand. Sew on a hemmed appliqué patch with discreet over-and-over stitch, or make a feature of the stitching – wool yarn looks great with felt, or try metallic threads. You could add embroidery, beads or sequins over your appliqué shapes.

REMODELLING

Clothes can be transformed with a little tweaking. Crop long trousers, or make skinny fits into Capri pants; take off cuffs to make short or three-quarter-length shirt sleeves; take up skirts to this year's length; adapt charity shop buys to suit your figure and style.

Taking up skirts and trousers
The key is making sure you've judged the new length correctly. Put on the shoes or boots you usually wear with the item, and use

safety pins or dressmaker's pins to hold in position. Don't be tempted to fit just one leg with trousers, and measure the other – they might have been different lengths to start with.

Avoid cutting off fabric unless you really have to, so you have the option of letting down again. With trousers, I often keep the existing hem as the bottom edge, turn that up and sew by hand. This will usually be too bulky or noticeable with a skirt, so you'll need to neaten the new raw edge with zigzag stitch, bias binding or tape. Leave a good, wide hem margin.

Beware of taking up a bias-cut skirt – it can be fiendishly difficult to get it to hang straight. With any skirt, pin it up first, place on a hanger to check the alignment, and then try it on (a friend is useful here, to judge and re-pin where necessary).

Lengthening
This is difficult with most trousers, unless you have a hem to let down – and one that hasn't got too worn or grimy. With jeans and twill trousers you could try adding a band or cuff in a similar weight of material. This is easiest, and tends to look best, with a straight-leg cut.

With skirts you can have more fun. For a quick fix, sew wide lace so it peeks out from under the bottom of the skirt. This works particularly well for skirts with some volume, such as those cut on the bias. Another idea is to add a ruffle around the hem (→ page 324).

Letting out
Most letting out (and taking in) is a tricky proposition best left to the experts, but there are cheats the amateur can attempt. For example, you can often shift collar and waistband buttons to give

Giving a skirt a bit of ruffle

Cut your chosen ruffle fabric into a straight band, in line with the grain of the material. Make its length one-and-a-half to twice the skirt's circumference (or seam together two pieces, each half that length), and its width the amount you want to add to the skirt's length, plus about 4cm/1½in for seam and hem allowances.

Run a line of zigzag stitching along what will be the top edge, to stop it fraying. Add a row of loose-tension machine stitching 1cm/½in in from this edge, or else use a medium running stitch (about 5mm/¼in long). Leave longish trailing ends – and try not to get them caught up in the stitching. Seam the two short ends together to make a circle. Press the seam and finish its edges with zigzag stitch. Pull on one thread of your loose-tension stitching to gather the ruffle. Check the band fits around the skirt's circumference and make the gathers as even as you can.

With both the skirt and ruffle the right way out, pin the ruffle under the skirts hem so that the gathering stitching is hidden. Make sure the side seams line up. Tack, then sew two lines of matching top-stitching one just in from the hem edge and the other to catch in the top of the ruffle.

Try on the skirt to check its length, then turn up a 5mm/¼in hem on the ruffle, press under, turn up again to give you the correct finished length and sew with a single line of machine top-stitching, or hem by hand.

an extra centimetre/inch or two of leeway. If a beloved cardigan becomes too tight to do up, try sewing pieces of ribbon under the bust or at the waist to close it with a tie instead. Unpick the buttons and sew ribbon round the neck and front if you want to disguise your tricky fix.

Taking in

Move buttons and hooks to improve the fit. On a double-breasted jacket, you can sometimes move all the buttons over to make a larger size look more fitted, but check first by wrapping it round you to ensure you don't look overly swaddled.

To bring in a blouse, try sewing ribbon into the side seams and then tying it at the back. With strappy tops you can simply tie a knot in the straps to see if this improves the look – then sew if you want to, although I sometimes leave the knots as a feature.

Needlecrafter's tip:

For inspiration, how-tos and a slice of life from sewers and knitters look at craft blogs such as http://angrychicken.typepad.com, www.yarnstorm.blogs.com, http://whipup.net and http:// soulemama.typepad.com.

Magic with T-shirts

Cotton and other fine jersey knits are great to cut into new shapes because, being knitted, they're fray-resistant. You'll need to be happy living with the raw edge, though, because these fabrics are hard to hem. Draw your shapes on first, preferably with dressmaker's chalk, which can be rubbed off. Here are some ideas to try.

✂ Cut the sleeves off on the diagonal from just by the underarm seam to make capped sleeves.

✂ Trim a shallow scoop from shoulder to shoulder, just beneath the neck edging, to make a boat neck, or slice down to make a V.

✂ Chop through both layers of an almost-too-tight T-shirt from one shoulder to the opposite underarm, and cut off the other sleeve, for an asymmetrical, one-shoulder style.

Home dyeing

It may take quite a bit of (usually hot) water, but with home dyeing age-greyed white shirts and faded tops can become vivid new wardrobe options. There are two ways to go – you could use commercial mixtures, such as Dylon, or experiment with vegetable peelings and wild plants. The first has more predictable outcomes on the whole, and a wider range of clear colours – so is probably best if you're reviving a garment and have a particular shade in mind. But the second is more fun – and greener, as you will be certain you are not using polluting or toxic synthetic chemicals.

Check with manufacturers or expert sources to make sure you are using the correct dye type for the material – in general, avoid multi-purpose dyes as often they are not very colourfast. Always try to remove stains (especially greasy ones) from fabrics before dyeing, and give clothes a wash. Use a mild detergent or soap, and try to use soft water, such as rainwater, or add some kind of water softening. Don't put in any fabric conditioner. If you are using a hand dye, rather than one that goes in the washing machine, squeeze and stir the material to distribute the colour evenly, and keep to small batches. Always use a bucket or pan that gives plenty of room – but don't risk dyeing the bath. You can buy 'cold water' dyes that work at around 40°C or below.

You can buy colour strippers to prepare already dyed garments, but this means another dose of chemicals. Instead, remember your school art lessons and combine colours, such as red and indigo to make purple, or yellow and blue for green. However, the results will be a bit of a gamble. Alternatively, you could opt to intensify a colour, by dyeing a red with a deep burgundy to enrich it, or turning a pale blue to a dark night sky.

Natural dyes

Before 1828, when coal-tar dyes were invented, all fabric colours were of plant, animal or mineral origin. Madder was used for the bright red of soldiers' coats, weld for a clear primary yellow and logwood for navy blue. Today, weavers and textile designers are starting to experiment with natural colours again. You can use anything from onion skins and teabags to blackberries and red cabbage. For hints and materials, see www.fibrecrafts.com and refer to books such as *The Craft of Natural Dyeing* by Jenny Dean and the *Woolgatherings* booklets, available from www.mulberrydyer.co.uk.

Dyer's tip:
Bear in mind that synthetic thread (which is used for most stitching these days) may come out a different colour, or may not take the dye at all.

TRANSFORMING

If your dress, skirt, T-shirt or any other item or clothing has reached the end of the mending, reviving, remodelling road, it's time to transform it into something else. Cutting up for dusters and cleaning cloths are the obvious ones.

Felted wool

What do you do with a jumper that's shrunk or gone out of shape beyond retrieval? You felt it! This gives a great material for appliqué and patching other jumpers' elbows, or the opportunity to transform the item into something totally different – such as a cushion cover (→ page 329). Felt doesn't fray, so it will save you time when it comes to sewing.

Delicate wools that require gentle treatment are the easiest. The first thing I tried to felt was washable lambswool that would take a normal 40°C wash. It never really felted properly, although it did come up with a rather nice fluffy finish. Your jumper should be at least 85 per cent wool.

You'll also need a pair of rubber gloves, wool-safe washing detergent, a bowl of piping hot water, a bowl of cold water and some ice cubes.

When felting wool, you do exactly what you usually avoid – which is change its temperature quickly. Dissolve the detergent in the piping hot water, dunk the jumper in and rub, squeeze and generally mistreat it. Wring out and lift into the cold water (add some ice cubes to keep it really cold), then do the same thing there.

Repeat about five times, or until the wool has matted into felt. If it's really not happening, try adding boiling water to your hot bowl, then leave until it's cool enough to handle the wool. Dry flat and finish off in the airing cupboard.

The washing-machine method
If you're felting several items, it can be easier to use the washing machine. Do a 90 °C wash and put in some towels or tea towels – they'll add friction, and also make the most of the hot wash. Also pop in a Magno Ball water-softener if you have one (→ page 229) to give even more pounding.

MAKE: *The cardigan cushion*

This is simple to put together because the fixing has already been done for you, in the form of the cardigan buttons. The back of the cardigan will make the front of the cushion cover – or you could use a section from another felted woolly. You might also try this method with a thick shirt.

You will need:

1 felted cardigan, or a cardigan front and another piece of felted knitwear
1 cushion pad
Tape measure
Paper, such as a newspaper sheet
Felt-tipped pen or pencil

Sharp scissors
Needle and thread
Sewing machine

1. Measure the cushion pad and make sure there's enough felted cardigan to fit around it. On the piece of paper, draw a square the size of the flattened cushion pad, plus about 1.5cm/½ in on each side for seam allowances.

2. Turn your cardigan inside out, with the buttons done up, and pin the pattern to it, making sure the buttons won't end up in a seam margin. Adjust so the line of buttons comes either in the centre of the cushion, or offset.

3. Cut through both layers of material – or cut once from the buttoned side of the cardigan and once from your other felted fabric. Pin and tack around the edges, with right sides together.

4. Machine-sew a seam around all four sides, about 1.5cm/½in in from the edge, with a tight stitch, then zigzag along the edges, just in case of fraying.

5. Open the buttons, turn the cover right way out and stuff the pad inside. If the cover pulls open between the buttons, add extra poppers.

What to do with old socks

These days, few of us have woolly socks that are worth darning, and holes in cotton and acrylic socks can be difficult to fix unless caught really small. But if you want to try it, there's a helpful video on how to darn by Greenfibres (www.greenfibres.com) on YouTube.

Otherwise, try making sock puppets. Pull the sock on your hand (or your child's hand) so the heel is on top of your knuckles. Push the toe end right in between your fingers and thumb so it makes a mouth. You could use felt to make a tongue and buttons for eyes, and even embroider a nose. If the heel is worn, here's what to do. Push the heel section inwards, cut ear shapes from felt, tuck into the fold and pin in place. Turn the sock inside out, and pin, tack and then sew a seam concealing the heel, sewing in the ears as you do so.

How to restore, revive and beautify clothes and fabrics

Get yourself a sewing kit and learn how to do some basic stitches – it really is an invaluable modern skill.

When clothes have accidents, don't throw them away – mend them.

Have the last laugh on moths by sewing up and disguising moth holes.

Be creative with braids, ribbons and badges.

Try minor alterations, such as shortening trousers – they can give old clothes a new life and bring unworn items out of the wardrobe.

Bring clothes back into fashion by cinching them in, chopping them off, or adding lengthening ruffles and cuffs.

See what you can do with an old T-shirt and a pair of scissors.

Bored with the colour? Then have a go at dyeing.

If its old life is really over, transform it into something totally different.

12

CREATING AN OFFICE AT HOME

L *ike me, many people now work from home, either full-time or for a day or so a week – and even if your house isn't your office, the likelihood is you'll have a computer (or more than one) for homework,*

researching holidays, blogging, organizing photos, social networking or playing games.

My office is in our attic bedroom. That's not supposed to be good for 'sleep hygiene', because the worry is you'll move straight from desk to bed, but with its views over the garden and Solsbury Hill (when I stand up), it's a very pleasant place to work. It's also making pretty good use of the lightest room in the house, which would otherwise be neglected during the day.

Working in the bedroom has made me think harder about my desk and what I have on it. Instead of a utilitarian computer cabinet I sit at a 1930s dressing table – battered, but it's unusual, and I love it. The top isn't always clear of work-junk, but it has decorative touches, such as a vintage tin stationery box, a Japanese cup and saucer and a pretty bag from a 'natural' perfumer to take the bits and pieces I want to keep but haven't got around to filing.

THE PEOPLE-FRIENDLY OFFICE

Just because you're working doesn't mean you need to recreate an impersonal office atmosphere.

☞ Choose a space that's comfortable to be in – the warmest room if you want to be cosy and keep down winter energy use, or one with a view that inspires.

☞ Is a tucked-in, cupboard-like corner really the best option? Think about giving rooms a double function: if your work is concentrated within school hours, for example, even a living room becomes a possibility. Some people like working at the kitchen table.

☞ If you have good, simple storage, you're less likely to leave work scattered around. I like cupboards, because you can shove everything in at the end of the day and it's out of sight.

☞ If you are working in a bedroom, keep the electronic equipment to a minimum. Try to site printers, broadband routers and old-fashioned cathode ray tube (CRT) monitors away from the sleeping area.

Furniture

You don't need a new desk to set up a new office. You may already have something that could do the job, such as a console table (they're made narrow, to fit in a hall) or a trestle that can be put away after use. Think about second-hand options – it doesn't have to be chunky grey office furniture. As well as local shops, markets and car-boot sales, try charities that take furniture donations. Quite often these run workshops to renovate what they receive and offer training, and will be happy for you to help fund their endeavours.

Alternatively, you could try some DIY restoration, giving a desk a fresh lease of life by revarnishing (use water-based varnish to reduce VOCs) or treating with a wood oil, such as those from Osmo (www.osmouk.com). For furniture in poor condition, painting can cover up many past sins as well as transform the whole look and feel of a piece.

If you are buying new (and this goes for any furniture), look for wood that is certified by the Forest Stewardship Council (www.fsc-uk.org) and choose local or European-grown timber ahead of popular tropical hardwoods. Buy to last, and buy something you like, so you'll be happy keeping it for a long time.

MDF could be an environmentally friendly option because it uses trimmings and powder that would otherwise be wasted. The problem is the formaldehyde that it can give off, so ask for formaldehyde-free options. Also, little MDF is recycled.

Home worker's tip:
For a no-cost office, check Freecycle (→ page 207) or look for local swapping forums, such as Recap Swap & Sell (www.recap.co.uk) in Cambridgeshire and Peterborough.

Healthier working

Make sure your chair gives you the support you need. You should be able
to place your feet flat on the floor, and sit square-on to the computer,
without having to twist.

Use a footrest or solid, non-slippery book to achieve the right height if
the chair isn't adjustable.

Ideally, your eyes should be in line with the top of the screen, and your
arms relaxed at the keyboard and mouse, so that your wrists can be
straight but not tense. Use a cushion to adjust your height relative to
the computer.

Working at a screen doesn't make your sight worse, although it can
highlight existing problems. If your eyes feel tired and dry, keep the
atmosphere humid with plants or a bowl of water by a radiator – and
don't have the heating too high.

Home worker's tip:
Remember to have breaks, and don't leave your hand hovering over
the mouse or trackpad as you read documents on screen (something
I catch myself doing). Frequent shorter breaks are better than a
longer rest every hour – try to take at least a couple of minutes off
every 20 minutes to half an hour.

Plants to clean your office air

Researchers from Columbia University in New York found that
children who live in leafy areas have lower rates of asthma. It could
be the trees filtering the air, or it could be playing outside more

(away from household pollutants), but some plants certainly have purifying properties and can remove small amounts of VOCs.

- *Any house plant* will use carbon dioxide and put oxygen back into the air, and can help create a more comfortable level of humidity in dry atmospheres. Plants also lift your spirits.
- *Peace lilies, spider plants and philodendrons* are particularly good at removing formaldehyde, according to a study by NASA and the Associated Landscape Contractors of America.
- *Gerberas and chrysanthemums* are among those more effective at removing benzene.
- *Bamboo palm, ficus and ivy* also help to purify air.
- *Avoid mould*, which can produce irritating spores, by not overwatering – let the soil surface dry between drenchings (check with a finger if the compost beneath is getting too dry).

SWITCHING OFF ELECTRONIC EQUIPMENT

If you work from home, it can be easy to let work-time spill over into rest-of-your-life-time, and that can also mean leaving computers, peripherals and phones on when you're not actually using them. Eighty-five per cent of the money spent on powering the world's computers is wasted on machines that aren't doing anything.

You can buy socket devices that shut everything down when you turn off the master equipment, but I'm not sure these are really worthwhile – you might just as well use an ordinary socket bank you have already and switch off at the plug. Unplug chargers when they've done their work. If you can feel that a charger or transformer is hot, or if it has a light on, it's using electricity even if it isn't charging anything.

Turn off your broadband when you don't need to be connected to the whole world, and definitely switch it off at the end of the working day. Unless you're printing right at that moment, turn the printer off standby too. Try to have a decent lunch break – and shut everything down when you do, switching off at the socket to make sure devices aren't still stealthily using power.

Home worker's tip:
There are currently worries about the health effects of wireless wi-fi networks because of radiofrequency radiation (RFR). You may prefer to use old-fashioned cabling for your home network instead, or limit the amount of time you keep it on – especially when there are children in the house. Scarily, there are also concerns about the electromagnetic radiation from baby monitors, see www.powerwatch.org.uk.

THINK BEFORE YOU PRINT

Sustainability consultant Envolve (www.envolve.co.uk), based in Bath, helps local businesses to be greener – especially by cutting their energy use and waste. Here are some of Envolve's tips to reduce your paper and ink impact.

☞ Do you really need a hard copy? With the search facilities on the web and on your computer, you'll probably be able to find information and documents more easily online and on your hard drive than on a piece of paper.

☞ Learn about your printer's settings. You can pre-programme your printouts, so set them to double-sided, black and white, draft quality as the default, and use this for all but important letters.

☞ If you need information from the web, try to avoid printing out lots of image-heavy pages. Instead, copy and paste the text into a word-processing document and adjust the font and type size to use less ink and paper. You can often save online shopping receipts as PDF files, so you don't have to print them at all – choose this among the printing options.

☞ Recycle inkjet cartridges, or donate them to charities, which can sell them for cash. Use refilled or remanufactured cartridges if your printer allows you to do so, and if you're buying a new printer, check that it's compatible with recycled versions. Good-quality recycled printer paper is cheaper and more widely available than it used to be – although you may need to ask for it in ordinary stationers.

Home worker's tip:

Shredded paper isn't good for recycling but it's great for compost: spread it among the green, wet waste, such as grass cuttings. Tear up chip-and-pin receipts and put them in the compost too for maximum security (who's going to want to delve in your heap of kitchen peelings and weed tops?). Hand-operated shredders are widely available.

Stationery advice

Out: Staples

In: Staple-less staplers and paperclips

Staple-less staplers cleverly cut and fold the paper to keep up to five or so
   pages together. Or try an old-fashioned hole-punch and treasury tags.

Out: New envelopes

In: Old envelopes

You can buy gummed labels to re-use envelopes, although you may need
   to hone your opening technique (try charity shops for an old-style
   paper knife). If you really need new, buy recycled, and use padded bags
   that have shredded paper wadding instead of bubble wrap, so they can
   be composted.

Out: Sticky notes

In: Backs of envelopes

If they can't be re-used, make envelopes into handy note-takers.

Out: Standard ballpoints

In: Recycled and compostable pens

There are all kinds of innovative options at eco suppliers such as
   www.greenstat.co.uk and www.nigelsecostore.com – or go retro
   with a lovely fountain pen and bottle of ink.

Out: CDs for backing up and sending files (→ page 211)

In: Flash memory, file-sending services and online file storage

Memory sticks that slot into your computer's USB port start at just a few
   pounds, and can offer up to 32GB of space, while some online file stores
   are free.

♦ **Home worker's tip:**
♦
♦ *You can get taken off junk mail lists by going to*
♦
♦ *www.mpsonline.org.uk for personally addressed mail, or emailing*
♦
♦ *optout@royalmail.co.uk for mail addressed to 'The Occupier' –*
♦
♦ *although this may mean you don't receive local authority*
♦
♦ *communications. Alternatively, decide who you do and don't want*
♦
♦ *to hear from at www.itsmypost.com*

REDUCING YOUR E-WASTE

E-waste, or WEEE as it's also known (Waste Electrical and Electronic Equipment), has become a mountainous issue, with estimates for the amount discarded globally each year ranging from 20 billion to 50 billion tonnes (→ page 214).

Much of the growth in e-waste is down to how frequently mobile phones and computers are upgraded. The average lifespan of a computer in developed countries is around two years. As I write this, my laptop has just passed its second birthday, and I'm determined to do what I can to keep it going for a good few more years yet – although by then the letters will probably have worn off all the keys.

Spring-cleaning your computer

One way to help prevent your PC ending up as one of the three million or so that are decommissioned each year is to clean it – carefully. If debris (such as pet hair) blocks the air vents, or components become covered in dust, your computer may overheat and even break down. Specialists recommend that you give equipment a spring clean at least once a year.

The outside

Before you start, back up your files, make sure there are no CDs or DVDs in the drives, unplug your computer and remove all the cables. Remove the battery from a laptop.

Step 1: You can use an ordinary vacuum cleaner to get rid of the worst dust, but avoid the screen. Place a thin, clean cloth such as muslin over the nozzle to stop loose keys being sucked up inadvertently.

Step 2: Wipe the casing of the box and monitor – and the outside of your printer and scanner – with a lint-free cloth dampened in water and well wrung out (never get liquid anywhere near the computer).

Step 3: Dust the screen lightly with a clean lint-free cloth (any grains of dirt could scratch). For the glass screen of a cathode ray tube (CRT) monitor, use a very mild solution of 1 teaspoon of vinegar in 250ml/½ pint/9fl oz water to dampen the cloth. For an LCD screen, use water only and wipe lightly from top to bottom.

Step 4: You can clean sticky, greasy fingermarks off the keyboard with a lint-free cloth dampened in a very mild solution of detergent. A cotton-wool bud or cuticle stick wrapped in a clean muslin or lint-free cloth is good for grimy key edges.

Step 5: Open up your mouse and check the rollers that make contact with the ball. Remove any hairs with tweezers and use a cotton-wool bud to polish grime off the rollers – a fingernail also works well.

The inside

You may prefer to leave the internal workings to the experts, but if you're feeling confident, remember these pointers – and always check the manual for instructions on how to dismantle your computer safely.

☞ Don't use a mains vacuum cleaner as the static could damage your PC. Portable battery-powered cleaners are OK.

☞ Steer clear of any circuit boards – concentrate on the casing and mechanical parts, such as the fans.

☞ Instead of a portable vacuum you could use an artist's brush and hold a cloth underneath to catch the dust and fluff.

☞ Tempting as it may be, avoid blowing dust out of hard-to-reach crevices as our breath contains water vapour, which could corrode components.

☞ Don't open a laptop.

Home worker's tip:

If you spill tea – or anything else – on your keyboard, turn off your computer immediately, unplug the keyboard and hold it upside down over a towel to get out the worst. Using a lint-free cloth, mop up as much of the remainder as you can, then leave the keyboard upside down to dry overnight. In the morning, take a deep breath and check that it still works.

Give your PC a makeover

Thinking of changing your computer? Then think again – you may not need as much power as you think. When buying new, bear in mind that laptops and LCD screens take less energy to run, and think about a refurbished model from retailers such as PC World, or find local refurbishers at www.itforcharities.co.uk.

☞ If you're running out of storage space, consider keeping an archive on an external drive or online file-storage server. Edit down folders of photos or videos, which take up a lot of space.

☞ If it's RAM memory that's the problem, a short-term solution is to limit the number of windows you have open and the number of applications you have running. You can buy extra memory, even for laptops.

☞ There are lots of web forums that can help you troubleshoot specific problems.

☞ Check software and operating system upgrades that may be available to fix bugs – although you might have to pay for these.

☞ You can easily replace laptop batteries, and plenty of stores on eBay offer lower-price clones – although these may not have the same lifetime or reliability. To extend your battery life, Apple suggests you don't keep it plugged in all the time; run your laptop on its battery between charges (www.apple.com/batteries). Look at your computer manufacturer's website for tips.

☞ For more serious issues and makeovers, find a local expert – it may cost a bit to get your problem sorted out, but it'll most likely be cheaper, and most definitely be greener, than buying a new piece of kit.

Extend the life of your mobile

My mobile phone is looking a little worn these days. Once shiny and silver, its paint is chipping off, and it even shows the wrong network logo since I switched. Luckily, I don't worry about being judged by my hand-candy, and the only time I'll swap to a new phone is when this one shows signs of giving up. Mind you, if your handset does go wrong, it may be possible to get it fixed.

For a new or refurbished phone, try www.ebay.co.uk/ ebayforcharity when buying. If you want to change network but not phone, you can unlock your mobile so it will take the new SIM card. The methods and codes can be found by delving around online (you can find many for free in forums) or, for more difficult cases, you could turn to a specialist.

Green business directory

You can look up the credentials of banks, phone companies and much more through www.ethiscore.com, which is a subscription service linked to *Ethical Consumer* magazine. (For green energy, → Chapter 3.)

Banks and building societies: Ethically guided and greener options include The Co-operative (www.co-operativebank.co.uk), Triodos Bank (www.triodos.co.uk) and the Ecology Building Society (www.ecology.co.uk).

Phone: For an ethically guided company, look at The Phone Co-op (www. thephone.coop), which also offers broadband and mobile packages.

ISPs and web hosting: The millions of server computers that make up the world's data centres collectively use a vast – and growing – amount of electricity. In the US, solar panels are springing up in California, and web giant Google has committed itself to a renewable-energy future (www.google.com/renewable-energy). In the UK, at present, choices are limited. Carbon-neutral www.greenisp.org.uk and ethical GreenNet (www.gn.apc.org) offer broadband and web hosting; or try family-run, solar-powered www.ecologicalhosting.com.

Home worker's tip:

If you need to travel abroad but don't want to fly, The Man in Seat Sixty-One (www.seat61.com) has extensive information to help you plan your journey by rail and sea.

How to make your office more eco-homely

Create a you-friendly space with eco-friendly fittings.

Re-purpose a table or dressing table as a desk, or look at second-hand options.

Work smart, sit tall and take plenty of short breaks from the screen.

Don't keep the computer, printer, broadband or scanner on if you're not using them right that minute.

Think before you print, and set your print settings to use the least paper and ink.

Prolong your PC's useful life by giving it some TLC.

Look hard at ways to improve your computer's performance before you embark on buying a new model.

Choose greener suppliers – from your bank account to your stationery.

13

SPECIAL OCCASIONS

*S*ome people might feel that following the green code has no place in celebrations – which are, by definition, about pushing the boat out, being generous, extravagant, and popping the champagne corks.

Those people could have a point. Who wants to be stingy and picky at a friend's birthday or wedding? Who wants to be fretting about carbon emissions and turning down the thermostat at Christmas (that's surely what January is for)?

But greener celebrations really aren't the contradiction in terms you might at first think. It may mean putting extra thought and effort into what you do – but you'll finish up with more delicious food, more personal presents, and a very special, individual party, or, in the case of a wedding, one that's a world away from an identikit hotel bash.

ENTERTAINING AT HOME

Thinking ahead. That's the key to stress-free home entertaining – and the way to avoid pre-packaged options and too much reliance on the deli. I'd suggest preparing at least two dinner-party courses pretty much completely in advance, so you'll be able to relax with guests. Follow the lead of many top chefs and cook with seasonal food, which will be tastier as well as greener.

Wine and party drinks

The advice with alcohol is to buy local if you can, to cut wine miles, and from smaller producers. You'll find organic wines in supermarkets but for a wider choice, including vegetarian and vegan, look at specialists such as www.vintageroots.co.uk and www.ethicalwine.com. Biodynamic methods in particular, which employ natural cycles, such as the phases of the moon, and tailored soil treatments, are producing some of the world's most sought-after bottles.

Put France above Chile on your favourites list, and don't forget about English wines, especially when it comes to champagne-method bubblies such as those from Limney Estate (www. davenportvineyards.co.uk). Vinceremos (www.vinceremos.co.uk) also stocks organic whiskies, liqueurs and grappa. For a talking point, you could make your own sloe gin or fruit brandy, while elderflower cordial and home-made lemonade will help to keep non-alcohol drinkers happy.

RECIPE: *Your own lemonade*

✳ ✳ ✳ ✳ ✳ ✳ ✳ ✳ ✳ ✳ ✳ ✳ ✳ ✳

This is based on a recipe I first made at school and later adapted at home. You can try variations such as lemon-and-lime or orange-and-lemon.

You will need:

4 lemons
100g/3½oz raw caster sugar
Water

Choose organic, unwaxed lemons. Scrub the fruit, then thinly pare the zest from two of them with a potato peeler. Put this in a pan with the caster sugar and enough water to cover, bring to the boil and simmer for a few minutes. Cool and strain into a jug. Squeeze all of the lemons and add the juice to the jug. Stir and dilute with water to taste. If you need to add more sugar, dissolve it first in a little warm water.

Four lemons should be enough for a jugful, but you can easily increase amounts and store in a screw-top bottle that you've washed thoroughly and sterilized in the oven by heating to about 100°C/200°F/gas mark ½, then leaving to cool.

RECIPE: *Oven-baked crisps*

� � � � � � � � � � � � � � �

Why not offer guests home-made crisps, especially if they're made from your own potatoes (→ page 173)?

You will need:

> *Plenty of potatoes washed but unpeeled*
> *Olive oil*
> *Sea salt*
> *Freshly ground black pepper*

Heat the oven to 220°C/425°F/gas mark 7. Cut the potatoes, leaving the skins on, into 5mm/¼in slices, pat dry, then brush both sides with a little olive oil and lay on a baking tray. Season and bake for 20 minutes, or until golden brown. You may need to turn them over about two-thirds of the way through. Take them straight out if you'd like some softness in the centre, or turn the oven off and leave them to dry for your own home-made crunchy oven crisps.

Party organizer's tip:
It's polite to offer napkins, and will save your guests' clothes – but try
to avoid paper ones. Patterned fabric serviettes will show the stains
less than plain ones. For a DIY option, you could hem squares of
bright fabric from a worn-out dress, or unfaded portions from old
cotton curtains or tablecloths.

Greener garden parties

Out: Patio heaters
In: Rugs and shawls
A pub patio heater emits about 4 tonnes of carbon dioxide a year – a tonne more than the average car. They're becoming an endangered species anyway.

Out: Disposable or electric barbecues
In: Sustainably sourced charcoal
For mega-barbies, liquid petroleum gas (LPG) is the greenest option, but locally sourced charcoal is technically carbon neutral. It also avoids the problems associated with imported charcoal, such as habitat destruction and child labour. Try BioRegional (www.bioregional.com), your local wildlife trust, or suppliers listed at www.allotmentforestry. com/maps/charsup.htm.

Out: Buying party crockery or chairs you'll hardly ever use
In: Borrowing from friends and neighbours
Try to avoid disposable plates and cutlery too (→ page 382).

Out: Lighting up your garden as though it's day
In: Solar-powered lights and a few candles
Try to find soy candles from a sustainable source – they're cleaner and
longer-lasting as well as more eco-friendly than paraffin wax. Browse
eco stores and suppliers such as www.hapibean.co.uk for tea lights.

Party organizer's tip:

*For a simple fly, wasp and mosquito repellent when eating outside,
cut a lemon in half lengthways, then spike whole cloves into the
cut surface. The spice and citrus emit a fragrance that the beasties
don't like.*

EASTER

It seems that Christmas is barely over these days before the
chocolate eggs are on the shelves, in all their colourful foil, plastic
and cardboard wrapping. There are plenty of organic options now,
and companies are starting to produce eggs with less packaging
(which is good for their profit margins as well as the planet).
Alternatively, you could make your own.

For chocoholics, Easter bunny-shaped chocolate cookies and
rice crispie or cornflake nests go down well. You can find Easter egg
moulds in cookware shops or online, where you'll also discover tips
for getting the best results.

Decorating your own eggs

Blowing eggs

This technique is best reserved for older children and those of a patient disposition. Shake the egg to break the yolk, then make a small hole in the top and bottom with a needle. Put your mouth or a straw to the hole and blow out the white and yolk (which you can scramble or use for an omelette). Wash the shell through with water and some vinegar, and leave to dry fully. You can adapt an egg carton as a stand to paint the shell – carefully.

Colouring hard-boiled eggs with natural dyes

The colours will be clearer with white-shelled eggs – although these are harder to find nowadays. First make the dye by boiling your chosen dyestuff (→ page 356) with water and white vinegar (which makes for a more vivid colour) for about half an hour or more. Then strain it. A rough guide is about 500ml/1 pint/18fl oz of water to 1 tablespoon of vinegar and a couple of cupfuls or handfuls of the dyestuff.

Take the eggs out of the fridge to warm up, then simmer – not too vigorously, so they're less likely to crack – for 10 minutes. (The red date stamp will wash off as they boil.) Pop an egg into your dye with a spoon and make sure it's covered. Leave until it's the shade you want, turning occasionally to ensure an even colour. Remove with the spoon and dry on a plate covered with a flattened paper grocery bag (kitchen roll can leave marks).

To create patterns, try wrapping rubber bands around the eggs, or drawing on them with crayon – or melted wax for older children – before dyeing. (Note that some of the dye may transfer to hands, clothes and furniture, so be careful where you put your eggs.)

WEDDINGS

The carbon footprint of a wedding is about 14.5 tonnes of CO_2 – more than the average European is responsible for in an entire year. Eco wedding planner Louise Moon (www.ecomoon.co.uk) suggests that couples initially aim to do 'just one thing' to make their wedding greener. This needn't be the cause of more stress – in fact, it can make your celebrations more individual, personal to you, and fun.

Five top ways to greener nuptials

Use local produce
Whether you're organizing the food through family, going to a restaurant or employing a catering company, focus on in-season specialities and organic where you can – maybe even friends' home-grown. Avoid air-freighted peaches and strawberries in the middle of winter.

Make it easy for guests to get there

Guest travel is one of the biggest culprits. Choose a venue close to where most of your guests live, or one that's easily accessible by public transport. You could hire a coach (or old-fashioned double-decker bus) to ferry groups there and back, instead of leaving them to use individual cars or taxis. Think about having the ceremony and reception at the same venue.

Be creative with wedding favours and stationery

If you decide to have favours, fun options include native trees to plant (www.wedding-tree-favours.com) and paper laced with wildflower seeds that can be planted and grown (www.elliepoopaper.co.uk). Cut it into flower or heart shapes and add raffia (which is biodegradable). Let guests reply to invites by email – you could even send a pretty e-vite; if you're having it designed, ask for a JPG or PDF file.

Appoint a tidying-up monitor

Try not to let caterers simply sweep everything into black bin liners, but recycle instead. If you set up recycling bins beforehand, it'll be even easier.

Be an eco-beautiful bride

Think about a gorgeous vintage dress, or ask a dressmaker to create something for you with vintage fabrics and lace. Look at natural and organic ranges for your make-up (*The Green Beauty Bible* by Sarah Stacey and Josephine Fairley is a handy resource), and carry a home-grown and tied bouquet (→ page 360).

Party organizer's tip:

For the last wedding we went to, I took flower confetti – dried blue,

pink and white delphinium flowers – that had been offered on

Freecycle. You can buy petal confetti ready in packets, or make some

from a local florist's past-their-best flowers, or overblown blooms in

a friend's garden.

Yurts and tipis

You could have a home-grown wedding in your garden, or a friend's. Louise recommends yurts and tipis as a really unusual option – they allow you to celebrate in the great outdoors and can be hired anywhere in the UK. Online sources include www.stunningtents.co.uk, www.tipis4hire.com and www.papakata.co.uk. But only go the yurt route in the summer, so you don't have to use heaters. If you're setting up in a field or at a farm venue, encourage your guests to camp there, and you'll minimize transport as well.

Ethical rings

Why not choose a family heirloom or vintage ring, or find a jeweller who'll craft you something individual with stones from a setting donated by a family member? If you're buying new, Canadian diamonds are conflict-free. Gold from ethical sources can be found via www.credjewellery.com, www.urthsolution.com or www.greenkarat.com (a US-based venture that arranges for gold to be recycled). Ethical brands and designers include Pippa Small, Fifi Bijoux, Ingle and Rhode, and Russell Simmons, who has set up a Diamond Empowerment Fund (www.simmonsjewelryco. com).

For more information on the issues around diamond and gold mining, see www.globalwitness.org and www.cafod.org.uk/ campaigning/unearth-justice.

Party organizer's tip:
You don't need to be a great pastry chef or artful icer to make your own wedding cake. Instead, try a cupcake version. Decorate enough cupcakes for your guests and arrange them on vintage cake-stands. At an informal gathering, you could even involve your guests – everyone gets to ice a cake and add sugar shapes or crystallized flower petals when they arrive.

The flowers

From daffodils, willow and catkins in earliest spring, to roses, cornflowers and peonies in summer, and chrysanthemums, berries and silvery honesty seedheads as autumn moves into winter, there are so many beautiful British-grown and native floral and foliage choices. However, about 90 per cent of cut flowers bought in the UK are imported.

- Look out for local growers and seasonal flowers. Near us, Bath Organic Blooms (www.bathorganicblooms.co.uk) grows poppies, scabious, corncockles and spring bulbs, while Sweet Loving Flowers (www.sweetlovingflowers.co.uk) is in the Dyfi valley, Wales. Also try Wiggly Wigglers in Herefordshire (www.wigglywigglers.co.uk) and in the east of England there's Country Roses (www.countryroses.co.uk). Ask your local independent florists and keep an eye out at farmers' markets.
- Try ordering direct from farms. Those in the Isles of Scilly (such as www.scillyflowers.co.uk) and Cornwall produce the earliest blooms.
- The Netherlands has been leading the way with organic flowers, but there are now more UK options. Explore the suppliers listed at www.organic-store.co.uk/organic-cut-flowers.html.
- If your heart is set on winter roses, make sure they're fairtrade (see www.fairtrade.org.uk/products). There is the issue of flower miles, but fairtrade does offer a better deal to African farmers.

MAKE: *Tie your own bouquet*

✳ ✳ ✳ ✳ ✳ ✳ ✳ ✳ ✳ ✳ ✳ ✳ ✳ ✳

Rachel Lilley runs a florist and flower school in Bath (www.rachellilley.com). These are her tips for making a hand-tied bouquet – gorgeous for a wedding.

You will need:

Long-stemmed flowers and some stiff-stemmed foliage
Scissors
String
1 plastic carrier bag or other tough, waterproof bag or cellophane
Newspaper, brown paper, magazine pages or re-used wrapping paper
Ribbon

1. Remove the lower foliage and any thorns and place each flower type in a separate pile.

2. Decide on your central flower – usually the largest bloom. Hold this in one hand at the point where you want to tie the bouquet (the higher up you hold it, the tighter the bouquet) and a second flower of the same type in your other hand.

3. Place the second bloom so its stem crosses over the first at the tying point and the flower heads are close together. Take hold of both stems with the first hand and move the flowers round a quarter turn. Repeat with a third flower of the same type, turning again in the same direction.

4. Continue placing flowers and turning the bouquet. Add different blooms and foliage stems in threes or fives to give a natural-looking, circular shape. The stems should start to form a spiral pattern. Looking at the bouquet in a mirror will help you to see where you need to adjust or add more flowers.

5. When you're happy, wind string three or so times around the point you've been holding and tie. Trim all the stems to the same length, snipping each at an angle.

6. For a wedding bouquet, stand it in water until the last moment. For a gift bouquet you want to last, put the stems into the plastic bag, or wrap plastic around the bottoms. Tie with string to make a pocket that will hold water, and trim to neaten.

7. If you are wrapping the flowers, gather your paper into a rough fan shape, then wrap around the bouquet and tie with more string or a ribbon. Carefully fill the water pocket with a jug, pouring the water down next to one of the central flowers.

CHRISTMAS

There's so much to feel worked up about in the festive season and so much to love. In a way, trying to be greener can put the enjoyment back into Christmas preparations – as long as you're not so overstretched that anything extra will make you tear your hair out.

Greener gifts

What really makes a difference is a thought-about gift that someone really wants and can use, from wonderful natural skincare products to a book or toy they've had their eye on. Then it won't end up at the back of a cupboard, but instead be enjoyed and perhaps even loved. So don't be afraid to ask friends and family what they really want – maybe everyone could do a letter to Santa at the start of December.

♥ If you sign up for the newsletters emailed out by green sites, from eco stores to charities, you'll receive all kinds of ideas for presents that have a smaller ecological footprint, are fairtrade or encourage greener living, or help others. Make sure to explain to the recipient why it's so great, or not everyone may appreciate the sentiment.

♥ Think about giving experiences rather than objects. (Dear Santa, this year I would like a furniture renovation course, or perhaps a day learning about herbs . . .) Make a gift of your time – friends with children might appreciate baby-sitting vouchers, or a relative might like a computer skills crash course.

♥ If you're giving an eco gadget, make sure it'll be appreciated and used, and make time to explain how it works. (Even eco gadgets take resources to manufacture and transport.)

♥ Why not give hand-made presents? Try clementine marmalade (→ page 146) or kilner jars filled with sweetmeats such as the festive brownies below, or make simple sewn gifts such as lavender bags (→ page 300) or cushion covers (→ page 329). You could cook or sew bulk batches and that's all of your friends and family sorted.

♥ Go vintage – second-hand bookshops or vintage stores and markets are lovely places to browse for out-of-the-ordinary presents.

RECIPE: *Chocolate and cranberry festive brownies*

✳ ✳ ✳ ✳ ✳ ✳ ✳ ✳ ✳ ✳ ✳ ✳ ✳ ✳ ✳

If you're making these as gifts, hold a few back and serve for dessert with a spoon of crème fraiche. Children love to help with these, maybe because they involve chocolate. Have some extra, broken into small pieces, to keep chocolate-loving mini-cooks happy. These quantities make about 15 squares.

Ingredients:

285g/10oz unrefined caster sugar

225g/8oz butter, preferably unsalted, cubed

150g/5½ oz plain or cooking chocolate (70 per cent cocoa solids)

3 large eggs plus one extra egg yolk

85g/3oz flour

85g/3oz cocoa powder

½ teaspoon baking powder

Small pinch of salt (leave out if you're using salted butter)

2 handfuls of fresh cranberries (if you're buying a packet, you can freeze the rest)

Heat the oven to 180°C/360°F/gas mark 4. Line a rectangular cake tin, about 15cm/6in by 30cm/12in., with unbleached baking parchment. Wash the cranberries.

Place the chocolate and butter in a heat-proof bowl over a small pan of simmering water. Make sure the bowl doesn't touch the liquid. Leave on a very low heat to melt – and resist the temptation to stir, or the chocolate may go grainy.

Whisk the eggs, extra yolk and sugar until light and mousse-like, then slowly add the buttery melted chocolate, mixing gently with a metal spoon. Sieve the flour and cocoa into the bowl, and fold in until the batter is a fairly even brown. Mix in the cranberries.

Pour the batter into your cake tin and roughly even out the top. Bake for 25 minutes – set the timer as it's crucial not to overcook brownies. Test by sticking a skewer into the centre. You want to see a bit of goo on it, but not wet cake mixture, if the skewer comes out clean, whip the brownies out straight away. If they're not cooked, add three minutes on the timer, then test again. Leave to cool completely before cutting into wedges.

Gift wrapping ideas

In the UK we use 8,000 tonnes of wrapping paper each Christmas, which amounts to around 50,000 trees. Some paper can be re-used for wrapping, or else kept for children's craft projects. Wrapping paper with metallic foils or shiny plastic finishes can't be put in the compost and isn't good for recycling either.

- Save brown and other paper carrier bags for presenting your gifts. Robust ones can be re-used several times. Brown paper and tissue paper can both look stylish with imaginative decoration, and they compost well. Try magazine pages for smaller gifts.
- Decorate plain wrappings with home-made gift tags, ribbon and lace ties (which can be salvaged for next year), and shapes cut from last year's wrapping-paper scraps.

✂ Try wrapping without tape – fold everything up and secure with ribbon or string, then the paper can be used again more easily. If you do need to stick, choose old-fashioned Sellotape (www.sellotape.com), made from tree cellulose, rather than plastic tape.

Party organizer's tip:

Try making your own cards – you could cut up ones from previous years. Or use fabric, magazine cut-outs, or anything else that inspires your artistic side. One hundred sheets of A4 recycled coloured card cost around £11 from www.greenstat.co.uk; trimmed to A5 that means 200 cards. Children's nursery or school artworks can be recycled into cards for relatives. Potato prints are fun – add stickers, or dust the still-wet paint with glitter.

Christmas trees and decorations

It's official: real trees are greener (unless you use your fake tree for eons). It's mainly because trees take carbon dioxide out of the atmosphere as they grow, rather than needing energy and petrol derivatives for their manufacture.

Look for a locally sourced tree. One year ours was delivered by environmentally friendly electric milk float. Try the search at http://pickyourownchristmastree.org/ukxmastrees.php, which also has tips on selecting and caring for cut trees. Check with your council for its post festive season tree recycling facilities.

Re-use tree decorations, or make some of your own, for example, by cutting shapes from the sumptuous thick paper catalogues that come through the post, punching a hole and hanging them from colourful embroidery silks (these also make great gift tags). Energy-efficient LED Christmas lights are now widely available, although we're still using our old not-so-green ones – I wouldn't feel right about retiring them until they go kaput.

Around the home, try natural decorations, such as traditional holly, ivy and mistletoe, together with other berries and evergreen foliage. An orange studded with cloves will give a Christmassy perfume, or you could choose a tree variety with scented foliage.

How to celebrate in green style

For food and wine, think local and find out your region's specialities – there are surprises even in big cities.

Make your outdoor entertaining more friendly to the environment by avoiding patio heaters.

If you're planning a wedding, do at least one thing to make it greener – maybe wear a dress made from vintage fabric, or with vintage trimmings, or hold the reception in a friend's garden.

Choose seasonal British flowers and support the UK's organic growers (or grow your own).

Dye an egg this Easter – use red cabbage for blue and beetroot for pink.

Give home-made presents – it's more personal as well as greener.

Buy a real tree from a nearby farm next Christmas.

14

A GREENER
START IN LIFE

Bringing *another person into the world is probably the worst thing we can do for our ecological footprint. It means another person's consumption, waste and carbon emissions, bearing in mind that if everyone* in the world lived as we do in the UK, it would take three earths to support us all.

On the other hand, having children is what makes many people think more deeply about the future of the planet and start to make different choices in their own lives. That was certainly the case with us.

Children also bring all sorts of possibilities for being creatively green, from baking to re-using materials for craft projects. Even scrappy odds and ends of torn-off wrapping paper can make collages and cards for nursery and school friends. Plastic food trays become paint palettes, and cardboard packets are transformed into robots and spaceships.

GREEN FIRST STEPS

At seven months pregnant I was busy trying to put the finishing touches to painting Ethan's nursery. Before that, I'd done my share of steaming off wallpaper and sanding the woodwork. I've found out since that these were probably the last things I should have been doing. Not only because, kneeling to paint the skirting boards, I cut off the circulation to my feet and became frantic that I was getting varicose veins. No – the main reason pregnant women should steer clear of the decorating is that you could be inhaling all kinds of chemicals, from lead if the existing paint is very old, to volatile organic compounds (VOCs), antifungals and a host of other synthetics in the new paint you're putting on, not to mention the adhesive fumes from laminate floors and formaldehyde that can come from MDF.

In the womb and as newborns, children are especially susceptible to chemical pollutants, partly because they are developing so quickly, and partly because their bodies are not yet able to break them down as effectively as adults. Scientists from around the world are agreed that some commonly found substances can have far-reaching effects on children's health – not only in infancy, but increasing the likelihood of diseases from diabetes to cancer later in life.

For checklists and articles backed up by an impressive scientific committee, take a look at US site Healthy Child Healthy World at http://healthychild.org. I also find the Nova Scotia Guide to Less Toxic Products, www.lesstoxicguide.ca, clear and helpful.

Parent's tip:

Advice to expectant mothers includes limiting intake of oily fish, such as mackerel and tuna, and avoiding swordfish, shark and marlin, because of the risk of mercury, dioxin and PCB (polychlorinated biphenyl) contamination.

LOW-VOC PAINTS AND NATURAL ALTERNATIVES

We started researching natural paints when we first moved into our house and decided to redecorate, but ended up using more conventional low-VOC instead. The reasons? The wider colour range (although natural paint options are improving all the time) and the unfamiliarity. Next time, I'm more determined to go natural. I would suggest trying to find a local decorator who's used to working with natural paints, or setting aside some time to enjoy experimenting with samples before you choose.

Low-VOC paints
These are widely available from DIY stores as well as specialists. Most are still based on acrylic or vinyl emulsions but are better for your health, and work like the paints you're used to. Choose water-based eggshell rather than synthetic oil-based wood paint.

Natural wall paints
These include casein (milk) paints, limewash distempers and clay-based paints that use naturally occurring pigments. Some emulsions, such as the Natural Paint Collection at www.greenbuildingstore. co.uk, are made with chalk and plant oils. Many natural paints have some kind of compromise, either including some VOCs, or some acrylic, or occasionally artificial pigments, but traditionally made limewashes and distempers are truly sustainable. Natural finishes are also breathable, so can help with damp problems if applied over a breathable surface (such as lime plaster). Depending on the paint you choose, they can

produce a lovely chalky finish or else a colourwash effect. You may need to mix them yourself, and bear in mind that limewash is caustic, so you will need goggles, gloves and overalls.

Natural oil-based paints

As an alternative to water-based synthetics, look for glosses based on natural oils and resins. However, they may include citrus oil, which can be an irritant.

Manufacturers

Websites to browse include Aglaia (http://naturalpaintsonline.co.uk), Aquamarijn (from www.constructionresources.com), Auro (www.auro.co.uk), earthBorn (www.earthbornpaints.co.uk), Livos (from www.ecomerchant.co.uk) and Rose of Jericho (www.rose-of-jericho.demon.co.uk). Farrow & Ball (www.farrow-ball.com) also produces limewash and distemper.

SMART NURSERY SOLUTIONS

There's nothing wrong with adapting furniture you already have for the nursery, or choosing second-hand (→ page 335), but if you're buying new, Germany and Scandinavia have some of the strictest environmental regulations, which is good news for children's furnishings. The mattress for Ethan's Flexa bed (part of a modular range designed to take children from toddlerhood to teens, see www.flexa.dk) fulfils the Oeko-Tex (www.oeko-tex.com) standard for textiles. It's made from non-allergenic natural fabrics that are free from harmful substances and produced responsibly. We didn't have to go to an obscure online source to find it – the bed was in the window of our main furniture store in Bath.

IKEA aims to apply the strictest local regulations across all the countries where it does business, and look out for the Nordic Swan eco-label on products (www.svanen.nu/Eng/).

Buying furniture that can be adapted – or repainted or refinished – as children grow up is a more sustainable approach than choosing one-year-and-it's-in-the-attic items. The Stokke Tripp Trapp from the Netherlands (www.stokke.com) has become a classic – as it converts from a baby's highchair to an ordinary seat at the table.

Baby mattresses and duvets

In his Moses basket and cot, I'm afraid to say, Ethan had the usual foam-plus-synthetic-covering mattress, but a number of companies now offer organic and natural-fibre options. These include latex (from the rubber tree, but bear in mind that some people have a latex allergy), coir fibre, mohair and cotton-filled – www.borndirect.co.uk has a selection. You can find organic and natural mattresses for adults, and mattress protectors, at www. naturalcollection.com.

For duvets and pillows, organic cotton fleece and organic Merino lambswool (see www.naturalhome-products.com) are alternatives to synthetic fibre or traditional down. The cotton can be washed at 60°C to kill dust mites, or use a neem oil treatment to ward them off.

If you know anyone who knits or crochets – or fancy taking it up yourself – ask for a blanket in organic cotton yarn, such as Lion Brand, available from www.rainbowsilks.co.uk (download free infant blanket crochet patterns from www.lionbrand.com), or Blue Sky from www.getknitted.com.

BREAST IS GREENEST

The World Health Organization recommends breastfeeding exclusively for the first six months, and then continuing alongside solid food until the age of two. It's the environmentally friendlier – as well as baby-friendlier – option, because you don't have all that formula manufacture and packaging. Breastmilk contains everything to fulfil your baby's nutritional requirements, and changes its composition over time to suit the stage of development. It helps boost the baby's immune system; it's convenient (you don't have to lug loads of equipment around); and it could protect you against pre-menopausal breast cancer and ovarian cancer.

There are scary findings about the toxic chemicals that have been detected in breastmilk, but be reassured that experts agree the benefits of breastfeeding far outweigh any risk presented by these small amounts. Toxic chemicals also move across the placenta during pregnancy, and this appears to have a much more significant effect on children's health and development. In fact, breastmilk may contain substances that actually work to reduce the impact of toxic substances. The best thing for your baby is to reduce your own exposure to hazardous chemicals.

Having said all this, some mothers find it difficult or impossible to breastfeed (I had problems myself). If this is the case, try not to be hard on yourself. Look into organic formulas and opt for glass bottles (available from www.greenbaby.co.uk).

Parent's tip:

For breastfeeding support, try organizations such as La Leche League (www.laleche.org.uk), the National Childbirth Trust (www. nctpregnancyandbabycare.com) and the Breastfeeding Network (www.breastfeedingnetwork.org.uk). Your local Sure Start may also be running initiatives (www.surestart.gov.uk).

THE GREAT NAPPY DEBATE

In the UK we use three billion nappies a year, and 90 per cent of those are disposables. In the introduction to this book I came clean about the fact that after nine months we ditched Ethan's re-usable nappies. In the end, we were beaten by the washing – every day, it seemed, we'd have a lineful, like little towelling pelts pegged in the sun. However, I now know that was because we didn't invest in enough – you need around 24 to give you breathing space, because newborns can need 10 to 12 changes a day.

A 2005 Environment Agency report (www.environment-agency.gov.uk) caused outrage by suggesting that disposable nappies, home-washed re-usables and nappy laundry re-usables were about the same in terms of environmental impact, with cloth nappies let down by the amount of energy needed to wash and dry them. The Women's Environmental Network (www.wen.org.uk), among others, argued that the report's assumptions were flawed (for example, it assumed a larger amount of energy used per wash than is the case with the current generation of washing machines and a temperature of 60°C).

You can find information about different types of cloth nappies, and advice on using them, from the Real Nappy Campaign (www.realnappycampaign.com) and from stockists such as Born (www.borndirect.com) and Green Baby (www.greenbabyco.com). My own top tip? Don't flush the liners even if they say you can – our drains got blocked.

The right nappy for you and your baby

Worried about chemicals
Go for re-usables, or greener disposables such as Nature Babycare (www.naty.com, available from Sainsbury's and Waitrose), Moltex Öko (www.moltex.de) or Tushies (www.tushies.com). Conventional single-use nappies can contain a non-biodegradable superabsorbent chemical gel and may have synthetic fragrance.

Focused on climate change
Disposables may well edge it on energy use. If you opt for re-usables, don't wash them above 60°C and ban that tumble dryer – use the airing cupboard instead in winter. A soak such as Bio-D's Nappy Fresh (www.biodegradable.biz) or percarbonate laundry bleach (→ page 42) means you could lower the wash temperature further.

No time to wash, but don't want disposables
You could try a nappy laundering service. They leave you clean nappies and wraps that hold everything in, plus a lidded bin; your baby messes up the nappies, the laundry collects them – perhaps even by eco-friendly rickshaw – and delivers fresh ones.

On a budget

You can save £500 or more on keeping a child in nappies by buying flat terry nappies instead of disposables. Look for second-hand from eBay or your local National Childbirth Trust branch (www.nct.org.uk). Incentive schemes can be located through Nappy Finder at www.realnappycampaign.com.

Concerned about landfill

Go for re-usables (although Tushies and Nature Babycare are biodegradable).

WASH CLOTHES BEFORE WEAR

The average 100 per cent (conventional) cotton T-shirt actually contains 73 per cent cotton. The rest is made up of chemicals, resins, fabric treatments and pesticides used in growing the cotton and making and storing the garment. I was shocked to discover this, and now try to wash all Ethan's clothes before he wears them. With second-hand, I often re-wash to try to get rid of any synthetic fragrances, but sometimes it takes a few goes before they've toned down – which shows how persistent the chemicals are. You could also try soaking overnight in a baking-soda solution before washing. The same advice applies to baby bedding and linen. (For more about organic and ethical clothing, → Chapter 10.)

Parent's tip:

As a first-time parent it's easy to think you have to buy a lot of special equipment, and make sure it's the top specification you can afford. While some things may make your life easier, a lot of the paraphernalia, from complicated sterilizers to dedicated

nappy-change bags, really isn't a necessity – as second-time parents

will tell you. Try to borrow and pass on what you can – many items

are needed for just a few months to a year.

PVC IN CHILDREN'S TOYS

Polyvinyl chloride (PVC) can contain all kinds of potentially nasty components, including phthalates, which make it flexible, nonylphenol and organotins. The worry is that such chemicals may leach out of the plastic, especially as it ages or is chewed.

The good news is that the European Union has completely banned several phthalates from all toys and childcare items, and restricted others so they don't appear in toys that could go in children's mouths. However, policing imports, especially from the Far East, could be a problem. Many high-street retailers and brands have either already banned or have pledged to remove hazardous chemicals from children's and household products, so check labels and ask customer-service departments.

Parent's tip:

There are many sources of fairtrade toys (such as Lanka Kade,

www.lankakade.co.uk) and toys made from renewable resources,

such as rubberwood, and from organic fabrics. Ask your local toy

shops, and look online. Toys to You (www.toys-to-you.co.uk) has a

recycling initiative on its site, so you can help to redirect some of the

13 million relatively new toys that end up in landfill each year.

Making your own toys

It's a joke among parents that if you give a young child a present they'll enjoy playing with the wrapping paper and the box as much as the toy inside. That may be an exaggeration, but it points up the way that children often don't need the sophisticated playthings we think they do. There are plenty of opportunities for play with simple items found around the house.

At the age of three Ethan's favourite pastimes included bouncing on our bed, clambering over the furniture and playing chasing games. Home-made squidgy modelling dough also keeps him happy for ages.

MAKE: *Home-made play dough*

✤ ✤ ✤ ✤ ✤ ✤ ✤ ✤ ✤ ✤ ✤ ✤ ✤ ✤ ✤

We usually make two different colours then mix a third from them. This dough seems to keep for a long time in an airtight container. I have a store of Body Shop body butter tubs (the company no longer does its own recycling, alas) that are handy for this – as well as for organizing my buttons and other sewing bits and pieces. I use a teacup for the measurements.

Ingredients:

> *1 cup flour*
> *½ cup fine table salt*
> *1 cup water*
> *1 tablespoon sunflower or other light oil*
> *1 teaspoon cream of tartar*

A few drops of vanilla essence

Two colours of food dye

Mix all the ingredients except the food dye in a saucepan (I like the vanilla essence because it reminds me of the commercial Play-Doh smell from my childhood). Cook over a low heat, stirring all the time so it doesn't burn. When the mixture forms a ball and comes away from the sides of the pan, take it off the stove. If it is too soft, cook it a little longer. Split into two balls (it'll be hot, so you may want to leave it to cool a while). Mix the dye colours into each ball initially with a spoon, and then by kneading.

If you're making just one colour, you can add the food dye at the beginning. At Ethan's school they also work in some glitter.

MAKE: *Blowing bubbles*

Bubble mixtures always seem to get poured out into the bath or on to the floor when there's still half a bottle left. Refill bubble bottles that have come home from small friends' parties with your own bubble mixture.

Ingredients:

300ml/½ pint/10½fl oz water

3–4 tablespoons concentrated eco washing-up liquid

1–2 tablespoons glycerine

Mix the ingredients together – this amount fits into a standard jam jar. Adjust the quantities according to how concentrated your washing-up liquid is. It may involve some trial and error. It's best to make up the mixture a few hours before you want to use it, so any bubbles have a chance to subside.

Parent's tip:

Many websites feature experiments, activities and crafts for children – mostly tried and tested by other parents. Try www.activityvillage.co.uk and www.creativekidsathome.com.

Birthday parties

Hopefully the days of the 'statement' children's party are numbered. Or perhaps I'm just dreaming. For Ethan's third birthday we tried to be responsible and sustainable – and then blew it all by hiring a bouncy castle.

♥ Make the cake yourself and you'll know what's going into it. You can find organic baking ingredients fairly easily – although not decorations such as Smarties or sugar sprinkles (yet). Eco-friendly party supplier Little Cherry (www. littlecherry.co.uk) has beeswax birthday candles.

♥ If you really have to get disposable plates and cups, opt for recycled paper or degradable ones made from reed, cornstarch, bamboo or palm leaves, plus wooden cutlery, through sources such as The Green Stationery Company (www.greenstat. co.uk), Goodlife (www.ecothefriendlyfrog.co.uk) or

www.nigelsecostore.com, then put them on the compost heap
after use. Even better, ask parents to bring a plate, bowl and cup
with their child – but be prepared to spend time reuniting lost
implements with their owners.

♥ Dispose of balloons responsibly, for the sake of wildlife, and
opt for latex balloons you blow up yourself over helium-filled
foil ones, as latex will in time degrade.

♥ Sort, re-use and recycle the wrappings, and use old wrapping
paper or magazine pages for Pass the Parcel.

♥ Make your own party bags by re-using and decorating brown
paper ones. Try to avoid plastic gifts and anything that's going
to break the second the visiting child is out the door (which will
also help to avert tears).

♥ You might organize a toy swap at the party, so each child goes
home with something new to them – although this could be
tricky with pre-schoolers, who are particularly attached to
what's 'theirs'.

♥ With imagination, plus a bit of time and odds and ends, your
garden, flat, local park or beach can become the backdrop for all
kinds of themes, games and adventures.

MINI ECO WARRIORS

Our children are the future custodians of the planet – so it's up to
us to help them learn from our mistakes.

♥ If you've started taking green steps, for your children it'll just be
normal. Even at two Ethan knew the difference between the

recycling, compost and rubbish bins – although he doesn't always choose the right one.

♥ For older children you may need an incentive scheme or some kind of competition, with prizes worth changing behaviour for. Perhaps you could use a mixture of 'little angel' incentives with a green tinge (such as a wind-up torch or camping trip), and 'little devil' treats (such as chocolate or a coveted battery-powered toy) that fulfil those cravings for a high-carbon lifestyle.

♥ Don't children just love catching you out when you do something wrong? This can be put to good use – set one in charge of making sure all the house electronics are switched off, and another in charge of checking the shower timings.

♥ Give them their own seeds and a patch of soil or pots to grow what they like. See Chapter 6 for projects and basics.

♥ Even urban areas have city farms where children can meet, feed and learn about animals and farming. Older children may even be able to help out.

Eco-Schools

Is your child's school an Eco-School? If not, encourage the head to sign up at www.eco-schools.co.uk. The programme encourages pupils, teachers and other staff, parents and governors to join in helping to gauge the school's impact on the environment, then work out an action plan to make improvements. It covers everything from recycling, energy and water saving, and transport, to healthy eating, litter and improving biodiversity in the school grounds (in other words, planting more trees and creating spaces to attract wildlife and butterflies). There are three awards to keep young and older minds focused and to recognize progress.

Make your school greener by...

Not driving there
If your school doesn't already run a walking bus scheme, take a look at www.thewalkingbus.co.uk.

Donating your scraps for crafts
Ask what would be useful – you may be able to give something from your business or hobby. Schools and projects can buy donated craft materials at low cost from scrapstores – www.childrensscrapstore.co.uk lists organizations around the UK.

Having Zero Waste packed lunches
Apples instead of chocolate bars, home-made sandwiches instead of bought snackboxes, home-made popcorn instead of crisps – see if your school will run no-waste lunchtimes for a day a week.

Helping to organize a fairtrade tuck shop
The one at our local infant school was started by Year 2 pupils – with some assistance.

Setting up a school vegetable plot
Growing vegetables can help children learn about seeds, where our foods come from, soil, beneficial insects – and then the harvest can make healthy school lunches. Join Garden Organic for Schools at www.gardenorganic.org.uk (it's free) or look up Growing Schools at www.growingschools.org.uk.

Creating a wildlife area

School grounds provide increasingly important wildlife habitats and could even become a setting for outdoor lessons in good weather. Your local wildlife trust (see www.wildlifetrusts.org) can help and advise.

Encouraging recycling at school as well as at home

Find resources for children at www.ollierecycles.com and www.recyclezone.org.uk.

Enjoying the natural world together

My mother's enthusiasm for the natural world – for birds and wildflowers, and the landscape – sparked my imagination as a child. I became fascinated, and even kept a nature diary. We still compare notes and look up the flowers we've seen on Cornish walks together.

But you don't need to know all the plant and insect names to enjoy nature. You can learn along with your children, and take digital photos – or specimens if appropriate – to identify from books or online. (You must never dig up wild plants.) A magnifying glass makes creepy-crawlies even more exciting, akin to 'garden monsters'.

In a medium-sized or larger garden you could have a wildflower meadow of native plants (you can find seeds online, from sources such as www.meadowmania.co.uk). Make sure you have some species that attract bees, butterflies and other insects. Consult one of the increasing number of books on

wildlife gardening, or see English Nature's online guide
(www.englishnature.org.uk).

If you have a small patch, there'll still be plenty of life in it. Log
seats, made from a section of tree trunk, double as insect homes –
lift one up and you could find anything from ants' nests and
woodlice to stag beetles. Otherwise, make the most of local parks
and nature reserves. Many areas of waste land in cities have been
reclaimed by enthusiasts to create wild spaces and reserves that
are great for hiding and adventure games as well as
nature-spotting.

Parent's tip:

For wildlife-watching ideas and projects, try the Shropshire Wildlife
Trust blog (http://shropshirewildlifetrust.ethink.org.uk) and
www.bbc.co.uk/breathingplaces, and join Woodland Trust Nature
Detectives (www.naturedetectives.org.uk).

Ladybird hotel

Provide ladybirds with a place to hibernate over the winter. There
are two ways to do it. One is to take an old tin, perhaps from tinned
tomatoes, and make sure the lid hasn't left any jagged edges. Clean
it thoroughly. Help children to fill it with used straws that you've
saved up, pushing them right down and making sure the tin is
completely packed. Trim off the spare ends so they're about level
with the mouth of the tin, then tie some string around the can to
hang it up.

Alternatively, children can collect up twigs, hollow stems, old straw and hay, and tie them into bundles with string.

Hang your ladybird hotels from tree branches, or else nestle them into a hedge or fence, a little way above the ground so they're less likely to get frosty. Ladybirds and other insects will appreciate the warmth over the winter, and then you can see what comes out into the spring sunshine.

Set up a bird feeder

You can buy all sorts of feeders and seed from pet shops, garden centres and specialists such as www.wigglywigglers.co.uk. In the winter, birds like a mix of nuts and seeds with fat, such as lard or white vegetable shortening, or else peanut butter, cheese and apple. Mould the ingredients in a shallow yogurt pot or cottage-cheese tub, then turn out and put on an existing bird table. Otherwise make a hole in the tub before you fill it, thread string through and tie a knot on the inside so you can hang it up.

The Royal Society for the Protection of Birds (www.rspb.org.uk) has more ideas, including making a seed feeder from a drink bottle.

Don't be tempted to leave out stale bread or rice, because these can swell in birds' stomachs. Try to keep feeders away from cats' favourite haunts, and don't forget birds need water too, especially in frozen winters and during summer dry spells.

How to raise the new green generation

Give babies a good start by trying to avoid hazardous chemicals during pregnancy and when they're newly born.

Make your nursery as sustainable and safe as possible, with good-quality second-hand furniture and baby-friendly, eco-friendly new buys.

Breast is best for feeding – if it's not going as planned, be sure to get some support.

Make your nappies greener nappies!

Have fun mixing home-made play dough and helping with craft projects.

Spend your time, rather than money and non-renewable resources, on making children's parties exciting.

Encourage your children's school to be a greener place, and try to avoid driving there.

Find ways to enjoy the natural world together.

Remember, your children will inherit the Earth – and they need to make a better job of looking after it than we have (so far).

ACKNOWLEDGEMENTS

Many people, many library visits, many websites and many ideas have contributed to this book. I would especially like to thank Victoria Millar, my partner in craft, who has helped me to revive my sewing skills and lent me her sewing machine (and felted cushion cover method). Also Tony Ashford, without whom our garden would be nowhere near what it is today, and who gave his valuable comments on my efforts to convey the basics of growing your own.

My gratitude goes to Jenny Ambrose at Enamore, Tad Korbusz at Living-Sense, florist Rachel Lilley, Jacqui Grainger and Veronica Parsons at Envolve, Ali Jennings of Curvemedia (www.curvemedia.co.uk), Louise Moon of EcoMoon, Mitch Tonks at FishWorks, Kirsty Righton at the Soil Association, Elizabeth Salter Green at CHEM Trust, Peter Ellis at Rose of Jericho and white goods specialist Andy Triggs, who contributed their expertise and cast their eyes over sections of the manuscript, and to Peter Andrews of Bath Organic Group. Also to all those who have asked a question, mentioned a tip, checked information, or helped with answers, in particular, Eliane Wilson.

Everyone at John Murray has been very supportive, especially my editors Eleanor Birne and Helen Hawksfield. Thanks to all those involved in the process of making this book – not forgetting my agent Simon Trewin.

Ms Harris's Book would not have happened without Clive and Ethan, my wonderful family. Thank you, Clive, for believing in me, and this, all the way through. Maybe you'll even get to read it one day . . .

INDEX

oven-roasted tomatoes recipe
126–7
Oxfam 210, 287

pachacuti.co.uk 295
packaging 354–5, 375
   food 126, 134–5, 160–1
   laundry detergent 252, 255
   plastic 202–3, 214
packed lunches 385
paint and varnish 28, 213, 336,
   372–3
paintbrushes 24
palm oil 117
pangrattato 152–3
pans 126, 127–8
pantries 112–15
paper 179, 340, 365–6, 383
parsley 171
parties 350–4, 382–3
Patagonia 291
patching 308, 311, 318, 319, 320
PC World 345
pectin 143–4
People Tree 288–9, 294
perchlorethylene 263
personal hygiene 29, 231–2,
   240
pest control 53–4, 164, 190–2
Pesticide Action Network 98
pesticides 28, 98, 104, 278,
   289–92, 378

PETA (People for the Ethical
   Treatment of Animals) 53
Phone Co-op 347
phones 70, 83–4, 210, 342, 346,
   347
pick-your-own 96, 366
pillows and pillowcases 46, 215,
   374
Pippa Small 359
pizza toppings recipes 155–6
plants 237, 337–8
plastic 202–3, 214, 216–20
   bags 98–101, 213, 215, 216,
      219
   bottles 228, 291
   containers 119, 206
play dough 380–1
polish 36, 41, 48
pollution 28, 109, 110
polychlorinated biphenyls (PCBs)
   109, 371
polyethylene terephthalate
   (PETE) 218–19
polyproylene 119, 219–20
polystyrene 220
polythene 119
polyvinyl choloride (PVC) 219,
   379
potatoes 160, 172–4, 175, 190,
   191, 194
poultry 106–9
pregnancy 33, 39, 109, 370–1